Data Structures

Theory, Problems and Applications

"We want that education by which character is formed, strength of mind is increased, the intellect is expanded, and by which one can stand on one's own feet..."

. . . Swami Vivekananda

"The meaning of education is to encourage in people a sense of self-introspection, the ability to grasp and to develop the capacity for constructive works..."

. . . Dr. S. Radhakrishnan

"Always surround yourself with the kind of people who can make you believe that you can do it..."

. . . R. S. Salaria

"I hear and I forget,
I see and I understand,
I do and I remember"

. . . Confucius

"Treat others the way you wish to be treated..."

. . . R. S. Salaria

Data Structures

Theory, Problems and Applications

R. S. Salaria

Alumnus of IIT, Delhi.
Certified Software Quality Professional, Govt. of India.
Sun Certified Programmer, SUN Microsystems, USA.
Sun Certified Trainer, SUN Microsystems, USA.

Former Head
Department of Computer Science & Engineering
Thapar University, PATIALA-147004. (Punjab)

KHANNA BOOK PUBLISHING CO. (P) LTD.

4C/4344, Ansari Road, Darya Ganj, New Delhi-110002
Ph: 011-23244447-48 E-mail: contact@khannabooks.com

Data Structures

R.S. Salaria

ISBN: 978-93-81068-32-8

Edition: 2011

Published by:

Khanna Book Publishing Co. (P) Ltd.

4C/4344, Ansari Road, Darya Ganj, New Delhi-110 002

Phone: 011-23244448 Telefax: 011-23244447

E-mail: contact@khannabooks.com

Website: www.khannabooks.com

Regd. Off: 1694-95, 1st Floor, Nai Sarak, Delhi-110006 (India)

Phone: 011-23283211 Telefax: 011-23256658

Printed in India by:

S.P.S. Printers & Binders, Delhi

Dedication

Dedicated to our
dearest parents,
daughters Surbhi & Mehak,
beloved readers, esteemed faculty, and
our country men/women at large.

Preface

This book is specially designed to serve as textbook for the students of BCA of Punjab Technical University, Jalandhar, and covers all the topics as prescribed in their syllabus.

The subject of data structures is of prime importance for the students of Computer Science and IT. It is of practical nature and requires thorough understanding of basics and concepts of the subject before putting them into practice.

It is important to mention here that the data structures are backbone of any kind of software. Software is designed to store, manage and manipulate the data ranging from a small volume to a huge volume. If the data is not organized properly and efficiently, the software will not be able to deliver the desired performance. Therefore, to build kind of software, we need to have thorough understanding of the basics and concepts of the subject of data structures.

I am certain that this book will enable you to achieve the desired objectives. During the writing of the book, special emphasis is given to keep the language very simple, best effort is made to include as many as illustrative example and to present them in a visual form.

Enjoy reading this book, and feel free to send your free and frank comments, suggestions, and positive criticism. Your valuable inputs will help me to improve and fine tune the book to meet your expectations.

. . . R. S. Salaria
Email : *rssalaria@yahoo.com*

Acknowledgements

It is my pleasure to take this opportunity to thank all those who have helped me directly or indirectly in the preparation of this book.

I would like to place on record and acknowledge the works of all those great authors whose work I have referred in the preparation of this book.

My very special thanks are reserved for honourable Dr. APJ Kalam, former President (popularly known as people's president), Republic of India, my role model, whose teachings fascinate me, make us believe that India is a great country, and we should take pride in the brand "Made in India".

I thank from the core of the heart for revered Dr. D.S. Chauhan, Vice-Chancellor, UP Technical University, Lucknow, for giving his blessings. He is always a source for inspiration for me, and I am very sure that he will continue to shower his blessing in future too.

I also thank Prof. C.M. Bahl, Managing Director, Rayat-Bahra Group of Institutes (having three campuses at-Mohali, Ropar and Hoshiarpur, in the state of Pubjab), and former Director, Computer Centre, Pubjab University, Chandigarh, for his continuous advice and encouragement that always motivates me to believe in greatness and doing great things.

I also own thanks to my kids, Surbhi Salaria and Mehak Salaria, whose valuable time I have taken away which I owe to them and should have spent with them.

Finally, I must thank my publisher, **Khanna Book Publishing Co. (P) Ltd.**, for their aggressive marketing and thus establishing the book as one of the best books on *Data Structures*.

— R. S. Salaria

Word of Advice for Students

My beloved students, I would like to remind you that we can categorize people as

People who watch the things happening,
People who look into how things are happening, and
People who make the things happen.

Now you are to find out where you fit-in and where you want to be.

I firmly believe that youth of our country is second to none, and this fact is recognized world wide.

Our honourable former president Dr. APJ Kalam (first and may be the last president known as *people's president*) has been saying at all the platform that in India there is no dearth of resources and talent, only thing we need to change is *the mindset* (we have to shed *chalta hai* attitude). He has set a vision for us to see India a developed country by 2020, and the basis for his vision is the talent of our youth.

Take some time to discover yourself and try to assess how much talent you possess. Utilize your period of study to harness that talent. I can assure you that you will have a great future.

I want to share a popular game with you which all of us used to play in our childhood. The game is of burning a peace of paper using a lens under the sun. When the lens and the paper are held stationery, it starts burning in a few seconds. However, if you keep moving either the paper or the lens, the paper will never burn. *Why it happens so?* The answer is simple – the light energy emitted by the sun is not focused. The same is with us. We have enough energy in ourselves, but we don't focus it, rather we waste it in meaningless acts. The next question arises is – *where to focus our energy?* The natural answer of this question should be – what you want to become in your life (that basically defines your goal). So you need to focus your entire energy on your goal, and surely you will achieve your goal.

I would also like to share with you a scene from the popular epic – *Mahabharta*. When Dronacharya, Guru of Pandvas, asked his disciples to aim at the eye of a fish hanged on a tree. All his disciples, except Arjuna, replied in a same manner – *Guru ji, we see a fish*. However, when the turn of Arjuna came, his reply was – *Guru ji, I see only the eye*. That is the kind of the focus you also need to develop in your life.

The next point is that when you have identified your goal, you need to identify the steps that you need to follow in order to accomplish your goal. Once the goal and the steps to accomplish your goal are identified, write them nicely on a piece of a paper and paste that paper at a place which you visit regularly. Whenever you will visit that place, the writing on the paper will remind you about your goal and what you have to do to achieve your goal.

The final word, you may set any goal for yourself and that may be of becoming a successful doctor, an engineer, an administrator or a businessman, but you must also try to be a *nice human being*. You know a nice human being is like a fruit of all seasons, and is welcome every where, anytime. I believe, the basic mantra to become a nice human being is too simple and can be stated as

"Treat the others the way you want to be treated, in other words, don't do anything with others which you wish others shouldn't do with you."

Enjoy your student life and make best use of it . . .

Wish you good luck and a nice time ahead.

. . . R. S. Salaria

Syllabus

Introduction to Data Structure: Basic concept of data, Problem analysis, algorithm complexity, Big O notation and time space trade off.

Stacks & Queues: Basics of stacks and queues, Recursion, Polish notation, circular Queues, priority Queues.

Linked Lists: Single linked list, circular linked list, doubly linked list and dynamic storage management, generalized list, Garbage Collection.

Trees: Definition & Concepts, Basic trees, Binary tree representations, threaded storage representation, binary tree traversals, and application of trees.

Searching and sorting: use of various data structures for searching and sorting, linear and binary search, insertion sort, selection sort, merge sort, bubble sort, quick sort, heap sort.

Contents at a Glance

Table of Contents

Chapter 1

Introduction to Data Structures

Learning Objectives

After reading this chapter, students will be able to

- explain the basic terms related to data organization
- differentiate between data and information
- explain the meaning of data type and various forms of data types
- define data structure and its scope
- describe the criteria for selection of appropriate data structure for modeling the data of a problem in hand
- differentiate between data type and data structure
- describe in various data structures
- describe in various operations that can be performed on data structures

1.1 INTRODUCTION

We know that the main memory is *volatile*, *i.e.*, it looses its contents when the system is turned off, whereas the secondary memory is *non-volatile*, *i.e.*, retains its contents unless overwritten with new ones. We also know that the processor can only process the data that is available in main memory. Therefore, if the data to be processed is not available in the main memory, then it has to be transferred from secondary memory to the main memory. Similarly, if the new data entered in the main memory under program control or intermediate and/or final results produced by the program are to be preserved for the future usc, thcy arc transferred from main memory to the secondary memory.

In order to represent and store data in main memory and/or secondary memory, we need an appropriate model. The different models used to organize data in the main memory are collectively referred to as *data structures*, whereas the different models used to organize data in the secondary memory are collectively referred to as *file structures*.

This chapter provides an overview of data structures and other related issues.

1.2 BASIC TERMINOLOGY OF DATA ORGANIZATION

This section introduces the basic terminology related to data organization. Every student must understand these terms.

Data – The term *data* simply refers to a value or set of values. These values may represent some observations from an experiment, some figures collected during some survey (such as *census*, *exit polls*, etc.), marks obtained by a student in an examination, etc.

Data item – A *data item* refers to a single unit of values. For example, *roll number*, *name*, *date of birth*, *age*, *address* and *marks in each subject* are data items. Data items that can be divided into sub items are called *group items* whereas those who can not be divided into sub items are called *elementry items*. For example, an address is a group item as it is usually divided into sub items such as *house number*, *street number*, *locality*, *city*, *pin code*, etc. Likewise, a *date* can be divided into *day*, *month* and *year*; a *name* can be divided into *first name* and *surname*. On the other hand, *roll number*, *marks*, *city*, *pin code*, etc. are normally treated as elementry items.

Entity – An *entity* is something that has certain *attributes* or *properties* which may be assigned values. The values assigned may be either numeric or non-numeric. For example, a student is an entity. The possible attributes for a student can be *roll number*, *name*, *date of birth*, *sex* and *class*. The possible values for these attributes can be *1234*, *Surbhi*, *12/03/1993*, *F*, *9*.

Each attribute of an entity has a defined set of values, called *domain*. For example, the domain for *sex* attribute consists of only *M* (for males) and *F* (for females) value.

Entity set – An *entity set* is a collection of similar *entities*. For example, students of a class, employees of an organization, products manufactured by a manufacturing unit, etc. forms an entity set.

Record – A *record* is a collection of related data items. For example, *roll number*, *name*, *date of birth*, *sex*, and *class* of a particular student such as *1234*, *Surbhi*, *12/03/1993*, *F*, *9*. In fact, a record represents an entity.

File – A *file* is a collection of related records. For example, a file containing records of all students in class, a file containing records of all employees of an organization. In fact, a file represents an entity set.

Key – A *key* is a data item in a record that takes unique values and can be used to distinguish a record from other records. It may happen that more than one data item has unique values. In that case, there exist multiple keys. But at a time, we may be using only one data item as a key, called *primary key*, that too depending on the problem in hand. The other key(s) are then known as *alternate key(s)*.

In some cases, there is no field that has unique values. Then a combination of some fields can be used to form a key. Such a key is known as *composite key*.

In worst case, if there is no possibility of forming a key from within the record, then an extra data item can be added to the record that can be used as a key.

Information – The terms *data* and *information* have been used to mean same thing. But actually information is more than just data. In simple terms, information is a processed data. Data is just a collection of values (raw data), from which no conclusions can be drawn. Thus data as such is not useful for decision making. When the data is processed, by applying certain rules, new generated data becomes information. This new generated data (information) conveys some meaning and hence can be used for decision-making. For more clarity, consider the next example.

Example 1.1:

An agricultural scientist wants to study the effect of a particular pesticide on a new variety of wheat. He uses a different amount of pesticide for different fields of wheat and notes down the yield of wheat in each field. Here, the amount of pesticide used and yield of wheat in each field represents data.

As such these values do not convey anything regarding the effect of pesticide on the yield. Next he applies the technique of correlation analysis to determine the correlation coefficient whose value lies in the range −1 to +1. This coefficient, which is also a value, conveys valuable information about the effect of pesticide on yield of wheat. If correlation coefficient is greater than 0, it means increased amount of pesticide has positive effect on the yield. If correlation coefficient is less than 0, it means increased amount of pesticide has negative effect on the yield. If correlation coefficient is equal to 0, it means increased amount of pesticide has no effect on the yield.

1.3 CONCEPT OF A DATA TYPE

A *data type* is a collection of values and a set of operations that act on those values. Whether our program is dealing with pre-defined data types or user-defined types, following two aspects must be considered:

- Set of values
- Set of operations

For example, consider an integer data type which consists of values {MININT, . . ., −3, −2, −1, 0, 1, 2, 3, . . ., MAXINT}, where MININT and MAXINT are the smallest and largest integers that can be represented by an integer type on a particular computer. The operations on integers include the arithmetic operations of addition (+), subtraction (−), multiplication (*), and division (/). There are also operations that test for equality/inequality and the operation that assign an integer value to a variable.

1.3.1 Primitive Data Type

A *primitive data type* is a data type that is *predefined*. The predefined data type is also known as *built-in data type*. These primitive data types may be different for different programming languages. For example, C & C++ programming languages provide *built-in* support for integers (*int, long*), reals (*float, double*) and characters (*char*).

The right hand side of the assignment statement can have a *value*, *a variable* or *an expression*. However, if several assignment statements appear in the same line, such as

```
Set k = 1, loc = 1, max = a_i
```

then they are executed from left to right.

Input/Output - Data may be input and assigned to variables by means of a *read* statement with the following format

```
Read: variable list
```

where the *variable list* consists one or more variables separated by comma.

Similarly, the data held by the variables and the messages, if any, enclosed in double quotes can be output by means of a *write* statement with the following format

```
Write: message and/or variable list
                or
Print: message and/or variable list
```

where the *message* and the variables in the *variable list* are separated by comma.

Execution of Instructions - The instructions in the algorithm are usually executed one after the other as they appear in the algorithm. However, there may be instances when some instructions are skipped or some instructions may be repeated as a result of certain conditions.

Calling a Sub Algorithm - To call a sub algorithm from the algorithm or sub algorithm, a special statement, called *call* statement (instruction) is used. This statement is used along with the name of the sub algorithm followed by the list of the parameters.

For example, the statement

```
Call FindLocation( a, n, loc )
```

calls sub algorithm named *FindLocation*, and having parameter list that comprises three names *a*, *n* and *loc*. The calling algorithm passes to it an array named *a* of size *n*, and the sub algorithm assigns the location of the largest element to *loc*.

1.3.2 User-Defined Data Type

A *user-defined data type* is one that user defines as per his/her own requirement. The programming languages provide support for creating user-defined data types. For various C and C++ languages support user-defined data types by means of structures (*struct*), unions (*union*), and enumerations (*enum*).

1.3.3 Abstract Data Type

An *abstract data type* is a data type that is organized in such a way that the specification of the values and the specification of the operations on those values are separated from the representation of the values and the implementation of the operations.

For example, consider *list* abstract data type. A *list* is basically a collection of elements which can be ordered or unordered. The primitive operations on a list may include adding new elements, deleting elements, determining number of elements in the list, and applying a particular process to each element in the list. Here, we are not concerned with how a list is represented and how the above mentioned operations are implemented. We only need to know that it is a list whose elements are of given type, and what can we do with the list.

1.4 DATA STRUCTURE DEFINED

A *data structure* is a logical model of a particular organization of data. The choice of a particular data structure depends on the following consideration:

- It must be able to represent the inherent relationship of the data in the real world.
- It must be simple enough so that it can process efficiently as and when necessary.

The study of data structures includes:

- Logical description of the data structure.
- Implementation of the data structure.
- Quantitative analysis of the data structure. This analysis includes determining the amount of memory needed to store the data structure and the time required processing it.

1.5 DESCRIPTION OF VARIOUS DATA STRUCTURES

This section introduces various data structures, which will be discussed in detail later in the book.

The various data structures are divided into following categories:

- ***Linear data structures*** – a data structure whose elements form a sequence, and every element in the structure has a unique predecessor and unique successor. Examples of linear data structures are *arrays*, *linked lists*, *stacks* and *queues*.
- ***Non-linear data structures*** – a data structure whose elements do not form a sequence, there is no unique predecessor or unique successor.. Examples of non-linear data structures are *trees* and *graphs*.

In the subsequent sections, we will have a look on these data structures.

1.5.1 Arrays

An *array* is a list of finite number of elements of same data type, *i.e.*, integers, reals or strings etc. The individual elements of an array are accessed using an index or indices to the array. Depending on the number of indices required to access an individual element of an array, arrays can be classified as:

- *One-dimensional array* or *linear array* that requires only one index to access an individual element of the array.
- *Two-dimensional arrays* that requires two indices to access an individual element of the array. In Mathematics, equivalent to two-dimensional array, we have a *matrix* and in business terminology we have a *table*.
- The arrays for which we need two or more indices are generally known as *multi-dimensional arrays*.

1.5.1.1 Linear Arrays

A *linear array* is a list of a finite number, say *n*, of homogeneous data elements such that

- The elements of the array are referenced by an index set consisting of *n* consecutive integer numbers.
- The elements of the array are stored in consecutive memory locations.

The number *n* of the elements is called the *size* of the linear array. In general, if *lb* is the smallest index, called the *lower bound*, and *ub* is the largest index, called *upper bound*, then size of the linear array is given by

```
size = ub - lb + 1
```

Note that the size of the array = *ub* if *lb* = 1. If not explicitly stated, generally we will consider the index set consists of 1, 2, 3, . . ., *n* or *ub*.

Suppose *a* is the name of the linear array with *n* elements, then its elements can be denoted as

$a_1, a_2, a_3, \ldots, a_n$	in mathematical notation
$a(1), a(2), a(3), \ldots, a(n)$	in BASIC and FORTRAN languages
$a[1], a[2], a[3], \ldots, a[n]$	in PASCAL language
$a[0], a[1], a[2], \ldots, a[n-1]$	in C/C++ and Java languages

The number *k* in *a*(*k*) or *a*[*k*] is called a *subscript* and *a*(*k*) or *a*[*k*] itself is called a *subscripted variable*.

> To be consistent with the C language notation, if an array has *n* elements for a given dimension, its index set will be considered as 0, 1, 2, . . ., *n*–1.

Example 1.2:

Consider a linear array *rn* consisting of roll numbers of 5 students of a particular class. This array can be pictured as shown in Figure 1.1.

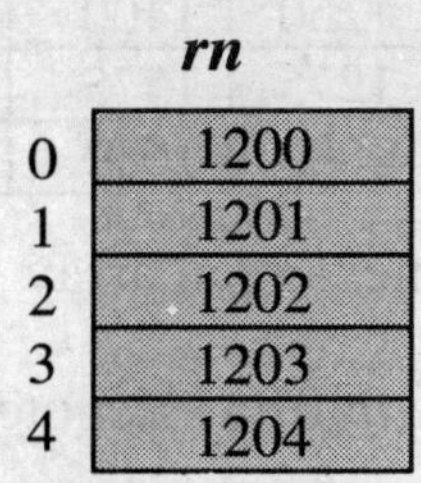

Figure 1.1: One-dimensional array *rn* storing roll numbers

Here *rn*[0] denotes 1200, *rn*[1] denotes 1201 and so on.

1.5.1.2 Two-dimensional Array

A two-dimensional array is a list of a finite number, say $m*n$, of homogeneous data elements such that

- The elements of the array are referenced by two index sets consisting of m and n consecutive integer numbers.
- The elements of the array are stored in consecutive memory locations.

The *size* of the two-dimensional array is denoted by $m \times n$ and pronounced as m by n.

Suppose b is the name of the two-dimensional array, then its element in *ith* row and *jth* column can be denoted as

b_{ij}	in mathematical notation
$b(i, j)$	in BASIC and FORTRAN languages
$b[i, j]$	in PASCAL language
$b[i][j]$	in C/C++ and Java languages

Example 1.3:

Suppose a manufacturing company has a chain of five stores and five departments in each store. The weekly sales for the company can be stored using two-dimensional array named *sale*. This array can be pictured as shown in the Figure 1.2.

sale

	0	1	2	3	4
0	2000	1200	1500	1000	1005
1	1500	1450	2010	1550	1250
2	1000	1250	1400	2000	3000
3	1250	1275	1575	3500	1750
4	5200	4000	1000	1200	1575

Figure 1.2: Two-dimensional array *sale* to storing sales

Here *sale*[0][0] denotes 2000, *sale*[0][1] denotes 1200, . . ., *sale*[4][4] denotes 1575.

In business terminology, a two-dimensional array is better known as a table, where as in mathematical terminology, it is known as a matrix.

1.5.2 Linked Lists

A *linked list* is a linear collection of data elements, called *nodes*. The linear order is maintained by pointers. Each node is divided into two or more parts. A linked list can be linear linked list (one-way list) or doubly linked list (two-way list).

1.5.2.1 Linear Linked List

In linear linked list, each node is divided in two parts:

- first part contains the information of the element.
- second part, called the *link field* or *nextpointer field*, contains the address of the next node in the list.

In addition, another pointer variable, say *head*, is used that contains the address of the first element of the list. The last element of the linear linked list has *NULL* value, pictured as *X*, in the *nextpointer* field to mark the end of the list. A Linear linked list can be traversed only in one direction.

Example 1.4:

The following figure shows a linear linked list with 4 nodes.

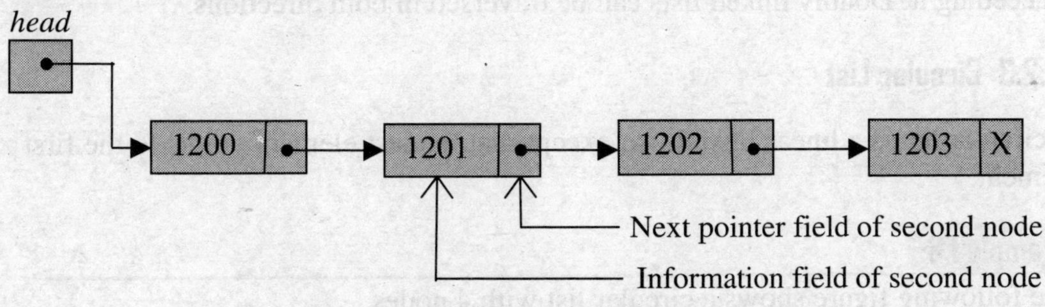

Figure 1.3: Linear linked list with 4 nodes

1.5.2.2 Doubly Linked List

In the doubly linked list, each node is divided into three parts:

- first part contains the information of the element,
- second part, called *previouspointer field*, contains the address of the preceding element in the list, and
- third part, called *nextpointer field*, contains the address of the succeeding element in the in the list.

Example 1.5:

The following figure shows a doubly linked list with 3 nodes.

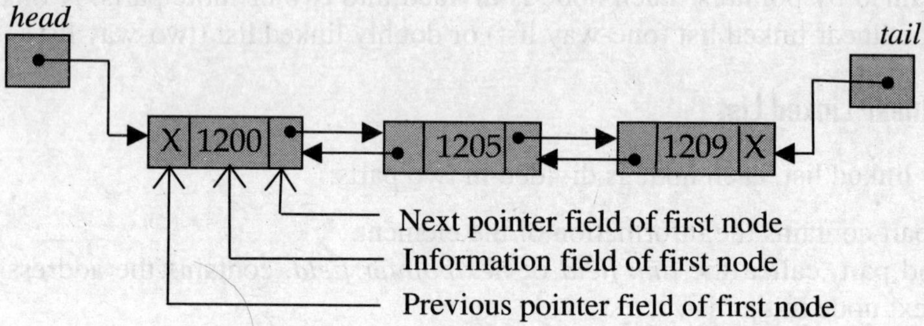

Figure 1.4: Doubly linked list with 3 nodes

In addition, two pointer variables, say *head* and *tail*, are used that contains the address of the first element and the last element of the doubly linked list, respectively. The first element contains *NULL* value in the *previouspointer* to indicate there is no element preceding it, and the last element of the linked list have *NULL* value in the *nextpointer* field to indicate that there is no element succeeding it. Doubly linked lists can be traversed in both directions.

1.5.2.3 Circular List

A circular list is a linear linked list, except that the last element points to the first element.

Example 1.6:

The following figure shows a circular list with 4 nodes.

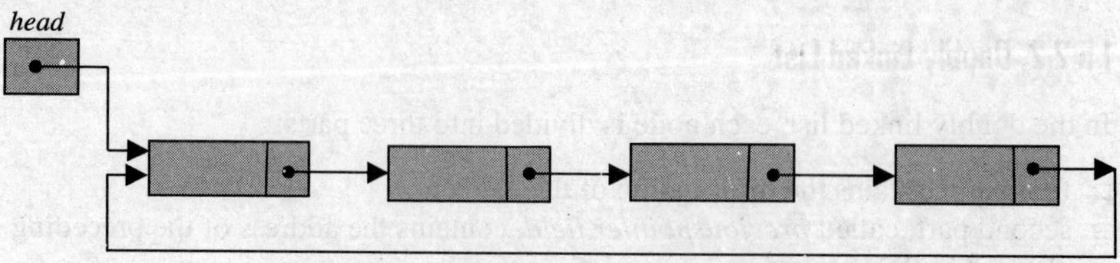

Figure 1.5: Circular list with 4 nodes

1.5.3 Stacks

A *stack*, also called a Last-In-First-Out (LIFO) system, is a linear list in which insertions and deletions can take place only at one end, called the *top*.

Example 1.7:

The following figure shows a stack with 6 elements.

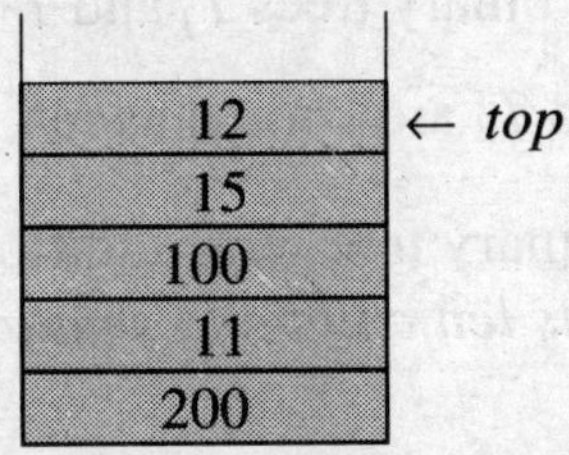

Figure 1.6: Stack with 6 elements

This structure operates in much the same way as stack of trays. If we want to place another tray, it can be placed only at the top. Likewise, if we want to remove a tray from stack of trays, it can only be removed from the top.

1.5.4 Queues

A *queue*, also called a First-In-First-Out (FIFO) or First-Come-First-Serve (FCFS) system, is a linear list in which insertions can take place at one end of the list, called the *rear* of the list, and deletions can take place only at other end, called the *front* of the list. This structure operates in much the same way a line of people waiting at a bus stop or at a cinema hall for their turn.

Example 1.8:

The following figure shows a queue containing 5 elements.

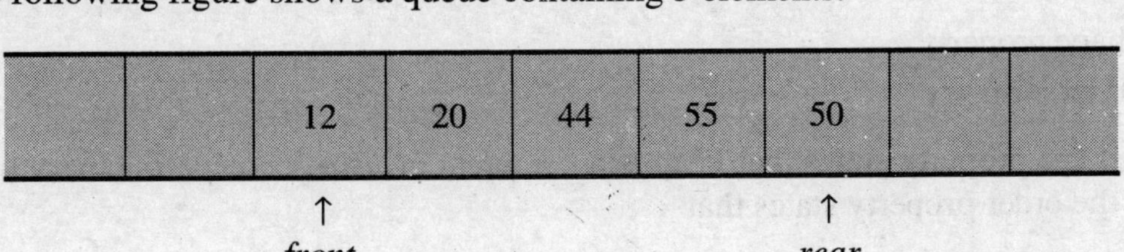

Figure 1.7: Queue with 5 elements

1.5.5 Trees

A *tree* is a data structure that represents a hierarchical relationship between various elements. A *binary tree* is a tree that can have utmost two children. Formerly, a binary tree T is defined as finite set of elements, called *nodes*, such that:

- Either T is empty, called the *null tree* or *empty tree*, or
- T contains a distinguished node R, called *root* of T, and remaining nodes form an ordered pair of binary trees T_1 and T_2.

Here the binary trees T_1 and T_2 are known as *left* and *right* subtrees, respectively.

A *binary search tree* is a binary tree with additional property — *the key value of any node N is larger than its left child and smaller than its right child.*

Example 1.9:

The following figure shows a binary tree and a binary search tree.

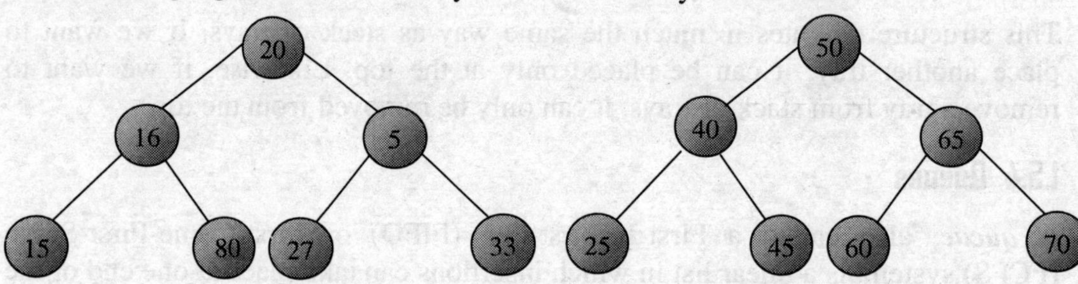

(*a*) Binary tree b) Binary search tree

Figure 1.8: Binary and binary search trees

1.5.6 Heaps

A *heap* is a binary tree that satisfies the following properties:

- Shape property
- Order property

The shape property states that heap is a *complete* or *nearly complete* binary tree. And the order property states that

- Either the element at any node is smallest of all of its children, called *min heap*, or
- Element at any node is largest of all of its children, called *max heap*.

A heap is represented in memory by sequential representation, *i.e.*, using linear arrays. The important applications of a heap structure are to implement priority queues in addition to being used for sorting an array, a technique popularly known as *heapsort*.

Example 1.10:

The following figure shows a *min heap* and a *max heap*.

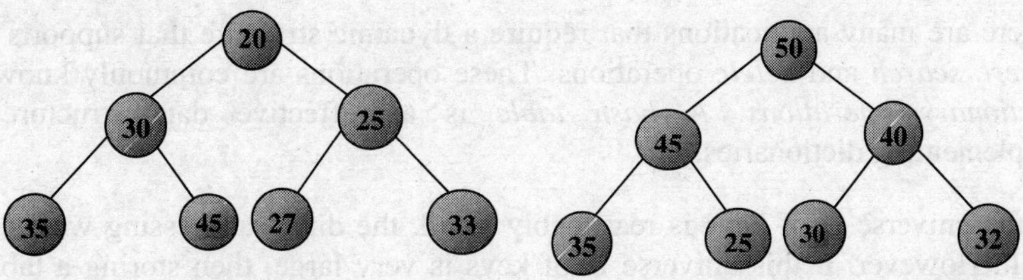

(*a*) Min heap (*b*) Max heap

Figure 1.9: Min and Max heaps

1.5.7 Graphs

A *graph G* is a ordered set (*V*, *E*), where *V* represent the set of elements, called *nodes* or *vertices* in graph terminology, and *E* represents the edges between these elements. This data structure is used to represent relationship between pairs of elements, which are not necessarily hierarchical in nature. For example, graphs may be used to show the air map, where the airline flies only between the cities connected by lines as shown in Figure 1.10.

Example 1.11:

The following figure shows the cities for which there is a direct flight.

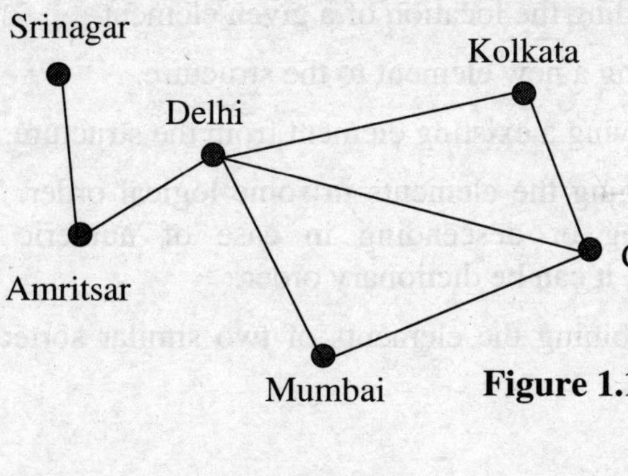

Figure 1.10: Airline Flights

In the above graph

V = { Srinagar, Amritsar, Delhi, Mumbai, Chennai, Kolkata }

E = { (Srinagar, Amritsar), (Amritsar, Delhi), (Delhi, Mumbai), (Delhi, Chennai),(Delhi, Kolkata),(Chennai, Kolkata),(Mumbai, Chennai) }

1.5.8 Hash Tables

There are many applications that require a dynamic structure that supports only *insert*, *search* and *delete* operations. These operations are commonly known as *dictionary operations*. A *hash table* is an effective data structure for implementing dictionaries.

If the universe U of keys is reasonably small, the direct addressing works very well. However, if this universe U of keys is very large, then storing a table of size $|U|$ will be impractical, or even impossible, given the memory available on a typical computer. If the actual set of keys K at a given time is very small relative to U, then most of the space allocated for table would be wasted.

A hash table requires much less storage than direct address table. Specifically, the storage requirement can be reduced to $O(|K|)$, even though searching for an element in the hash table requires constant time.

1.6 COMMON OPERATIONS ON DATA STRUCTURES

The various operations that can be performed on different data structures are described below:

- ***Traversal*** – Accessing each element exactly once in order to process it. This operation is called *visiting* the element.
- ***Searching*** – Finding the location of a given element.
- ***Insertion*** – Adding a new element to the structure.
- ***Deletion*** – Removing a existing element from the structure.
- ***Sorting*** – Arranging the elements in some logical order. This logical order may be ascending or descending in case of numeric key. In case of alphanumeric key, it can be dictionary order.
- ***Merging*** – Combining the elements of two similar sorted structures into a single structure.

SUMMARY

In this chapter, we have learnt about the

- basic terms related to data organization.
- concept of data type.
- primitive and abstract data types.
- definition of data structure.
- different factors that influence the choice of a particular data structure for a given problem.
- different data structures with suitable examples.
- different operations that can be performed on these data structures.

REVIEW EXERCISES

1. How the subject of *file structures* is different from the subject of *data structures*?
2. Explain the terms: *data*, *elementary item*, *entity*, *primary key*, *domain*, *attribute* and *information*. Also give example in support of your answer.
3. What is difference between *data* and *information*?
4. What is a *data type*? Differentiate between *primitive data type* and *abstract data type*.
5. What is a *data structure*? What are the factors that influence the choice of a particular data structure?
6. What are the areas of study under the domain of data structures?
7. How non-linear structures are different from linear data structures?
8. Describe, in brief, the various data structures.
9. Describe the various operations that, in general, can be performed on different data structures.

Chapter 2

Introduction to Algorithms

Learning Objectives

After reading this chapter, students will be able to

- define an algorithm and sub-algorithm
- explain the characteristics of a good algorithm
- describe the notation used to express algorithms
- describe various control structures
- explain the algorithm complexity and its components
- explain the time-space trade-off among algorithms
- express the complexity of algorithms using Big Oh notation
- describe the categories of algorithms on the basis of Big Oh notation
- explain the limitations of Big Oh notation
- explain the concept of recursion
- understand and work with popular recursive functions
- develop algorithm for any given problem

2.1 INTRODUCTION

The development of algorithms for manipulating the data structures is a major feature of this book. Basically, an algorithm is a description of the various steps involved in finding the solution of a particular problem.

In general, a problem can have a *direct solution* or an *iterative solution*. In the direct solution, there are fixed steps, which are not repeating, that we apply to arrive at the solution of the problem. However, in iterative solution, there certain steps within the algorithm that may have to be repeated (iterated).

This chapter describes the algorithms, the notation used to express the algorithms, the algorithmic complexity, and Big Oh (O) notation to express algorithmic complexity.

2.2 ALGORITHM DEFINED

An *algorithm* is a finite set of steps defining the correct solution of a particular problem. An algorithm can be expressed in English like language, called *pseudocode*, in a programming language, or in the form of a flowchart. In this book, we will describe the algorithms by numbering the steps which are executed in increasing order unless otherwise specified by the decision making for selecting particular step(s) or by repeating certain step(s).

However, what ever approach we use to express the algorithm, each algorithm must satisfy the following criteria:

- ***Input*:** There are zero or more values which are externally supplied.
- ***Output*:** At least one value is produced.
- ***Definiteness*:** Each step must be clear and unambiguous.
- ***Finiteness*:** If we trace the steps of an algorithm, then for all cases, the algorithm must terminate after a finite number of steps.
- ***Effectiveness*:** Each step must be sufficiently basic that it can in principle be carried out by a person using only paper and pencil. In addition, not only each step is definite, it must also be feasible.

Example 2.1:

Consider one-dimensional array $a[0{:}n-1]$ of real values, and we want to find the location of its largest element.

Solution:

Suppose that the location of the largest element is stored in variable *loc* and the variable *max* is used to keep track of the largest element. The problem can be solved as follows:

We begin with the assumption that the first element is the largest element, so initialize *loc* to 0 and *max* to a_0, *i.e.*, $loc = 0$ and $max = a_0$. We then compare *max* with each successive element a_k. If a_k is greater that *max*, we then update *loc* and *max* as $loc = k$ and $max = a_k$, respectively. The final value of *loc* gives the location of the largest element.

Algorithm 2.1

Let $a[0{:}n-1]$ be one-dimensional array with *n* real values. This algorithm finds the location *loc* of its largest element. The variable *i* is used as index variable, and *max* as temporary variable to store the current largest element.

```
1. Read: n                          // enter value of n
2. Repeat step 3 For i = 0 to (n-1) in steps of +1
3.     Read: ai                     // enter elements of array
   Endif
4. Set max = a0                     // take first element as largest
5. Set loc = 0                      // set location of element to 0
6. Repeat step 7 For i = 1 to (n-1) in steps of +1
7.     If (ai > max ) then          // compare next element with 'max'
          Set max = ai              // take this element as current largest
          Set loc = i               // update location of largest element
       Endif
   Endfor
8. Write: "Location of the largest element = ", loc
9. Exit
```

Algorithm 2.1 has its own input statements as well as output statements. That type of algorithm, when implemented, can run on its own. But in most of the cases, when the problem is large and complex, we divide the given problem into small manageable independent sub problems, which can be solved separately. Finally, we integrate the solution of all those sub problems to get the solution of the given problem in hand.

Further, to find the solution of each sub problem, we develop algorithm for it, called *sub algorithm,* which when implemented can't run on its own. They have to be called either by a main algorithm or by another sub algorithm. So for the calling purpose, we assign them a name and a parameter list through which they will communicate with the calling algorithms.

In Example 2.1, if we assume that the array is in memory, and we want to develop sub algorithm that finds and returns the location *loc* of the largest element to the main algorithm, then formal presentation of this sub algorithm may look as follows:

Algorithm 2.2

FindLocation(*a*, *n* , *loc*)

Here $a[0:n-1]$ is an one-dimensional array with n values in memory. This sub algorithm finds and returns the location *loc* of its largest element. The variable i is used as index variable, and *max* as temporary variable to store the current largest element.

```
1. Set max = a0                  // take first element as largest
2. Set loc = 0                   // set location of element to 0
3. Repeat step 4 For i = 1 to (n-1) in steps of +1
4.     If (ai  > max ) then      // compare next element with 'max'
          Set max = ai           // take this element as current largest
          Set loc = i            // update location of largest element
       Endif
   Endfor
5. Return
```

Then, the problem of finding the largest element of the given array can be solved as shown in algorithm 2.3.

Algorithm 2.3

Let $a[0:n-1]$ be one-dimensional array with n real values. This algorithm finds the location *loc* of its largest element.

```
1. Read: n                             // enter value of n
2. Repeat step 3 For i = 0 to (n-1) in steps of +1
3.     Read: ai                        // enter elements of array
   Endfor
4. Call FindLocation( a, n, loc )      // call sub algorithm
5. Write: "Location of the largest element = ", loc
6. Exit
```

2.3 ALGORITHMIC NOTATION

In this section, we will discuss the format (notation) to be used to express (describe) the algorithm and sub algorithm. This format is explained with reference to example 2.1, algorithms 2.1, 2.2 and 2.3.

Format for the formal presentation of the algorithm consists of following two parts:

- First part describes the input data, the purpose of the algorithm and identifies the variables used in the algorithms.
- Second part is composed of sequence of instructions that lead to the solution of the problem.

However, in case of sub algorithms, the format for the formal presentation of the sub algorithm consists of following three parts:

- First part is sub algorithm header that contains the name of the sub algorithm and a parameter list. Applicable to sub algorithms only.
- Second part describes the purpose of the algorithm.
- Third part is composed of sequence of instructions that lead to the solution of the sub problem.

Following conventions are used:

Comments - Each instruction may be followed by a comment. The comments begin with a double slash, and the explain the purpose of the instruction, such as

```
// this is a sample comment
```

Appropriate use of comments enhances the readability of the algorithm, which in turn helps in maintaining the algorithm.

Variable Names - For variable names, we will use italicized lowercase letters such as a *max*, *loc*, etc., whereas for defined constants, if any, we will use uppercase letters.

Assignment Statement - The assignment statement will use the notation as

Set $max = a_i$

to assign the value of a_i to *max*.

Completion of the Algorithm

The algorithm is completed with the execution of the last instruction. However, the algorithm can be terminated at any intermediate state using the *exit* instruction.

Completion of the Sub Algorithm

The sub algorithm is completed with the execution of the *return* instruction.

2.4 CONTROL STRUCTURES

An algorithm is made up of the following basic control (logic) structures that have been proved to be sufficient for expressing a solution, and hence for writing any computer program:

1. Sequence
2. Selection (*If*, and *If . . Else* and *Else If* ladder)
3. Iteration (*For* and *While*)

Sequence logic is used for performing instructions one after another in sequence. Thus, for sequence logic, instructions are written in the sequence in which they are to be executed. The flow of logic is from top to bottom.

```
:
:
instruction-1

instruction-2

instruction-3
:
:
```

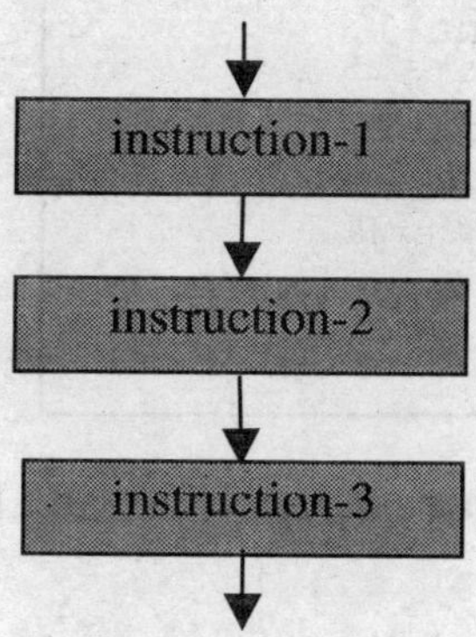

Figure 2.1: Syntax and logic flow for sequence structure

Selection logic, also known as decision logic, is used for making decision. It is used for selecting a proper path out of the alternative paths in the program logic. Decision logic is depicted as either *If*, *If - Else* structure or *Else If* ladder.

```
    :
    :
If ( expression ) then
    statement
Endif
    :
    :
```

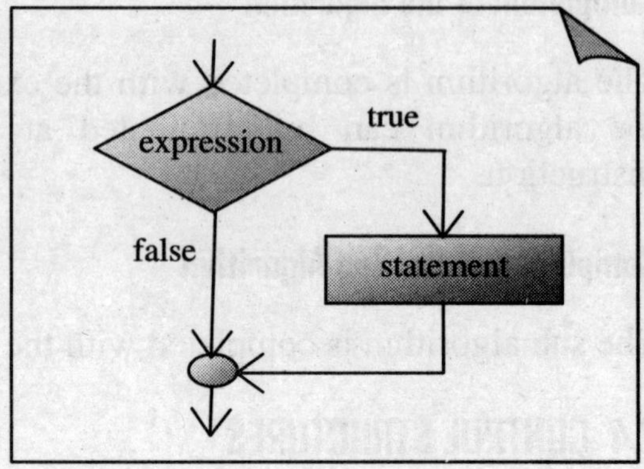

Figure 2.2: Syntax and logic flow for *If* selection structure

The *If* construct says that if the expression is true, then execute statement else (if the expression is false) skip over the statement.

```
    :
    :
If ( expression ) then
   statement-1
Else
   statement-2
Endif
    :
    :
```

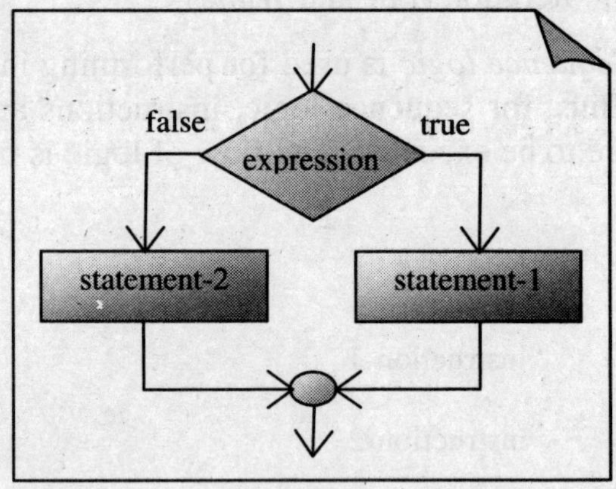

Figure 2.3: Syntax and logic flow for *If – Else* selection structure

The *If - Else* construct says that, if the expression is true, then execute statement-1, else (if the expression is false) execute statement-2.

Depending on the outcome of the expression being tested, if there are multiple alternatives (execution paths), the *Else If* ladder is a very handy construct.

```
If ( expression-1 ) then
   statement-1
Else If ( expression-2 ) then
   statement-2
Else If ( expression-3 ) then
   statement-3
        ⋮
Else If ( expression-n ) then
   statement-n
Else
   statement-s
Endif
```

Figure 2.4: Syntax of *else if* Ladder

The expressions are evaluated in order, and if any expression is true then the statement block associated with it is executed, and this terminates the whole chain. The last *else* part handles *none of the above* or default case where none of the specified expressions are satisfied.

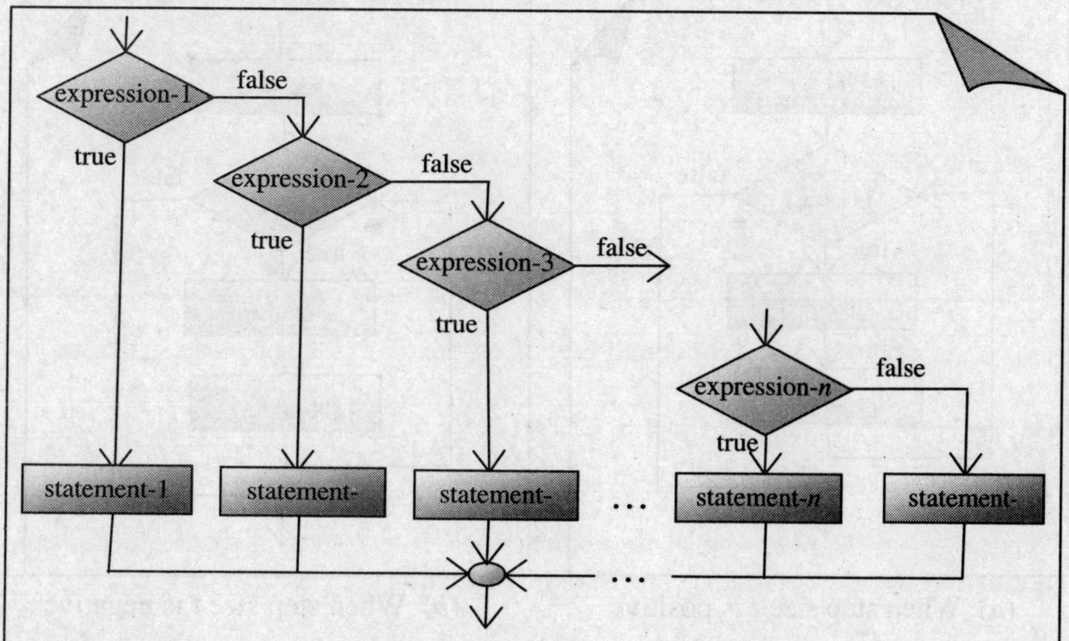

Figure 2.5: Logic flow of *else if* ladder

Iterative logic is used to produce loops when one or more instructions are to be executed several times depending on some expressions. It uses three loop structures called *For* and *While*.

```
   :
   :
For k = r to s in steps of t
   statement
Endfor
   :
   :
```

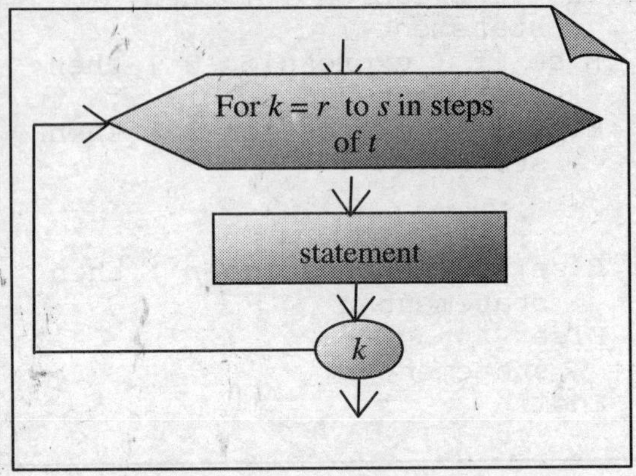

Figure 2.6: Syntax and logic flow for *For* iterative structure

It uses an index variable *k* to control the loop. Here *r* is called the initial value, *s* is called the final value and *t* is called the step size, which may be positive (increment) or negative (decrement).

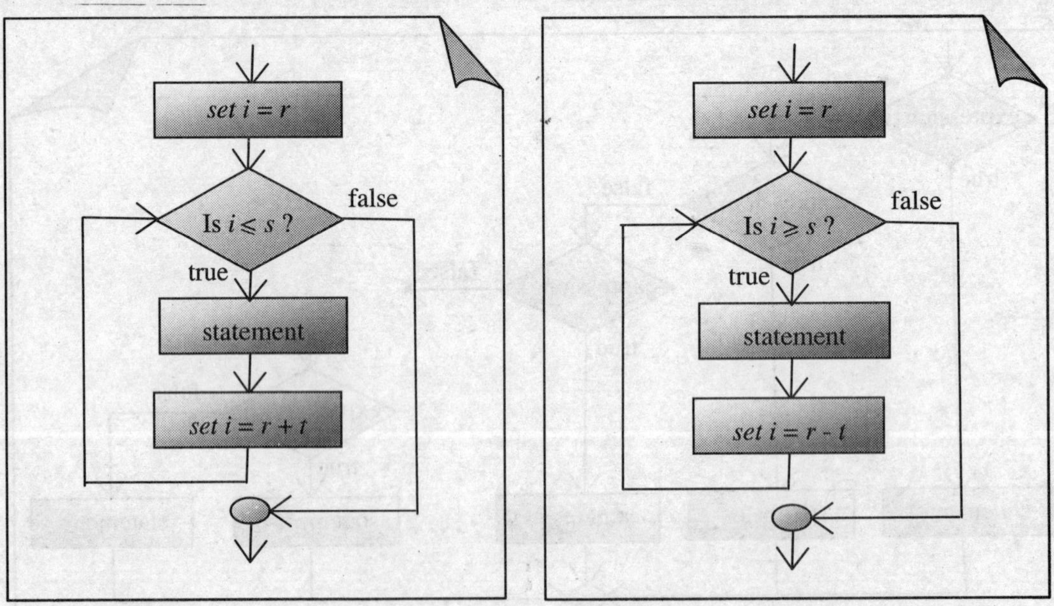

(*a*) When step size *t* is positive (*b*) When step size *t* is negative

Figure 2.7: Logic flow to show internal working of *For* iterative structure

```
    :
    :
While ( expression )
    statement
Endwhile
    :
    :
```

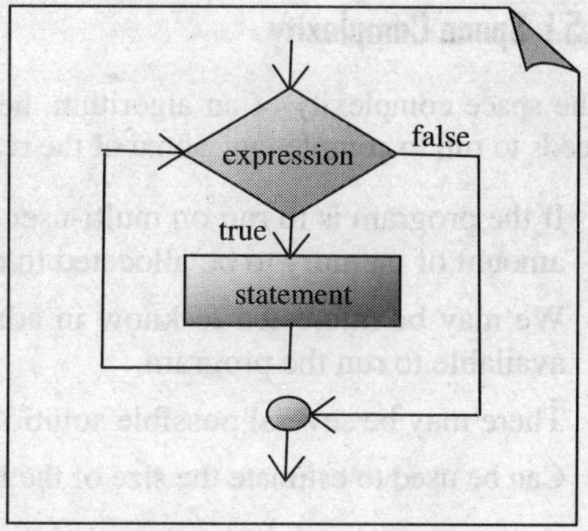

Figure 2.8: Syntax and logic flow of *While* iterative structure

The *For* loop is used when the number of iterations is known, where as the *While* loop is used when the number of iterations is not known.

2.5 ALGORITHM COMPLEXITY

There are basically two aspects of computer programming:

- One is the data organization, *i.e.*, the data structures to represent the data of the problem in hand, and is the subject of the present text.
- The other one involves choosing the appropriate algorithm to solve the problem in hand. Data structures and algorithms are inseparably linked. Once one has developed a firm base in programming techniques required to represent information, it is logical to proceed to more theoretical study of ways to manipulate it.

As an algorithm is a sequence of steps to solve a problem, there may be more than one algorithm to solve a problem. The choice of particular algorithm depends on following considerations:

- Performance requirements, *i.e.*, *time complexity*
- Memory requirements, *i.e.*, *space complexity*

Performance requirements are usually more critical than memory requirements; hence, in general, it is not necessary to worry about memory unless they grow faster than performance requirements. Therefore, in general, the algorithms are analyzed only on the basis of performance requirements, *i.e.*, running-time efficiency.

2.5.1 Space Complexity

The space complexity of an algorithm, hence program, is the amount of memory it needs to run to completion. Some of the reasons for studying space complexity are:

- If the program is to run on multi-user system, it may be required to specify the amount of memory to be allocated to the program.
- We may be interested to know in advance that whether sufficient memory is available to run the program.
- There may be several possible solutions with different space requirements.
- Can be used to estimate the size of the largest problem that a program can solve.

The measure the space complexity, we compute the amount of memory needed for instructions, for constants, simple variables and fixed size structured variables.

2.5.2 Time Complexity

The time complexity of an algorithm is the amount of time it needs to run to completion. Some of the reasons for studying time complexity are:

- We may be interested to know in advance that whether the program will provide a satisfactory real-time response. For example, an interactive program, such as an editor, must provide such a response. If it takes even a few seconds to move the cursor one page up or down, it will not be acceptable to the user.
- There may be several possible solutions with different time requirements.

To measure the time complexity accurately, we can count the all sort of operations performed in an algorithm. If we know the time for each one of the primitive operations performed on a given computer, we can easily compute the time taken by an algorithm to complete its execution. This time will vary from system to system.

Our intention is to estimate the execution time of an algorithm irrespective of the computer on which it will be used. Hence, the more reasonable approach is to identify the key operation and count such operations performed till the program completes its execution. A key operation in our algorithm is an operation that takes maximum time among all possible operations in the algorithm. The time complexity can now be expressed as a function of number of key operations performed.

2.5.3 Time-Space Trade-off

The best algorithm, hence best program, to solve a given problem is one that requires less space in memory and takes less time to complete its execution. But in practice, it is not always possible to achieve both of these objectives. As said earlier, there may be more than one approach to solve a same problem. One such approach may require more space but takes less time to complete its execution while the other approach requires less space but takes more time to complete its execution. Thus, we may have to sacrifice one at the cost of the other. That is what we can say that there exits a *time-space* trade among algorithms.

Therefore, if space is our constraint, then we have to choose a program that requires less space at the cost of more execution time. On the other hand, if time is our constraint such as in real time systems, we have to choose a program that takes less time to complete it execution at the cost of more space.

In the analysis of algorithms, we are interested in the *average case*, the amount of time a program might be expected to take on typical input data, and in the *worst case*, the amount of time a program would take on the worst possible input configuration.

2.5.4 Expressing Space and Time Complexity

Space and/or time complexity is usually expressed in the form of a function $f(n)$, where n is the input size for a given instance of the problem being solved.

Expressing space and/or time complexity as a function $f(n)$ is important because of following reasons:

- We may be interested to predict the rate of growth of complexity as the size of the problem increases.
- To compare the complexities of two or more algorithms solving the same problem in order to find which is more efficient.

The most important notation used to express this function $f(n)$ is *Big Oh* notation, which provides the upper bound for the complexity.

> Since in modern computers, the memory is not a severe constraint, therefore, our analysis of algorithms will be on the basis of time complexity.

2.6 BIG Oh NOTATION

Big Oh is a characterization scheme that allows measuring the properties of algorithms such as performance and/or memory requirements in a general fashion.

The algorithm complexity can be determined ignoring the implementation dependent factors. Eliminating constant factors in the analysis of the algorithms does this. Basically, these are the constant factors that differ from computer to computer. Clearly, the complexity function $f(n)$ of an algorithm increases as n increases. It is the rate of increase of $f(n)$ that we want to examine.

Suppose, $f(n)$ and $g(n)$ are functions defined on positive integer number n, then function $f(n) = O(g(n))$, read as "f of n is big oh of g of n", or as "$f(n)$ is of the order of $g(n)$", if there exists positive constants c and n_0, such that $f(n) \leq c \times g(n)$ for all values of $n \geq n_0$. That is, for all sufficiently large amount of input data ($n > n_0$), $f(n)$ will grow no more than a constant factor than $g(n)$. Thus g is an upper bound, except for a constant factor c on the value of f for all suitably large n, *i.e.*, $n \geq n_0$. While providing an upper bound function g for f, we will use only simple functional forms. These typically contain a single term in n with a multiplicative constant of one.

Table 2.1: Some examples

$g(n)$	$f(n) = O(g(n))$
20	$O(1)$ *i.e.*, Constant
$\frac{1}{2}n^2 + 3$	$O(n^2)$
$500n^2 - 25$	$O(n^2)$
$n^3 + n^2 - 1$	$O(n^3)$
$5n^3 + 3n + 6$	$O(n^3)$

Note that the exact constant values do not matter and that the relationship $f(n) \leq c \times g(n)$ may not hold for small input sizes. Since the purpose of *Big Oh* notation is to compare the algorithms in a general fashion, the anomalies that appear for small input sizes are ignored.

Table 2.2: Rate of growth of some standard functions

n \ $f(n)$	$\log_2 n$	n	n^2	n^3	2^n	$n\log_2 n$
5	3	5	25	125	32	15
10	4	10	100	10^3	10^3	40
100	7	100	10^4	10^6	10^{30}	700
1000	10	10^3	10^6	10^9	10^{300}	10^4

Observe that the logarithmic function $\log_2 n$ grows most slowly, whereas the exponential function 2^n grows most rapidly, and the polynomial function n^k grows according to the exponent k.

2.6.1 Categories of Algorithms

Based on *Big Oh* notation, the algorithms can be categorized as follows:

- Constant time (O(1)) algorithms
- Logarithmic time (O(log$n$)) algorithms
- Linear time (O(n)) algorithms
- Polynomial time (O(n^k), for $k > 1$) algorithms
- Exponential time (O(k^n), for $k > 1$) algorithms

Many algorithms are O($n$log$n$).

2.6.2 Limitations of Big Oh Notation

Big Oh notation has two basic limitations:

- It contains no consideration of programming effort.
- It masks (hides) potentially important constants.

As an example of later limitation, imagine two algorithms, one using $500000n^2$ time, and the other n^3 time. The first algorithm is O(n^2), which implies that it will take less time than the other algorithm which is O(n^3). However, the second algorithm will be faster for $n < 500000$, and this would be faster for many applications.

With these factors in mind, the Big Oh notation will be applied to determine algorithm complexity in this book.

2.7 CONCEPT OF RECURSION

A powerful concept in the development of programs is the ability for a function to refer to itself to solve a problem. This control technique, called *recursion* is an important concept in computer science and is convenient for a variety of problems that would be difficult to solve using iterative constructs such as *for, while* and *do – while* loops. Recursion is used extensively in many of the data structures and algorithms in the present text. Recursive functions can be directly implemented in either of the modern high-level programming language such C/C++/C#/Java. This section introduces recursion and illustrates the recursion through various illustrative examples.

2.7.1 Recursion Defined

In mathematics and computer science, recursion means self -reference. A recursive function, therefore, is a function whose definition is based upon itself. In other words, a function containing either a call statement to itself or a call statement to another function that may eventually may result in a call statement back to the original function, then that function is called a recursive function.

In order that the program should not continue indefinitely, a recursive function must have the following properties:

1. There must be certain criteria, called *base criteria*, for which the function does not call itself.
2. Each time the function does call itself (directly or indirectly), it must be closer to the base criteria, *i.e.*, it uses an argument(s) closer than the one it was given.

A recursive function with these two properties is said be well-defined.

Depth of Recursion

Suppose P is a recursive function. During the execution of a program, which contains P, we associate *level number* with each execution of P as follows. The original execution of P is assigned level 1; and each time P is executed because of recursive call, its level is one more than the level of execution that had made the recursive call.

The *depth* of a recursive function P with given set of arguments refers to the maximum level number of P during its execution.

2.7.2 Examples of Recursive Functions

Let us take some examples of recursive functions.

2.7.2.1 Factorial Function

The factorial of a positive number *n*, written as *n*!, is the product of the positive integers from 1 to *n:*

$$n! = 1.2.3...(n\text{-}2).(n\text{-}1).n \qquad \text{where} \qquad 0! = 1$$

Thus the definition of the iterative version of the factorial function can be written as

$$n! = \begin{cases} 1 & \text{if } n = 0 \\ \prod_{i=1}^{n} i & \text{if } n > 0 \end{cases}$$

From this definition, we have

0! = 1	1! = 1	
2! = 1.2 = 2	3! = 1.2.3 = 6	
4! = 1.2.3.4 = 24	5! = 1.2.3.4.5 = 120	and so on.

Observe that

$$4! = 4.3! = 4.6 = 24 \qquad \text{and} \qquad 5! = 5.4! = 5.24 = 120$$

And this is true for every positive integer *n*; that is

$$n! = n.(n\text{-}1)!$$

Thus, the factorial function can be defined recursively as

$$n! = \begin{cases} 1 & \text{if } n = 0 \\ n.(n-1)! & \text{if } n > 0 \end{cases}$$

This definition of *n*! is recursive, since it refers to itself when it uses (*n*-1)!.

Since, the value of *n*! is explicitly given when *n* = 0. Thus 0 is the base value for *n*. Also, the value of *n*! is defined in terms of a smaller value of *n* which is closer the base value. Thus the factorial function is well defined.

Example 2.2:

Let us compute 4! using recursive definition. This computation requires following steps:

1) 4! = 4.3!
2) 3! = 3.2!
3) 2! = 2.1!
4) 1! = 1.0!
5) 0! = 1
6) 1! = 1.1 = 1
7) 2! = 2.1 = 2
8) 3! = 3.2 = 6
9) 4! = 4.6 = 24

In other words, the above computations can be described in the following steps:

1. This step defines 4! in terms of 3!, so to compute 4!, we need to compute first 3!. Thus we have to postpone the computation of 4! until we compute 3!. This postponement is shown by indenting the next step.
2. This step defines 3! in terms of 2!, so we postpone computing 3!, until we compute 2!.
3. This step defines 2! in terms of 1!, so we postpone computing 2!, until we compute 1!.
4. This step defines 1! in terms of 0!, so we postpone computing 1!, until we compute 0!.
5. This step explicitly compute 0!, since 0 is the base value, and it equals 1.
6. Backtrack and compute 1! using the value of 0!.
7. Backtrack and compute 2! using the value of 1!.
8. Backtrack and compute 3! using the value of 2!.
9. Backtrack further and compute 4! using the value of 3!.

Observe that we backtrack in the reverse order of the original postponed computations. This type of postponed processing lends itself to the use of *stacks*. A stack data structure is described in *Chapter 5*.

In the above example, step 1 belongs to level 1, because it is original call to compute 4!. Hence step 2 belongs to level 2, step 3 belongs to level 3, step 4 to level 4, step 5 to level 5.

On the other hand, step 6 belongs to level 4, since it is the result of a return from level 5. In other words, step 6 and step 4 belongs to same level of execution.

Similarly, step 7 and step 3 belongs to same level, step 8 and step 2 to same level, and step 9 and step 1 to same level number, *i.e.*, level number 1.

Following algorithm computes *n*! recursively.

Algorithm 2.4

Factorial(*result*, *n*)

Recursive sub algorithm that computes the factorial of a positive integer number *n*. It returns its value in the variable *result*.

```
1. If ( n = 0 ) then
      Set result = 1
      Return
   Endif
2. Call Factorial(result, n–1)
3. Set result = n * result
4. Return
```

2.7.2.2. Positive Exponential Power Function

Like factorial function, similar iterative and recursive definitions exist for computing the positive exponential power of a number. Its iterative version is

$$x^n = \begin{cases} 1 & \text{if } n = 0 \\ \prod_{i=1}^{n} x & \text{if } n > 0 \end{cases}$$

where as its recursive version is

$$x^n = \begin{cases} 1 & \text{if } n = 0 \\ x.x^{n-1} & \text{if } n > 0 \end{cases}$$

Following algorithm computes x^n recursively.

Algorithm 2.5

Power(*result, x, n*)

Recursive sub algorithm that computes the positive exponential power *n* of a number *x*. It returns its value in the variable *result*.

```
1. If ( n = 0 ) then
      Set result = 1
      Return
   Endif
2. Call Power(result, x, n-1)
3. Set result = x * result
4. Return
```

2.7.2.3 Fibonacci Numbers

A very important sequence, *Fibonacci sequence,* usually denoted by $F_0, F_1, \ldots, F_n$, is as follows:

0, 1, 1, 2, 3, 5, 8, 13, . . .

That is, $F_0 = 0$ and $F_1 = 1$ and the subsequent terms are the sum of the two preceding terms.

For example, the next term in the above sequence is

$8 + 13 = 21$

A formal definition for Fibonacci number F_n is:

$$\text{fib}(n) = \begin{cases} n & \text{if } n \le 1 \\ \text{fib}(n-1) + \text{fib}(n-2) & \text{if } n > 1 \end{cases}$$

Notice that the recursive definition of the Fibonacci numbers differs from the recursive definitions of the factorial function and positive exponential power function in the sense that it refers to itself twice.

Next algorithm computes F_n recursively.

Algorithm 2.6

FibonacciNumber(*fib*, *n*)

Recursive sub algorithm that computes *n*th Fibonacci number F_n. It returns its value in variable *fib*. Here *fib1* and *fib2* are used as temporary variables.

```
1. If ( (n = 0) or (n = 1) ) then
      Set fib = n
      Return
   Endif
2. Call Fibonacci(fib1,n-2)
3. Call Fibonacci(fib2,n-1)
4. Set fib = fib1 + fib2
5. Return
```

2.7.2.4 Greatest Common Divisor

To find greatest common divisor (GCD) of two positive integers *m* and *n*.

Figure 2.9 demonstrates the continued division method to find the GCD of two positive integer numbers. You must have observed that in successive divisions, the divisor of the previous division becomes dividend, remainder of becomes divisor, and division is again carried out. This process is carried out till the reminder becomes zero, and the current divisor is taken as GCD of the given integer numbers.

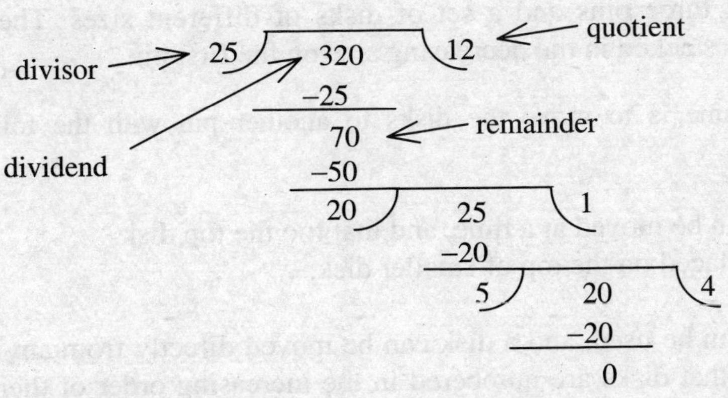

Figure 2.9: Illustration of computational procedure for HCF

A formal definition for GCD is:

$$\gcd(m,n) = \begin{cases} n & \text{if } m \,\%\, n = 0 \\ \gcd(n, m\%n) & \text{if } m \,\%\, n \neq 0 \end{cases}$$

Following algorithm computes *GCD* recursively.

Algorithm 2.7

GCD(*m, n, result*)

Recursive sub algorithm to compute GCD of *m* and *n*. It returns its value in variable *result*.

```
1. If ( m % n = 0 ) then
       Set result = n
       Return
   Else
       Call GCD(n, m % n)
   Endif
2. Return
```

2.7.2.5 Towers of Hanoi

Another famous recursive problem is the *Towers of Hanoi*. This is actually a game consisting of three pins and a set of disks of different sizes. The game starts with the disks stacked in the decreasing size on the first pin.

The aim of this game is to move the disks to another pin with the following constraints:

- Only one disk can be moved at a time, and that too the top disk.
- No disk can be placed on the top of smaller disk.

All the three pins can be used, and a disk can be moved directly from any pin to other one. Assume that disks are numbered in the increasing order of their size. In order to design a general algorithm for solving this problem with *n* disks from pin A to pin C using third pin B, let us look at some examples using few disks.

Case 1: *Given one disk only*

In this case, which is the *base case*, the disk can be directly moved from pin A to pin C as shown in Figure 2.10.

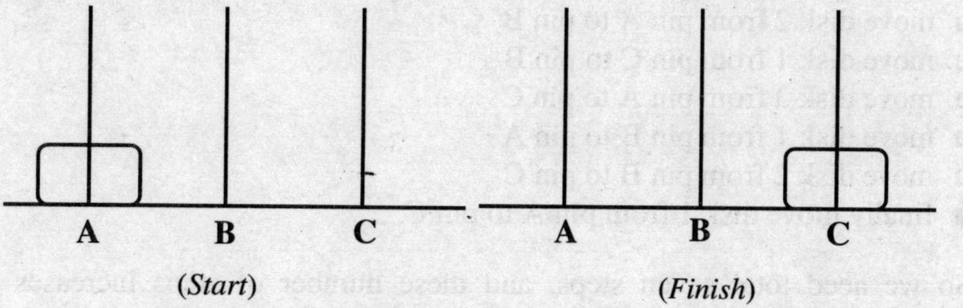

Figure 2.10: Tower of Hanoi for one disk

Case 2: *Given two disks*

In this case, first move disk 1 to pin B, then move disk 2 to pin C. The last step places the disk 1 on the top of disk 2 in pin C.

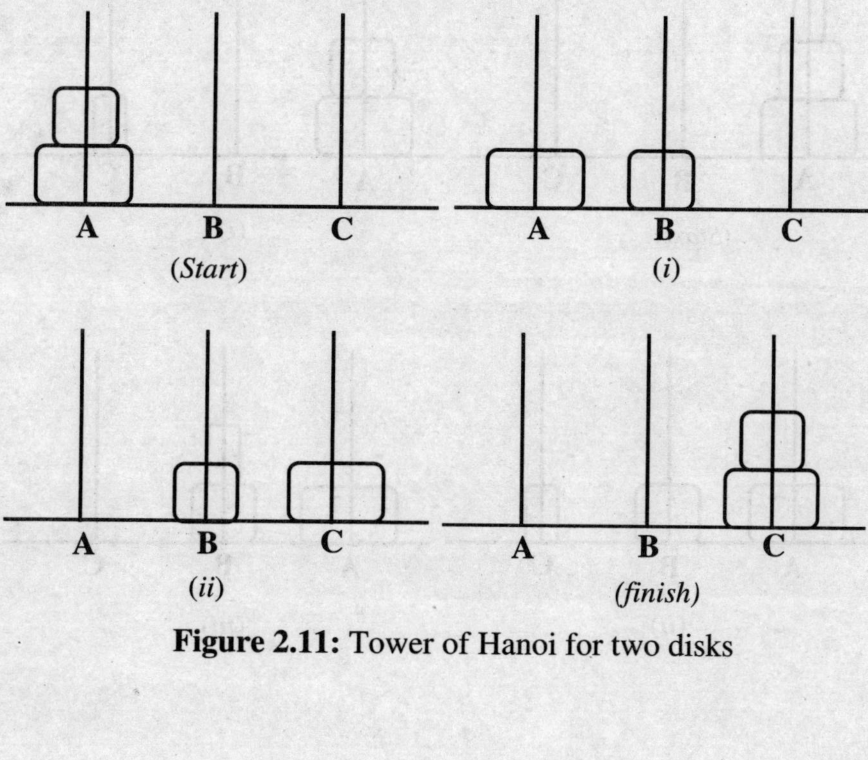

Figure 2.11: Tower of Hanoi for two disks

Case 3: *Given three disks*

In this case, the problem becomes little complex. Proceed as follows:

- move disk 1 from pin A to pin C
- move disk 2 from pin A to pin B
- move disk 1 from pin C to pin B
- move disk 3 from pin A to pin C
- move disk 1 from pin B to pin A
- move disk 2 from pin B to pin C
- finally move disk 1 from pin A to pin C

So we need total seven steps, and these number of steps increases with the increase of number of disks.

These steps are illustrated below.

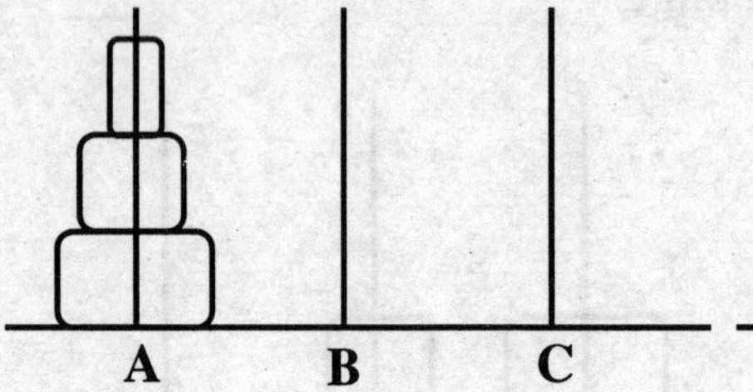

(*Start*)

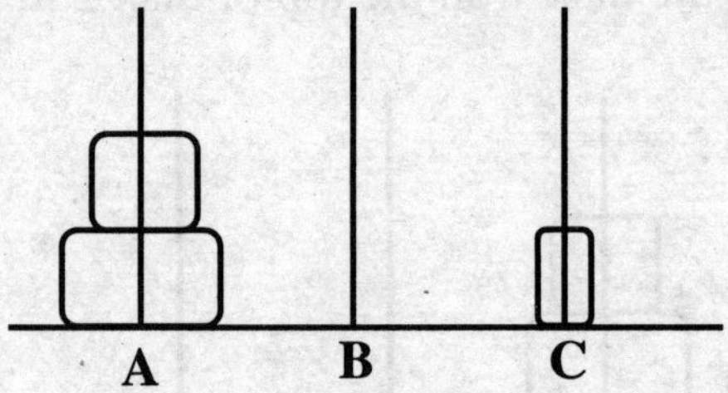

(*i*)

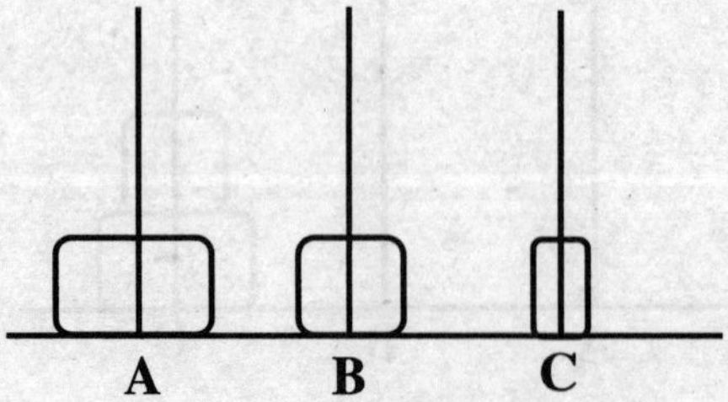

(*ii*)

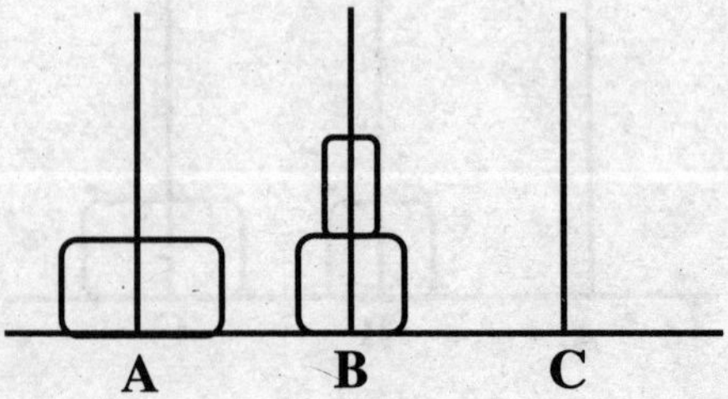

(*iii*)

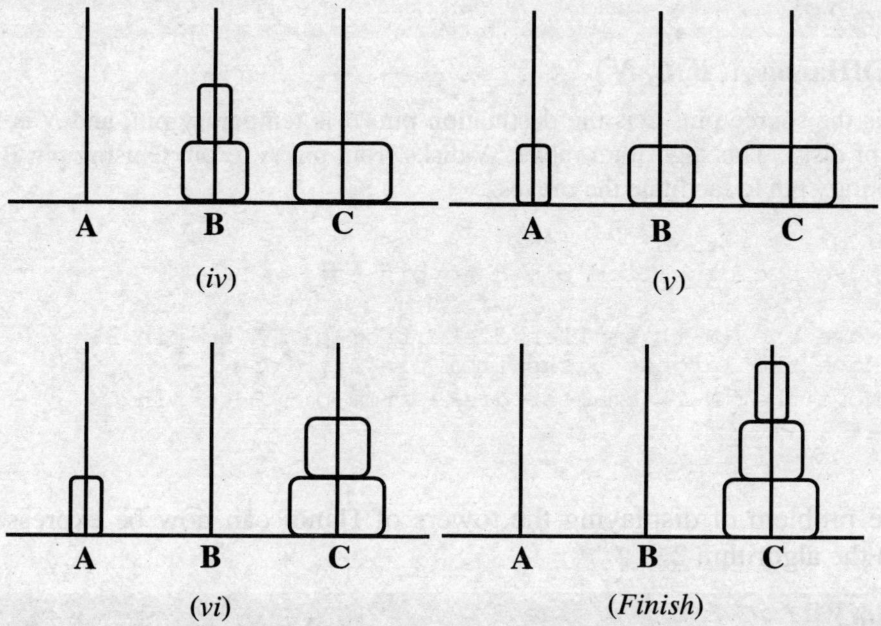

Figure 2.12: Tower of Hanoi for three disks

Having examined the above cases with two or three disks, the following observations can be made:

- In order to move the largest disk from pin A to pin C, we must move the smaller disks that are on the top to pin B.
- Then move the largest disk from pin A to pin C.

Once the largest disk has been moved, we must move, in the similar manner, all the smaller disks to pin C.

We can now describe recursively the required steps needed to move *n* disks from pin A to pin C using pin B as given below:

```
If ( N = 1 ) then
   Move the disk from pin A to pin C
Else
   Move the (N–1) smaller disks from pin A to pin B
   Move the largest disks from pin A to pin C
   Move the (N–1) smaller disks from pin B to pin C
Endif
```

Algorithm 2.8

TowerOfHanoi(*A, B, C, N*)

Here *A* is the source pin, *C* is the destination pin, *B* is temporary pin, and *N* is the number of disks. This algorithm moves *N* disks from pin A to pin C using pin B as the temporary pin to facilitate the moves.

```
1. If ( N = 1 ) then
      Move the disk from pin A to pin C
   Else
      Move the (N-1) smaller disks from pin A to pin B
      Move the largest disks from pin A to pin C
      Move the (N-1) smaller disks from pin B to pin C
   Endif
2. Exit
```

Then, the problem of displaying the towers of Hanoi can now be expressed as shown in the algorithm 2.9.

Algorithm 2.9

Here *N* is the number of disks. This algorithm calls algorithm 2.8 to play the Tower of Hanoi game.

```
1. Read: N                 // enter value of N
2. If ( N < 1 ) then       // test value of N
      Write: "Illegal Input . . ."
   Else
      Call TowerOfHanoi( A, B, C, N )
   Endif
3. Exit
```

2.8 RECURSION, ITERATION OR . . .?

When there are number of ways of solving a problem, the obvious question that arises is *"Which one should be selected?"*. There is no set of pre-defined rules to select a particular way; however, we must consider the following issues:

1. Processing time taken.
2. Computer memory used.
3. Time taken to develop the program.
4. Time taken to debug the program.
5. Time to maintain the program.

As a generalization, recursive solutions tend to do well in categories 3, 4, and 5. Because recursive solutions tend to be simple and small, the time and to modify the programs later on is less than the time needed for non-recursive solution of the same problem, if it does exists.

On the other hand, in general, recursive solutions do not tend to do well in their use of computer processing time and the amount of computer memory they require. When we are writing and running programs on our own computer, we often don't care about the time that a program takes to run as long as it gets finished in a reasonable amount of time. We usually don't care about the memory utilization if the program doesn't require more than the amount of memory that is available in our own computer. However, when we are programming for an environment that allows several programs to execute concurrently (multitasking) or that allows several users to work concurrently (multi-user), we should be very careful about the use of shared processor time and the computer memory resources.

There is no simple formula for obtaining the answer to the question of which one of several solutions for a problem is best. Even, if we have accurate statistics for each of the above categories, it isn't obvious how to compare the sets of numbers. Factors such as predicted life span of the program, frequency of usage, relative importance of the program, and cost of programming and processing must enter into the decision procedure. The field of *Software Engineering*, which beyond the scope of present text, attempts to address categories 3, 4, and 5. The field of *Algorithm Design and Analysis* attempts to address the theoretical aspects of categories 1 and 2, which is also beyond the scope of present text.

2.9 SUPPLEMENTARY PROBLEMS

Problem 2.1:

Formulate an algorithm to display the nature of roots of a quadratic equation of the type

$$ax^2 + bx + c = 0$$

provided $a \neq 0$.

Solution:

We know that the roots of the quadratic equation are given by the formula:

$$x_{1,2} = \frac{-b \pm \sqrt{b^2 - 4ac}}{2a}$$

where the expression $b^2 - 4ac$ is known as the discriminant.

Depending on sign of the discriminant, there are three possibilities for the roots;

1. If $b^2 - 4ac < 0$, then the root are imaginary.
2. If $b^2 - 4ac = 0$, then the roots are real and equal.
3. If $b^2 - 4ac > 0$, then the roots are real and distinct.

The complete algorithm will look like

Algorithm 2.10

This algorithm finds the nature of roots of the given quadratic equation. The user supplies the values of *a*, *b* and *c*, and the algorithm display the message indicating the nature of the roots.

```
1. Read: a, b, c
2. Set disc = b²-4ac
3. If ( disc < 0 ) then
      Write: "Roots are imaginary"
   Else If ( disc > 0 ) then
      Write: "Roots are real and distinct"
   Else
      Write: "Roots are real and equal"
   Endif
4. Exit
```

Problem 2.2:

Fibonacci sequence is given below:

0 1 1 2 3 5 8 13 21 . . .

Formulate an algorithm to generate the above sequence up to the term less than or equal to 100.

Solution:

Observe that, leaving first two terms, each term is obtained as the sum of the immediately preceding two terms.

If we use variable *previous* for previous term, *current* for current term, *next* for next term, and setting *previous* and *current* to values 0 and 1 respectively, *i.e.*, first two terms of the sequence, then the entire sequence can be generated by using the following recurrence relation

> *next* = *previous* + *current*
> replace *previous* by *current*
> replace *current* by *next*

The complete algorithm will look like

Algorithm 2.11

This algorithm generates the fibonacci sequence the term less that or equal to 100. It takes no input from the user.

```
1. Set previous = 0, current = 1
2. Write previous, current
3. Set next = previous + current
4. Repeat steps 5 to 8 While ( next ≤ 100 )
5.    Write: next
6.    Set previous = current
7.    Set current = next
8.    Set next = previous + current
   Endwhile
9. Exit
```

Problem 2.3:

Program to find whether the given positive number *n* is a prime number or not.

Solution:

A positive integer number is said to be prime if it divisible by 1 and itself only, *i.e.*, it cannot be factorized. In addition, to this definition, an even number except 2 is not a prime number.

Therefore, our test criteria becomes

1. If *n* is greater than 2 and is even then *n* is not a prime number.
2. If test at step 1 fails, then we try to divide number *n* by factors $k = 3, 5, 7, \ldots \sqrt{n}$. Therefore, if *n* is divisible by any value of *k*, number *n* is not a prime number.
3. If test at step 2 also fails, then *n* is a prime number.

The following algorithm implements this criterion.

Algorithm 2.12

This algorithm checks whether the given number *n* is prime or not. The number *n* will be supplied by the user as input.

```
1. Read n
2. If ( ( n > 0 ) and ( n % 2 = 0 ) then
      Write: n, "is not a prime number"
      Exit
   Endif
3. Set m = √n
4. Set k = 3
5. Repeat steps 6 and 7 While ( k ≤ m )
6.    If ( n % k = 0 ) then
         Write: n, "is not a prime number"
         Exit
      Endif
7.    Set k = k + 2
   Endwhile
8. Write: n, "is a prime number"
9. Exit
```

Problem 2.4:

Income tax for individuals is computed on slab rates as follows:

Income	Tax Payable
Upto Rs. 1,00,000/-	Nil
From Rs. 1,00,001/- to Rs. 2,00,000/-	10% of the excess over Rs. 1,00,000/-
From Rs. 2,00,001/- to Rs. 3,00,000/-	20% of the excess over Rs. 2,00,000/-
Above Rs. 3,00,000/-	30% of the excess over Rs. 3,00,000/-

Develop an algorithm that reads the income and prints the income tax due.

Solution:

Note the following:

- If the income is upto Rs. 1,00,000/- only, then the tax is *nil.*
- If the income is in the range of Rs. 1,00,001/- to Rs. 2,00,000/-, then the tax is 10% of the amount in excess of Rs. 1,00,000/-.
- If the income is in the range of Rs. 2,00,001/- to Rs. 3,00,000/-, then the tax is 10% of Rs. 1,00,000/- (Rs. 10,000/-) for a slab of Rs. 1,00,001 to Rs. 2,00,000/- plus 20% of the amount in excess of Rs. 2,00,000/-.
- If the income is more than Rs. 3,00,000/-, then the tax is 10% of Rs. 1,00,000/- (Rs. 10,000/-) for a slab of Rs. 1,00,001 to Rs. 2,00,000/- plus 20% of Rs. 1,00,000/- (Rs. 20,000/-) for a slab of Rs. 2,00,001 to Rs. 3,00,000/- plus 30% of the amount in excess of Rs. 3,00,000/-.

Let us have hands on by computing the tax if the given income is

(*i*) Rs. 2,50,000/- (*ii*) Rs. 1,75,000/- (*iii*) Rs. 3,20,000/-

Tax Computations for income of Rs. 2,50,000/-

For first Rs. 1,00,000/-	Tax is Nil
For next Rs. 1,00,000/-	Tax is 10,000/- (@ 10%)
For next Rs. 50,000/-	Tax is 10,000/- (@ 20%)
Total Tax due	**Rs. 20,000/-**

Tax Computations for income of Rs. 1,75,000/-

For first Rs.1,00,000/-	Tax is Nil
For next Rs. 75,000/-	Tax is 7,500/- (@ 10%)
Total Tax due	**Rs. 7,500/-**

Tax Computations for income of Rs. 3,20,000/-

For first Rs. 1,00,000/-	Tax is Nil
For next Rs. 1,00,000/-	Tax is 10,000/- (@ 10%)
For next Rs. 1,00,000/-	Tax is 20,000/- (@ 20%)
For next Rs. 20,000/-	Tax is 6,000/- (@ 30%)
Total Tax due	**Rs. 36,000/-**

The following algorithm implements this criterion.

Algorithm 2.14

This algorithm computes the income tax due on the gross salary, as per the specified policy.

```
1. Read: income
2. If ( income <= 100000 ) then
      Set tax = 0
   Else If (income <= 200000 ) then
      Set tax = ( income - 100000 ) *0.1
   Else If (income <= 300000 ) then
      Set tax = 10000 + ( income - 200000 ) *0.2
   Else
      Set tax = 30000 + ( income - 300000 ) *0.3
   Endif
3. Write: "Income tax payable = ", tax
4. Exit
```

SUMMARY

In this chapter, we have learnt about the

- algorithms and sub-algorithms.
- algorithmic notation.
- algorithm complexity, its objectives and various factors contributing to it.
- big Oh notation.
- time-space tradeoff.
- categories of algorithms based on Big Oh notation.
- limitations of Big Oh notation.
- important concept of recursion.
- depth of recursion.
- popular recursive problems and recursive algorithms for these problems.

REVIEW EXERCISES

1. What is an *algorithm*? What is the criterion that every algorithm must satisfy?
2. What is a *sub-algorithm*? How is it helpful?
3. Describe various control structures.
4. What is *algorithm complexity*? What is the need of measuring the complexity of an algorithm?

5. What do you mean by *time-space trade-off* among algorithms?
6. When we way that each step of the algorithm must be definite, what does it mean?
7. Which notation is popularly used to express the complexity of an algorithm?
8. Describe the *Big Oh* notation.
9. Name the different categories of algorithms based on *Big Oh* notation.
10. What are the limitations of *Big Oh* notation?
11. Describe recursion.
12. What is meant by depth of recursion?
13. Give the recursive definition of combination function $C(n, r)$.

PROGRAMMING EXERCISES

1. Formulate an algorithm to compute the roots of a quadratic equation of the type

   $$ax^2 + bx + c = 0 \qquad \text{provided } a \neq 0.$$

2. Fibonacci sequence is given below:

   0 1 1 2 3 5 8 13 21 . . .

   Formulate an algorithm to generate first n terms of this sequence.
3. Formulate an algorithm to print all prime numbers between m and n, where $m < n$.
4. Formulate an algorithm to find the least common factor (LCF) of two positive integer m and n. [**Hint:** Compute GCF using long division as in problem 13, use formula, $LCF(m,n) = \dfrac{m \times n}{GCF(m,n)}$]
5. Formulate an algorithm to evaluate a polynomial of type

   $$a_n x^n + a_{n-1} x^{n-1} + a_{n-2} x^{n-2} + ... + a_2 x^2 + a_1 x + a_0$$

   where $a_n \neq 0$. This is n^{th} degree polynomial.
6. Formulate an algorithm to find the sum of m integers starting from nth integer.
7. Suppose an amount p is deposited in a commercial bank, which pays compound interest at the rate of r% annually, for n years. Formulate an algorithm that prints the amount in account after each year.

8. A department store places an order with a company for *n* pieces of miners, *m* pieces of toasters, and *p* number of fans. The cost of items are as follows:

Item Description	Price per Unit (in Rupees)
Miners	1,500
Toaster	200
Fan	450

The discount allowed for various items are 5% for miners, 15% for fan, and 10% for toaster. The company charge 10% as sales tax on all items on net value after deducting the discount. Formulate an algorithm that reads *m*, *n*, and *p* and computes the amount to be paid by the store.

9. An employer plans to pay a bonus to all employees, where number of employees is 50. A bonus of 10% is to be paid to employees with earning at least Rs. 2000/- and 20% of the earning to others. The input contains name and earnings of an employee and the desired output is name and bonus to be paid to the employee. Draw flowchart or formulate algorithm or write pseudocode, whichever is your choice, for logical steps needed to accomplish the above task.

10. Formulate an algorithm to obtain solution of following pair of equations:

$ax + by = c$

$px + qy = r$ assuming that *a*, *b*, *c*, *p*, *q*, and *r* are non-zero.

11. The number 1991 is a palindrome because it is the same number when read forward or backward. Formulate an algorithm to find whether the given number *n* is palindrome or not.

12. The monthly telephone bill is to be computed as follows:

    Minimum Rs. 200 for upto 100 calls
    plus Rs. 0.60 per call for next 50 calls
    plus Rs. 0.50 per call for next 50 calls
    plus Rs. 0.40 per call for any call beyond 200 calls.

    The input contains name of the customer and number of calls made and the desired output is the name and telephone bill to be paid by the customer. Draw a flowchart for logical steps needed to accomplish the above task.

13. Program to check whether given +ve integer number is an Armstrong number.

    [**Hint:** A positive integer number is an Armstrong number if the sum of cubes of its digits equals the number itself. For example, number 153 is an Armstrong number since $1^3 + 5^3 + 3^3 = 1 + 125 + 27 = 153$]

14. Suppose the postal rates for mailing letters are as follows:

    Rs. 0.50 per 10 grams for the first 50 grams,
    Rs. 0.40 per 10 grams for the next 100 grams,
    Rs. 0.25 per 10 grams for the next 250 grams, and
    Rs. 25 per kilogram for letters weighing more than 400 grams.

    Write a program that prompts for weight of a letter and prints the postage to be paid.

15. The *Ackerman* function is defined recursively, for all non-negative values of m and n, as follows:

$$A(m,n) = \begin{cases} n+1 & \text{if } m = 0 \\ A(m-1,1) & \text{if } m \neq 0 \text{ but } n = 0 \\ A(m-1, A(m,n-1)) & \text{if } m \neq 0 \text{ and } n \neq 0 \end{cases}$$

    Find $A(1,3)$.

❑ ❑ ❑

Chapter 3

Arrays

Learning Objectives

After reading this chapter, students will be able to

- explain the concept of arrays
- explain the way arrays are represented in memory
- explain the way elements of an array are accessed
- explain the operations performed on arrays
- explain the limitations of arrays
- explain the application of linear arrays
- develop algorithms for performing any kind of operation on arrays

3.1 INTRODUCTION

An *array* is a collection of homogeneous data elements (i.e. elements of same type) described by a single name. Each element of an array is referenced by a subscripted variable formed by affixing to the array name a subscript or index enclosed in parentheses. The term subscript has the same meaning as in the mathematical notations. If single subscript is required to reference an element of an array, the array is known as *one-dimensional array* or *linear array*, and if two subscripts are required to reference an element, the array is known as *two-dimensional array*, and so on. Analogously, the arrays whose elements are referenced by two or more subscripts are called *multi-dimensional arrays*.

This chapter describes the different types of arrays and various operations that can be performed on arrays.

3.2 LINEAR ARRAYS

A linear array *a* is a list of a finite number *n* of homogeneous data elements such that

- The elements of the array are referenced by an index set consisting of *n* consecutive integer numbers.
- The elements of the array are stored in consecutive memory locations.

The number *n* of the elements is called the *size* of the array. In general, if *lb* is the smallest index called the *lower bound*, and *ub* is the largest index called *upper bound*, then size of the array is given by

```
size = ub − lb + 1
```

Note that the size of the array = *ub* if *lb* = 1.

Suppose *a* is the name of the linear array of size *n*, then its *k*th elements is denoted as

a_k	in subscript/mathematical notation
$a(k)$	in BASIC and FORTRAN languages, called parentheses notation
$a[k]$	in Pascal, C/ C++ and Java languages, called bracket notation

The number *k* in $a(k)$ or $a[k]$ is called a *subscript* and $a(k)$ or $a[k]$ is itself called a *subscripted variable*.

> In the present text, we will be using the bracket notation as it is also used in C/C++ languages, the languages of your implementation. Further, if an array is declared with size *n*, then its lower bound *lb* will be taken as 0 and upper bound *ub* as (*n*–1).

Index set is dependent on language being used to implement arrays. For example

- In BASIC language or FORTRAN language, if arrays size is *n*, the index set consists of 1, 2, 3, . . ., *n*.
- In Pascal language, we have to specify the lower bound and upper bound for the array.
- In C/ C++ and Java languages, if array size is *n*, the index set consists of 0, 1, 2, . . ., *n*–1.

3.2.1 Representing Linear Arrays in Memory

Recall that the memory of the microcomputer is simply a sequence of addressed locations as pictured in Figure 3.1.

Let *a* be a linear array with *n* elements. As arrays are stored in consecutive memory location, the system need not keep track of the address of every element of *a*, but needs to keep track of the address of first element only. The address of the first element is also known as the *base address* of the array, and is denoted by *base*(*a*).

Using this base address, the computer computes the address of the *k*th element, *loc*(*a*[*k*]), using the following formula:

$$loc(a[k]) = base(a) + w\,(k - lb) \qquad \text{in general}$$

$$loc(a[k]) = base(a) + w * k \qquad \text{in C/C++ languages}$$

where *w* is the number of bytes per storage location for one element of the array. Observe that the time taken to compute *loc*(*a*[*k*]) is essentially the same for any value of *k*.

Hence, computer takes same time to access any element of the array. Furthermore, by giving any value to *k*, one can access any element of the array without scanning other elements of array *a*.

Example 3.1:

Consider that array a is declared as array of integers with size 10, and its first element is stored at memory address 1197, *i.e.*, its base address is 1197, as pictured in Figure 3.2. We know that an integer number requires two bytes of memory, therefore, address of the element for $k = 3$, where k can take values from 0 to 9, is given by

$loc(a[3]) = 1197 + 2 * 3 = 1201$ [Example of C/C++ implementation]

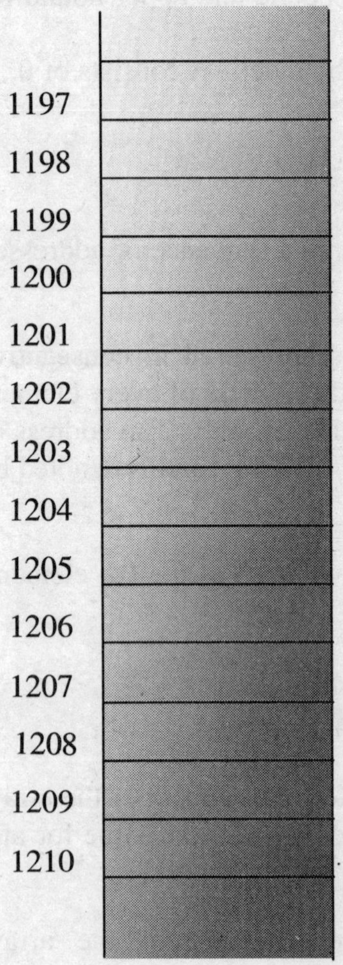

Figure 3.1: Computer Memory Map

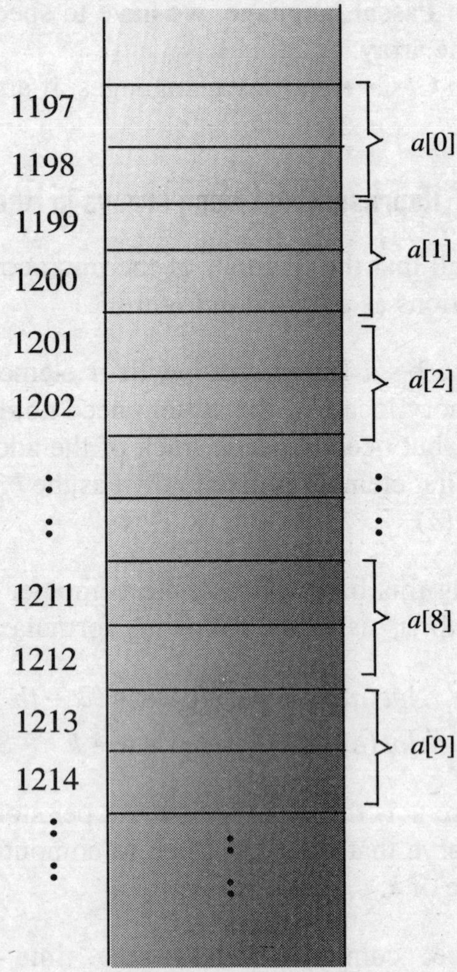

Figure 3.2: Storage of array *a* of integers

3.2.2 Operations on Linear Arrays

All the operations (traversal, search, insertion, deletion, sorting, and merging) introduced in *Chapter 1* can be performed on linear arrays. Their implementation is described below.

3.2.2.1 Traversal Operation

Traversing is the process of visiting each element of the array exactly once. Traversal of a linear array is very simple and straightforward. As elements of linear array can be accessing directly, only we have to vary an index from lower bound to upper bound in steps of one to access individual elements in order.

The following algorithms summarize the various steps. The algorithm 3.1*a* uses *While* structure to setup a loop while algorithm 3.1*b* uses *For* structure for setting up a loop.

Algorithm 3.1a

TraverseLinearArray(*a*, *n*)

Here *a* is a linear array of size *n*. This algorithm traverses the array and applies the operation *process* to each element of the array.

```
1. Set i = 0                              // Initialize counter
2. Repeat steps 3 and 4 While i ≤ (n−1)
3.     Apply process ( a[i] )             // visit element
4.     Set i = i + 1                      // increment counter
   Endwhile
5. Exit
```

Algorithm 3.1b

TraverseLinearArray(*a*, *n*)

Here *a* is a linear array of size *n*. This algorithm traverses the array and applies the operation *process* to each element of the array.

```
1. Repeat step 2 For i = 0 to (n−1) in steps of +1
2.     Apply process ( a[i] )          // visit element
   Endfor
3. Exit
```

Performance Analysis

As you must have observed in the above code that to access the elements the index is varied from lower bound to upper bound. Also we know that the time to access individual element is same irrespective of its position in the array. Therefore, for an array of size *n*, *for* loop executes *n* times. Thus, the traversal operation on linear arrays is $O(n)$ operation.

3.2.2.2 Search Operation

Searching is the process of finding the location of given element in the linear array. The search is said to be successful if the given element is found i.e. the element does exists in the array; otherwise unsuccessful.

There are two approaches to search operation:

- Linear search
- Binary search

The algorithm that one chooses generally depends on organization of the array elements. If the elements are in random order, then one have to use linear search technique, and if the array elements are sorted, then it is preferable to use binary search technique. These two search techniques are described in the next sections.

3.2.2.2.1 Linear Search

Given no information about the array *a*, the only way to search for given element *item* is to compare *item* with each element of *a* one by one. This method, which traverses *a* sequentially to locate *item* is called *linear search* or *sequential search*.

Algorithm 3.2

LinearSearch(*a*, *n*, *item*, *loc*)

Here *a* is a linear array of size *n*. This algorithms finds the location of the element *item* in linear array *a*. If search ends in success it sets *loc* to the index of the element; otherwise it sets *loc* to –1.

```
1. Set i = 0                        // Initialize counter
2. Repeat steps 3 and 4 While ( i ≤ (n–1) )
3.     If ( a[i] = item ) then
          Set loc = I               // element found at location i
          Exit
       Endif
```

```
4.     Set i = i + 1              // increment counter
   Endwhile
5. Set loc = −1                   // element not found
6. Exit
```

Performance Analysis

In the best possible case, the *item* may occur at first position. In this case, the search operation terminates in success with just one comparison. However, the worst case occurs when either the item is present at last position or missing from the array. In the former case, the search terminates in success with n comparisons. In the later case, the search terminates in a failure with n comparisons. Thus, we find that in worst case the linear search is $O(n)$ operations.

3.2.2.2.2 Binary Search

Suppose the elements of the array A are sorted in ascending order (if the elements are numbers) or dictionary order (if the elements are strings). The best searching algorithm, called *binary search,* is used to find the location of the given element. We do use this approach in our daily life. For example, suppose we want to find the meaning of the term *modem* in a computer dictionary. Obviously, we don't search page by page. We open the dictionary in the middle (roughly) to determine which half contains the term being sought. Then for the subsequent search one half is discarded, and we search in the other half. This process is continued till either we have located the required term or that term is missing from the dictionary, which will indicated by the fact that at the end we will be left with only one page.

Example 3.2:

To illustrate the working of the binary search technique, consider the following sorted array A with 7 elements

3, 10, 15, 20, 35, 40, 60

and we want to search element 15.

Solution:

Given Array *a*

a[0]	a[1]	a[2]	a[3]	a[4]	a[5]	a[6]
3	10	15	20	35	40	60

To start with, we take *beg* = 0, *end* = 6, and compute location of middle element as

$$mid = (beg + end) / 2 = (0 + 6) / 2 = 3$$

Since *a*[*mid*], *i.e.*, *a*[3] ≠ 15, and *beg* < *end*. We start next iteration.

As *a*[*mid*] = 20 > 15, therefore, we take *end* = *mid* – 1 = 3 – 1 = 2, where as *beg* remains unchanged. Thus

$$mid = (beg + end) / 2 = (0 + 2) / 2 = 1$$

Since *a*[*mid*], *i.e.*, *a*[1] ≠ 15, and *beg* < *end*. We start next iteration.

As *a*[*mid*] = 10 < 15, therefore, we take *beg* = *mid* + 1 = 1 + 1 = 2, where as *end* remains unchanged.

Since *beg* = *end*, again compute location of the middle element as

$$mid = (beg + end) / 2 = (2 + 2) / 2 = 2$$

Since *a*[*mid*], *i.e.*, *a*[2] = 15, the search terminates on success.

The element is found at index 2.

Algorithm 3.3

BinarySearch(*a*, *n*, *item*, *loc*)

Here *a* is a linear array of size *n*. This algorithms finds the location of the element *item* in sorted (ascending) linear array *a*. If search ends in success it sets *loc* to the index of the element; otherwise it sets loc to –1. Here variables *beg* and *end* to keep track of the first element and last element of the array to be searched, and variable *mid* is used as index of the middle element of the array under consideration.

```
1. Set beg = 0
2. Set end = n-1
```

```
3. Set mid = ( beg + end ) / 2
4. Repeat steps 5 and 6 While ((beg ≤ end) and (a[mid] ≠ item))
5.     If ( item < a[mid] ) then
           Set end = mid-1
       Else
           Set beg = mid+1
       Endif
6.     Set mid = ( beg + end ) / 2
   Endwhile
7. If ( beg > end ) then
       Set loc = -1                 // element not found
   Else
       Set loc = mid                // element found at location mid
   Endif
8. Exit
```

Performance Analysis

In each iteration, the search is reduced to one half of the array. Therefore, for n elements in the array, there will be $\log_2 n$ iterations or recursive calls. Thus, the complexity of binary search is $O(\log_2 n)$. This complexity will be same irrespective of the position of the element, even if it is not present in the array.

3.2.2.3 Insert Operation

Insertion refers to the operation of adding an element to existing list of elements. After insertion the size of the linear array is increased by factor of one. Insertion is possible only if the memory space allocated is large enough to accommodate the additional element. Inserting an element at the end of the linear array can be done very easily. However, to insert an element at any other location, the elements are to be moved downward to new locations to accommodate the new element and keep the order of other elements. The term *downward* refers to locations with larger subscripts.

3.2.2.3.1 Inserting at Given Position

Suppose we want to insert an element at position k. In this case, first we have to move elements starting from kth position down by one position in order to accommodate the element at kth position.

Algorithm 3.4

InsertAtGivenPosition(***a, n, item, k*** **)**

Here *a* is a linear array of size *n*. This algorithm inserts new element *item* at index *k*. The size of the array is also increased by 1.

```
1. Set i = n-1                       //Initialize counter
2. Repeat steps 3 and 4 While ( i ≥ k )
3.    Set a[i+1] = a[i]              //move element down (towards higher index)
4.    Set i = i - 1                  //decrement counter
   Endwhile
5. Set a[k] = item                   // insert the new element at index 'k'
6. Set n = n + 1                     // increase the size of the array
7. Exit
```

3.2.2.3.2 Inserting in a Sorted Array

Let us assume that array under consideration is sorted on ascending order. In this case, the best possible approach is to move the elements of the array down one by one till the first element of the array less than the element to be inserted is encountered. Then the new element is inserted to the right of this element. For example, if the element at the *i*th index is less than the element to be inserted, then the new element is inserted at index (*i*+1)th index.

Algorithm 3.5

InsertInSortedArray(***a, n, item*** **)**

Here *a* is a linear array of size *n* that is sorted in ascending order. This algorithm inserts new element *item* at its desired position so that array remains sorted. The size of the array is also increased by 1.

```
1. Set i = n-1                       // Initialize counter
2. Repeat steps 3 and 4 While ( item < a[i] ) and ( i ≥ 0 )
3.    Set a[i+1] = a[i]              // move element down (towards higher index)
4.    Set i = i - 1                  // decrement counter
   Endwhile
5. Set a[i+1] = item                 // insert the new element at its position
6. Set n = n + 1                     // increase the size of the array
7. Exit
```

In the test condition of *While* structure, an additional condition ($i \geq 0$), is added to avoid the index falling to a negative value. When *i* becomes equal to –1, it means that the new element is smaller that all the elements in the array, therefore, it must be inserted at the first position.

Performance Analysis

The best possible case occurs when the *item* is inserted at the last position. In this case, no element is moved down. The worst case occurs when the element is to be inserted at the first position. In this case, all the elements (n in number) are moved down. Therefore, while loop executes n time, each time moving one element down. Thus, complexity of insertion operation is $O(n)$, *i.e.*, linear time.

3.2.2.4 Delete Operation

Deletion refers to the operation of removing an element from existing list of elements. After deletion the size of the linear array is decreased by factor of one. Like insertion operation, deleting an element from the end of the linear array can be done very easily. However, to delete an element from any other location, the elements are to be moved upward in order to fill up the location vacated by the removed element. The term *upward* refers to locations with smaller subscripts.

3.2.2.4.1 Deleting from Given Position

Suppose we want to delete an element from position k In this case, we have to move elements starting from (k+1)th position up by one position to fill the hole created by deleted element from kth position.

Algorithm 3.6

DeleteFromGivenPosition(*a, n, k, item*)

Here a is a linear array of size n. This algorithm removes element at index k and assigns it to variable *item* that may be required for further processing. The size of the array is also decreased by 1.

```
1. Set item = a[k]
2. Set i = k                // Initialize counter
3. Repeat steps 4 and 5 While ( i < (n-1) )
4.    Set a[i] = a[i+1]    // move element up (towards lower index)
5.    Set i = i + 1         // increment counter
   Endwhile
6. Set n = n - 1            // decrease the size of the array
7. Exit
```

3.2.2.4.2 Deleting from a Sorted Array

In this case, first we have to find the position, say *k*, from where the given element is to be deleted and then starting from (*k*+1)th position, the elements are moved up by one position in order to fill the hole created at *k*th position.

Algorithm 3.7

DeleteFrom SortedArray(*a*, *n*, *item*)

Here *a* is a linear array of size *n* that is sorted in ascending order. This algorithm removes element *item* from the sorted array. This algorithm calls algorithm *BinarySearch* to find the location, say *loc*, of item in the array. The size of the array is also decreased by 1.

```
1. Call BinarySearch( a, n, item, loc )
2. Set i = loc                  // Initialize counter
3. Repeat steps 4 and 5 While ( i < (n-1) )
4.     Set a[i] = a[i+1]        // move element up (towards lower index)
5.     Set i = i + 1            // increment counter
   Endwhile
6. Set n = n - 1                // decrease the size of the array
7. Exit
```

Performance Analysis

The best possible case occurs when the *item* is deleted from the last position. In this case, no element is moved up. The worst case occurs when the element is deleted from the first position. In this case, almost all the elements (*n*–1 in number) are moved up. Therefore, the while loop executes *n*–1 times, each time moving one element down. Thus, the complexity of deletion operation is also O(*n*), *i.e.*, linear time.

3.2.2.5 Sort Operation

Sorting is the process of arranging the elements of the array in some logical order. This logical order may be ascending or descending in case of numeric values or dictionary order in case of alphanumeric values. We do, almost, use this process daily in our routine activities. For example, we do arrange our class notes in increasing order of date in order to refer them quickly later on. Like this there are many situations, which you can enumerate.

In this section, we will discuss one very popular technique, *Bubble sort*, to sort an array *a* with *n* elements in ascending order. More sorting methods, as per the syllabus, are discussed in *Chapter 8*.

Bubble Sort Method

The Bubble sort method requires $(n-1)$ pass to sort an array. In each pass every element $a[i]$ is compared with $a[i+1]$, for $i = 0$ to $(n-k)$, where k is the pass number and if they are out of order, *i.e.*, if $a[i] > a[i+1]$, they are swapped. This will cause the largest element move or bubble up. Thus after the end of first pass the largest element in the array will be placed in nth position, and on each successive pass, the next largest element is placed at position $(n-1)$, $(n-2)$, $(n-2)$, ..., 4, 3, 2, respectively.

For more clarity, carefully examine the following steps.

Pass 1.

Step 1. If $a[0] > a[1]$ then swap $a[0]$ and $a[1]$.
Step 2. If $a[1] > a[2]$ then swap $a[1]$ and $a[2]$.
⋮
Step n–1. If $a[n-2] > a[n-1]$ then swap $a[n-2]$ and $a[n-1]$.

Pass 2.

Step 1. If $a[0] > a[1]$ then swap $a[0]$ and $a[1]$.
Step 2. If $a[1] > a[2]$ then swap $a[1]$ and $a[2]$.
⋮
Step n–2. If $a[n-3] > a[n-2]$ then swap $a[n-3]$ and $a[n-2]$.

⋮

Pass *k*.

Step 1. If $a[0] > a[1]$ then swap $a[0]$ and $a[1]$.
Step 2. If $a[1] > a[2]$ then swap $a[1]$ and $a[2]$.
⋮
Step n–k. If $a[n-k+1] > a[n-k]$ then swap $a[n-k+1]$ and $a[n-k]$.

⋮

Pass *n*–1.

Step 1. If $a[0] > a[1]$ then swap $a[0]$ and $a[1]$.

After (n-1) passes, the complete array will be sorted in the desired order.

Example 3.3:

To illustrate working of bubble sort method, consider the sorting of the following array in ascending order.

30 25 45 60 10 35

Solution:

Note that, the output of a given pass becomes the input for the next pass. The sorting process is self explanatory. In each pass, one element, shown as shaded, reaches to its final position.

Given array can be shown as

a[0]	*a*[1]	*a*[2]	*a*[3]	*a*[4]	*a*[5]
30	25	45	60	10	35

Pass-1:

a[0]	*a*[1]	*a*[2]	*a*[3]	*a*[4]	*a*[5]
(30)	(25)	45	60	10	35

(*a*) Compare *a*[0] and *a*[1]. Since *a*[0] > *a*[1] (30 > 25), swap them.

a[0]	*a*[1]	*a*[2]	*a*[3]	*a*[4]	*a*[5]
25	(30)	(45)	60	10	35

(*b*) Compare *a*[1] and *a*[2]. Since *a*[1] < *a*[2] (30 < 45), no swap.

a[0]	*a*[1]	*a*[2]	*a*[3]	*a*[4]	*a*[5]
25	30	(40)	(60)	10	35

(*c*) Compare *a*[2] and *a*[3]. Since *a*[2] < *a*[3] (40 < 60), no swap.

a[0]	*a*[1]	*a*[2]	*a*[3]	*a*[4]	*a*[5]
25	30	40	(60)	(10)	35

(*d*) Compare *a*[3] and *a*[4]. Since *a*[3] > *a*[4] (60 > 40), swap them.

a[0]	*a*[1]	*a*[2]	*a*[3]	*a*[4]	*a*[5]
25	30	40	10	(60)	(35)

(*e*) Compare *a*[4] and *a*[5]. Since *a*[4] > *a*[5] (60 > 35), swap them.

a[0]	*a*[1]	*a*[2]	*a*[3]	*a*[4]	*a*[5]
25	30	40	10	35	60

Thus, after first pass, the largest element, 60, has moved to its final position. However, the rest of the numbers, which may have changed their positions, are yet to be sorted. The shaded part shows the elements that have been sorted.

For the remaining passes, only comparisons and swaps, if required, are shown.

Pass-2:

a[0]	*a*[1]	*a*[2]	*a*[3]	*a*[4]	*a*[5]	Action
(25)	(30)	40	10	35	60	No swap
25	(30)	(40)	10	35	60	No swap
25	30	(40)	(10)	35	60	Swap
25	30	10	(40)	(35)	60	Swap
23	30	10	35	40	60	

After second pass, the second largest element, 40, has moved to its final position.

Pass-3:

a[0]	a[1]	a[2]	a[3]	a[4]	a[5]	Action
(20)	(30)	10	35	40	60	No swap
20	(30)	(10)	35	40	60	Swap
20	10	(30)	(35)	40	60	No swap
20	10	30	35	40	60	

After third pass, the third largest element, 35, has moved to its final position.

Pass-4:

a[0]	a[1]	a[2]	a[3]	a[4]	a[5]	Action
(20)	(10)	30	35	40	60	Swap
10	(20)	(30)	35	40	60	No Swap
10	20	30	35	40	60	

After fourth pass, the fourth largest element, 30, has moved to its final position.

Pass-5:

a[0]	a[1]	a[2]	a[3]	a[4]	a[5]	Action
(10)	(20)	30	35	40	60	No swap
10	20	30	35	40	60	

After fifth pass, the fifth largest element, 20, has moved to its final position. And we are left with only element 10, as you can see it is in its final position.

Thus, the array is completely sorted in 5 passes.

Figure 3.3: Illustration of Bubble sort method

Algorithm 3.8

BubbleSortBasic(***a***, ***n*** **)**

Here *a* is a linear array with *n* elements in memory. This algorithm sorts the elements in the ascending order. It uses a temporary variable *temp* to facilitate the exchange of two values and variable *i* to is used as loop control variable.

```
1. Repeat steps 2 and 3 For k = 1 to (n-1) in steps of +1
2.     Repeat step 3 For j = 0 to (n-k-1) in steps of +1
3.         If ( a[j] > a[j+1] ) then
               Set temp = a[j]
               Set a[j] = a[j+1]
               Set a[j+1] = temp
           Endif
       Endfor
   Endfor
4. Exit
```

Performance Analysis

As explained above, after $(n-1)$ passes, the array will be sorted in ascending order. As you must have noticed, the first pass requires $(n-1)$ comparisons, the second pass requires $(n-2)$, ..., kth pass requires $(n-k)$, and the last pass requires only one comparison. Therefore, total comparisons are

$$f(n) = (n-1) + (n-2) + (n-3) + \ldots + (n-k) + \ldots + 3 + 2 + 1$$
$$= n(n-1)/2 = O(n^2)$$

3.2.2.6 Merge Operation

Merging is the process of combining the elements of two similar structures (linear arrays) into a single structure. Suppose that two arrays are unsorted, we can combine them end to end, *i.e.*, we can first put elements of array *a* into third array *c*, and then the elements of the second array *b* are placed after it in array *c* as pictured in Figure 3.4.

Array *a*	12	40	–3	2					
Array *b*	15	5	7	10	60				
Array *c*	12	40	–3	2	15	5	7	10	60

Figure 3.4: Merging end-to-end

In many cases, we may have sorted arrays and our aim is to combine them in such a way that the combined array is also in the sorted order. One straightforward approach is to join them end to end and then sort the combined array, but this approach in not efficient and economical. Therefore the best approach is to compare the elements of the given array, and based on this comparison; decide which element should go first to the third array. This process is illustrated in Figure 3.5, for arrays sorted in the ascending order.

Array *a*	12	40	–3	2					
Array *b*	15	5	7	10	60				
Array *c*	–3	2	5	7	10	12	15	40	60

Figure 3.5: Merging of sorted arrays

In case of sorted arrays, to start with, compare first element of array *a* (-3) with the first element of array *b* (5), and put the smallest of these (–3) into array *c*. since first element of array *a* is put in array *c*, next we compare second element of array *a* (2) with the first element of array *b* (5), since 2 is the smallest, put it into *c*. next compare third element of *a* (12) with first element of *b* (5), since 5 is the smallest, put it into *c*. next compare third element of *a* (12) with second element of *b* (7), since 7 is the smallest, put it into *c*, and so on., and when one array is exhausted, the elements of the other array are copied one by one to *c*. to accomplish the above task, we use counters to keep track of the current element which is a candidate to go in *c*, and the position in *c* where it will be stored.

Algorithm 3.9

MergingSortedArrays(*a, m, b, n, c*)

Here *a* and *b* are sorted (ascending) linear arrays of size *m* and *n*, respectively. This algorithm merges these arrays, by comparing their elements, into array c, which will be of size *m+n*. It uses variables *na* and *nb* to keep track of the respective elements of arrays *a* and *b*, and a variable *nc* to keep track of index in array *c* where the incoming element (either from array *a* or *b*) will be stored.

```
1. Set na = 0, nb = 0, and nc = 0
2. Repeat steps 3 and 4 While ( ( na ≤ m ) and ( nb ≤ n ) )
3.     If ( a[na] < b[nb] ) then
           Set c[nc] = a[na]
           Set na = na + 1
       Else
```

```
        Set c[nc] = a[nb]
        Set nb = nb + 1
     Endif
4.   Set nc = nc + 1
  Endwhile
5. If ( na = m ) then              // array a is exhausted
     Repeat While ( nb < n )
        Set c[nc] = b[nb]
        Set nb = nb + 1
        Set nc = nc + 1
     Endwhile
  Else                             // array b is exhausted
     Repeat While ( na <= m )
        Set c[nc] = b[na]
        Set na = na + 1
        Set nc = nc + 1
     Endwhile
  Endif
6. Exit
```

Performance Analysis

The input to this algorithm consists of the total number r (= $m + n$) of elements of a and b. each comparison assigns an element to array c, which eventually has r elements. According the number $f(r)$ of comparison cannot exceed r:

$$f(r) \leq r = O(r)$$

which means, the merging algorithm can be run in linear time.

3.2.3 Applications of Linear Arrays

Linear arrays are one of the primitive data structures. These are used represent all sorts of lists. In addition, these are used implement other data structures such as *stacks*, *queues*, *heaps*, etc.

3.2.4 Limitations of Linear Arrays

The main limitations of linear arrays are

1. The prior knowledge of number of elements in the linear array is necessary.
2. These are static structures. Static in the sense that whether memory is allocated at compilation time or runtime, their memory used by them cannot be reduced or extended.

3. Since the elements of these arrays are stored in consecutive locations, the insertions and deletions in these arrays are time consuming. This is because of moving down or up to creates a space of new element or to occupy the space vacated by the deleted element.

3.3 TWO-DIMENSIONAL ARRAYS

A two-dimensional array is a list of a finite number $m*n$ of homogeneous data elements such that

- The elements of the array are referenced by two index sets consisting of m and n consecutive integer numbers.
- The elements of the array are stored in consecutive memory locations.

The *size* of the two-dimensional array is denoted by $m \times n$ and pronounced as m by n.

Suppose b is the name of the two-dimensional array, then its element in the ith row and jth column is denoted as

b_{ij}	in mathematical notation
$b(i, j)$	in BASIC and FORTRAN languages
$b[i, j]$	in Pascal language
$b[i][j]$	in C/C++ and Java languages

Two-dimensional arrays are called *matrices* in mathematics and *tables* in business applications. A two-dimensional $m \times n$ array a is pictured as a rectangular pattern of m row and n columns, where the element a_{ij} appears in row i and column j. Figure 3.6 pictures two-dimensional array a of size 3×4.

	Col #0	Col #1	Col #2
Row #0	a_{00}	a_{01}	a_{02}
Row #1	a_{10}	a_{11}	a_{12}
Row #2	a_{20}	a_{21}	a_{22}

Figure 3.6: Picturing a two-dimensional array *a*

3.3.1 Representing Two-dimensional Array in Memory

Let a be a two-dimensional $m \times n$ array. Though a is pictured as a rectangular pattern with m row and n columns, it is represented in memory by a block of $m*n$ sequential memory locations. However, the elements can be stored in two different ways —

- **Column major order** – the elements are stored column by column i.e. m elements of the first column and stored in first m locations, elements of the second column are stored in next m locations, and so on.
- **Row major order** – the elements are stored row by row i.e. n elements of the first row and stored in first n locations, elements of the second row are stored in next n locations, and so on.

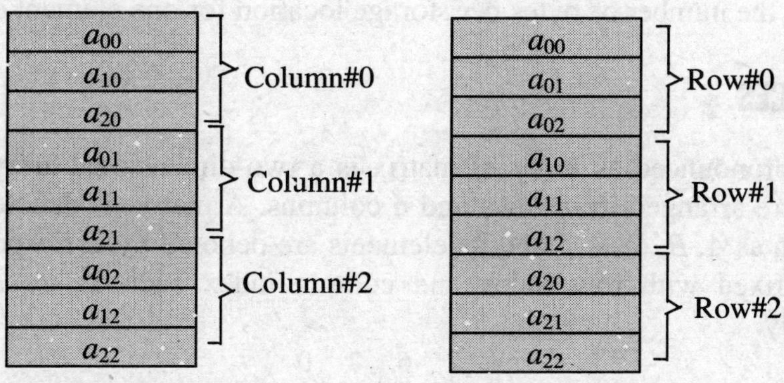

(*a*) Column major order (*b*) Row major order

Figure 3.7: Representation of two-dimensional array a of size 3×3 in memory

---

In C/C++ programming languages, the storage order is row-major order.

Let us consider a two-dimensional array a of size $m \times n$. Further consider that the lower bound for the row index is *lbr* and for column index is *lbc*.

Like linear array, system keeps track of the address of first element only, *i.e.*, the *base address* of the array.

Using this base address, the computer computes the address of the element in the *i*th row and *j*th column, i.e., *loc(a[i][j])*, using the following formulae:

Column Major Order

$loc(a[i][j]) = base(a) + w\,[\,m\,(\,j - lbc\,) + (i - lbr\,)\,]$ in general

$loc(a[i][j]) = base(a) + w\,(\,m \times j\ + i\,)$ in C/C++ languages

Row Major Order

$loc(a[i][j]) = base(a) + w\,[\,n\,(\,i - lbr\,) + (j - lbc\,)\,]$ in general

$loc(a[i][j]) = base(a) + w\,(\,n \times i\ + j\,)$ in C/C++ languages

where *w* is the number of bytes per storage location for one element of the array.

3.4 MATRICES

An $m \times n$ (pronounced as *m* by *n*) matrix is a two-dimensional array whose *m.n* elements are arranged in *m* rows and *n* columns. A matrix is denoted by capital letters such as *A*, *B*, *C*, . . ., and its elements are denoted by corresponding lower letters suffixed with row index and column index such as a_{ij}, b_{ij}, c_{ij}, . . ., respectively.

$$\begin{pmatrix} 2 & 6 & 2 & 0 \\ 3 & 5 & 0 & 9 \\ 8 & 6 & 7 & 1 \\ 4 & 1 & 4 & 9 \end{pmatrix}$$

Figure 3.8: A 4×4 matrix

Matrices are often used to organize data for business and scientific applications. It has been proved that many scientific and engineering problems can be solved efficiently if they are expressed using matrices.

Operations most commonly performed on matrices are transpose, addition or sum, subtraction or difference, and multiplication or product.

Transpose of $m \times n$ matrix *A* is an $n \times m$ matrix *B* (denoted as A^T) with the property

$$b_{ij} = a_{ji} \qquad \text{for } 0 \le i \le n-1 \text{ and } 0 \le j \le m-1$$

Algorithm 3.10

MatrixTranspose(*a, b, m, n*)

Here *a* and *b* are matrices of size *m*×*n*. The algorithm computes the transpose of matrix *a* and stores in matrix *b*. It uses two variables *i* and *j* as control variables.

```
1. Repeat step 2 For i = 0 to (m-1) in steps of +1
2.     Repeat step 3 For j = 0 to (n-1) in steps of +1
3.         Set b[j][i] = a[i][j]
       Endfor
   Endfor
4. Exit
```

The sum of two matrices is defined only when the two matrices are compatible, *i.e.*, have the same number of rows and columns. The sum of two *m*×*n* matrices *A* and *B* is a third *m*×*n* matrix *C* such that

$$c_{ij} = a_{ij} + b_{ij} \qquad \text{for } 0 \le i \le m-1 \text{ and } 0 \le j \le n-1$$

Algorithm 3.11

MatrixAddition(*a, b, c, m, n*)

Here *a, b* and *c* are matrices of size *m*×*n*. The algorithm computes the sum of elements of matrices *a* and *b*, and stores their sum in matrix *c*. It uses two variables *i* and *j* as control variables.

```
1. Repeat step 2 For i = 0 to (m-1) in steps of +1
2.     Repeat step 3 For j = 0 to (n-1) in steps of +1
3.         Set c[i][j] = a[i][j] + b[i][j]
       Endfor
   Endfor
4. Exit
```

Like sum, the difference of two matrices is also defined only when the two matrices are compatible. The difference of *m*×*n* matrix *B* from an *m*×*n* matrix *A* is a third *m*×*n* matrix *C* such that

$$c_{ij} = a_{ij} - b_{ij} \qquad \text{for } 0 \le i \le m-1 \text{ and } 0 \le j \le n-1$$

The product, *A***B*, of a *m*×*n* matrix *A* and a *q*×*p* matrix *B* is defined only when the number of columns in *A* equals the number of rows in *B*,. When $n = q$, the product is a *m*×*p* matrix *C* such that

$$c_{ij} = \sum_{k=1}^{n-1} a_{ik} b_{jk} \qquad \text{for } 0 \le i \le m-1 \text{ and } 1 \le j \le p-1 \text{ or } n-1$$

Algorithm 3.12

MatrixMultiplication(***a, b, c, m, n, p*** **)**

Here *a* is a matrix of size *m*×*n*. *b* is a matrix of size *n*×*p*, and *c* is a matrix of size *m*×*p*. This algorithm computes the product of elements of matrices *a* and *b*, and stores their product in matrix *c*. It uses three variables *i*, *j* and *k* as control variables.

```
1. Repeat steps 2 to 4 For i = 0 to (m-1) in steps of +1
2.    Repeat steps 3 to 4 For j = 0 to (p-1) in steps of +1
3.       Set c[i][j] = 0         // initialize to 0
4.       Repeat step 5 For k = 0 to (n-1) in steps of +1
5.          Set c[i][j] = c[i][j] + a[i][k] * b[k][j]
         Endfor
      Endfor
   Endfor
6. Exit
```

3.5 SUPPLEMENTARY PROBLEMS

Problem 3.1:

Suppose an array SUM[-20..20] is stored in memory with base address 1000. What will be address of element SUM[-5]? Assume that 2 bytes of memory is required for the storage of each element.

Solution:

The general formula to compute the address for the above array is

$$loc(a[k]) = base(a) + w\,(\,k - lb\,)$$

In our problem, the name of array is *SUM* and value for *k* is -5, *w* = 2, therefore above formula becomes

$$loc(SUM[-5]) = base(SUM) + 2 \times [\,(-5) - (-20)\,]$$

$$= 1000 + 2 \times [\,-5 + 20\,]$$

$$= 1000 + 2 \times 15 = 1030$$

Problem 3.2:

Consider the following statement is C/C++ languages

```
float data[50];
```

If the base address of array *data* is 2000, what will address of the 20th element of the array?

Solution:

The formula to compute the address in C++ is

$$loc(a[k]) = base(a) + w \times k$$

Since the data type is *float*, and we know that for an element of type float, 4 bytes of memory is required, therefore $w = 4$. We are required to find the address of the 20th element. Note that the index of the 20th element is 19, since the first element is stored at index 0, therefore value for k is 19.

The formula becomes

$$loc(data[19]) = base(data) + 4 \times 19$$

$$= 2000 + 4 \times 19 = 2076$$

Problem 3.3:

Suppose an array MAT[-10..10][-10..10] is stored in memory with base address 1000. What will be address of element MAT[-5][2] if the array MAT is stored on row-major order? Assume that 2 bytes of memory is required for the storage of each element.

Solution:

The formula for address calculation when a 2D array is stored on row-major order is

$$Loc(MAT[i][j]) = base(MAT) + w\ [\ n\ (\ i - lbr\ ) + (\ j - lbc\ )\ ]$$

In our problem, $n = 21$, $w = 2$, $lbc = -10$, $lbr = -10$, therefore, the above formula reduces to

$$Loc(MAT[-5][2]) = 1000 + 2 \times [21 \times (-5 - (-10)) + (2 - (-10))]$$

$$= 1000 + 2 \times [21 \times 5 + 12]$$

$$= 1000 + 2 \times 117 = 1000 + 234 = 1234$$

Problem 3.4:

Consider the following statement is C++

```
float mat[20][20];
```

If the base address of array *mat* is 2000, what will address of the element *mat*[5][4]of the array?

Solution:

Note that a 2D array is stored on row-major order in C++. Also the lower bound for each index is 0. Since the data type is *float*, and we know that for an element of type float, 4 bytes of memory is required, therefore $w = 4$.

Thus the formula for address calculation

$$loc(a[i][j]) = base(a) + w\ (n \times i\ + j\ )$$

becomes

$$loc(mat[5][4]) = base(mat) + 4 \times\ (20 \times 5\ + 4)$$

$$= 2000 + 4 \times (100 + 4)$$

$$= 2000 + 4 \times 104$$

$$= 2416$$

SUMMARY

In this chapter, we have learnt about the

- basics of arrays.
- representations of linear array in memory.
- various operations performed on linear arrays.

- applications of linear arrays.
- limitations of arrays.
- representations of two-dimensional array in memory.
- matrices and various operations on them.

REVIEW EXERCISES

1. What is an array? What are different types of arrays?
2. Give an example to show the usefulness of arrays.
3. How a linear array is represented in memory?
4. How a two-dimensional array is represented in memory?
5. Name some areas of application of two-dimensional arrays.
6. What are the limitations of arrays?

PROGRAMMING EXERCISES

1. Formulate an algorithm and then write a program to remove all duplicate elements from a linear array.
2. Formulate an algorithm and then write a program that interchanges the first element with the last element, second element with the second last element, and so on.
3. Formulate an algorithm and then write a program that computes and prints sum of squares of the reciprocal of each row of a matrix X of size $m \times n$.
4. Formulate an algorithm and then write a program that computes and prints sum of squares of the reciprocal of each column of a matrix X of size $m \times n$.
5. Formulate an algorithm and then write a program that computes the transpose of a square matrix A of size $n \times n$. Note that the transpose of the matrix is to be stored in the original matrix itself not in a separate matrix.
6. Given a matrix A of size $n \times n$, formulate an algorithm and then write a program that computes the sum of elements above the main diagonal; *i.e.*, those elements a_{ii} for which $i < j$.
7. Given a matrix A of size $n \times n$, formulate an algorithm and then write a program that computes the the sum of elements below the main diagonal; *i.e.*, those elements a_{ii} for which $i > j$.

8. A square matrix A of size $n \times n$ is said to be upper triangular if element $a_{ij} = 0$ for $i > j$. Formulate an algorithm and then write a program that checks whether the matrix is upper triangular or not.
9. A square matrix A of size $n \times n$ is said to be lower triangular if element $a_{ij} = 0$ for $i < j$. Formulate an algorithm and then write a program that checks whether the matrix is lower triangular or not.
10. A square matrix A of size nxn is said to be symmetric if element $a_{ij} = a_{ji}$ for all values of i and j. Formulate an algorithm and then write a program that checks whether the matrix is symmetric or not.
11. A $m \times n$ matrix is said to have a *saddle point* if some entry $a[i][j]$ is the smallest value in row i and the largest value in column j. Formulate an algorithm and then write a program that finds the saddle point if one exists.

❑ ❑ ❑

Chapter 4

Linked Lists

Learning Objectives

After reading this chapter, students will be able to

- explain the concept of linked lists
- distinguish between various types of linked lists
- explain the way linked lists are represented in memory
- write algorithms and programs for performing operations on linked lists
- explain the applications of linked lists

4.1 INTRODUCTION

Intuitively all of us know what a list is? Almost everyday, we use lists of all kinds, such as list of items to be purchased from market, list of addresses, list of references, etc. Lists are very useful and are common data structures. Formerly, a list can be described as a homogeneous collection of elements, with a linear relationship between the elements. The lists can be *unordered* – their elements be placed without a particular order, or *ordered* – their elements are placed in a particular order.

Stacks and *queues* are lists whose elements are ordered according to the time when they are added to them. The lists can also be ordered by the value. For example, a list of names of students can be ordered alphabetically, and a list of grades of student's can ordered numerically (in ascending or descending order). The *value-ordered* lists are frequently referred to as *sorted lists*.

When the elements in a value-ordered list are records rather than scalar data, their logical order is determined by one of the fields in the record, the *record key*. For example, a list of students in a class can be ordered alphabetically by name or numerically by roll number. In the first case, the name field of the record is the key; in the second case, the roll number field is the key. Such value-ordered lists are also called *key-ordered-lists*.

In this chapter, we will learn about the lists that are maintained in memory by means of linked lists.

4.2 LINKED LISTS

A *linked list* is a linear collection of data elements, called *nodes*. The linear order is given by pointers. Each node is divided into two or more parts.

A linked list can be of the following types:

- Linear linked list or one-way list
- Doubly linked list or two-way list
- Circular linked list
- Header linked list
- Two-way header list

In this chapter, we will discuss linear linked lists and doubly linked in details, and introduce other kinds of lists briefly.

4.3 LINEAR LINKED LIST

In a *linear linked list*, also called *singly linked list* or *one-way list*, each node is divided in two parts:

- first part contains the information of the element, and
- second part, called the *link field* or *nextpointer field*, contains the address of the next node in the list.

In addition, another pointer variable, for example *head*, is used that contains the address of the first element of the list. The last element of the linked list have *NULL* value in the *nextpointer* field (usually pictured as ×) to mark the end of the list. Figure 4.1 shows a linear linked list with 4 nodes.

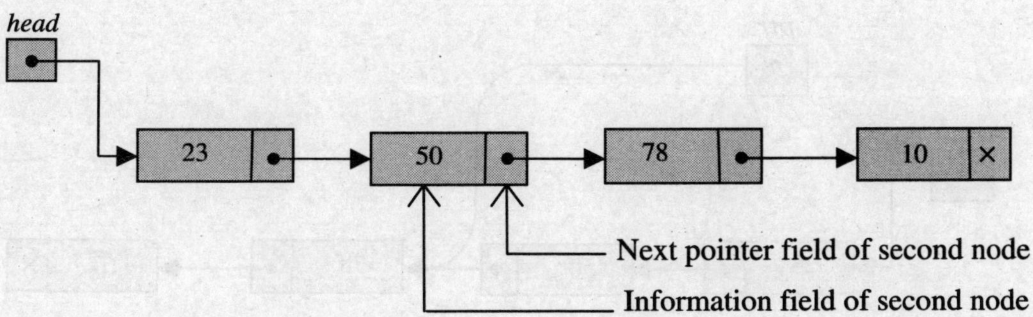

Figure 4.1: Linear linked list with 4 nodes

4.3.1 Representation of Linear Linked List

Let *LLIST* be a linear linked list. Then in order to represent *LLIST* in memory, we will use a record (structure), called *node*, with two fields – first one we will call *info* that will be used to hold information part, and the second we will call *next* that will be used to hold the next pointer field of the node. In addition, we will also use a *head* variable that holds the address of the first node, *i.e.*, location of the beginning of the list. A special value denoted by *NULL*, will be used to indicate the end of the list, *i.e.*, the *NULL* value in the next pointer field of a node will indicate that it is the last node of the list.

4.3.2 Operations on Linear Linked Lists

In this section, we will describe operations on linear linked lists.

4.3.2.1 Traversing

To traverse a linear linked list (*LLIST*), a temporary variable *ptr* is used to point to the node currently being processed. To start, the variable *ptr* is initialized to *head*, *i.e.*, the location of the first node of the *LLIST*. Apply process to the information part (*ptr->info*). Advance the *ptr* by using the assignment *ptr = ptr->next*, so that ptr now points to the next node. This process is continued till value of *ptr* becomes *NULL*, which signals the end of the *LLIST*. The algorithms 4.1 summarizes the various steps required for traversing a linear linked list *LLIST*.

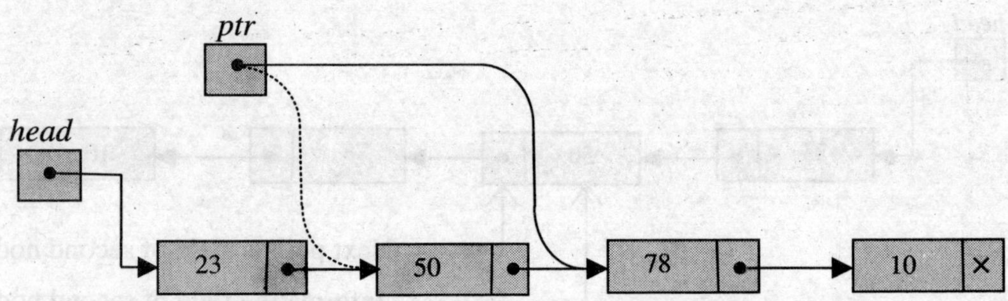

Figure 4.2: Visualization of step, Set *ptr = ptr->next*

Algorithm 4.1

Traverse(***LLIST*** **)**

Here *LLIST* is a linear linked list in memory. This sub algorithm traverses *LLIST*, applying an operation *process* to each element of the *LLIST*. The temporary variable *ptr* is used to point to the node currently being processed.

```
1. Set ptr = head
2. Repeat steps 3 and 4 While ( ptr ≠ NULL )
3.    Apply process to ptr->info
4.    Set ptr = ptr->next
   Endwhile
5. Return
```

4.3.2.2 Searching

In linear linked lists, only linear searching is possible. This is one of the limitations of linked lists as there is no way to find the location of the middle element of the list. Further, the list may be sorted or unsorted.

List is Unsorted

We traverse the list from the beginning, and compare each element of the list with the given element, say *item*, to be searched. If the match occurs, the location of the element is returned. If we reach the end of the list, and no match is found, then *NULL* value is returned to indicate the element is not in the list.

Algorithm 4.2

SearchInUnsorted(***LLIST*, *item*, *loc*** **)**

Here *LLIST* is a unsorted linear linked list in memory. This sub algorithm find the location, *loc*, of the first node where *item* first appears in *LLIST* or sets *loc* to *NULL* to indicate that *item* was not present in the *LLIST*.

```
1. Set ptr = head
2. Repeat steps 3 and 4 While ( ptr ≠ NULL )
3.     If ( item = ptr->info ) then
           Set loc = ptr
           Return
       Endif
4.     Set ptr = ptr->next
   Endwhile
5. Set loc = NULL
6. Return
```

List is Sorted

If the list is sorted (say in ascending order), then we traverse the list from the beginning, and compare each element of the list with element, say *item*, to be searched. If the match occurs, the location of the element is returned. If we reach the element that is greater than *item* or end of the list, then *NULL* value is returned to indicate the element is not in the list.

Algorithm 4.3

SearchInSorted(***LLIST, item, loc*** **)**

Here *LLIST* is a sorted (in ascending order) linear linked list in memory. This algorithm find the location, *loc*, of the first node where *item* first appears in *LLIST* or sets *loc* to *NULL* to indicate that *item* was not present in the *LLIST*.

```
1. Set ptr = head
2. Repeat steps 3 to 5 While ( ptr ≠ NULL )
3.      If ( item = ptr->info ) then
           Set loc = ptr
           Return
        Endif
4.      If ( ptr->info > item ) then
           Set loc = NULL
           Return
        Endif
5.      Set ptr = ptr->next
   Endwhile
6. Set loc = NULL
7. Return
```

MEMORY MANAGEMENT

The maintenance of linked lists in memory requires insertion of new nodes and deletions of existing nodes. Therefore, there is need of some mechanism which provides free memory space for the new nodes. In similar way, there is a need of mechanism whereby the memory space of deleted nodes is returned to the free pool of memory for future use.

As you may be aware that the operating system manages all the resources of a computer systems that include memory management. As part of the memory management, operating system keeps track of memory in use and the memory that is available, called *free pool/store*, for future use.

Garbage Collection

Suppose some memory space becomes available when some nodes are deleted or the entire list if deleted from memory in a program. Clearly, we want that the memory space to be available for future use. One way to do this is that add the memory space to the free store immediately.

However, this method may be too time-consuming for the operating system.

Practically, the operating system uses following approach — it periodically collects the deleted space into the free store. Any technique that does this collection is called *garbage collection.*

Operating system, usually, performs garbage collections following two steps:

1. In the first step, the operating system runs through memory and tags all those memory cells that are currently in use.
2. In the second step, the operating system runs through memory and collects all the untagged memory cells in the free store.

Operating system may perform garbage collection in either of the following cases:

1. only when some minimum amount of memory or no memory at all is left in the free store; or
2. the CPU is idle and has time to do the collection.

The garbage collection is invisible to the programmer. Any further discussion on the garbage collection is beyond the scope of this text.

Overflow and Underflow

A situation may arise when we want to insert new data into a data structure but no space is available, *i.e.*, the free store is empty. This situation is called *overflow*. In the case of linked list, this case will occur when operating system will not be able to allocate space for a new node.

Similarly, a situation may arise when we want to delete data from a data structure that is empty. This situation is called *underflow*. In the case of linked list, this case will occur when *head = NULL*, and there is a deletion of node.

The programmer must handle these situations and output appropriate messages to indicate the occurrence of such situations, and take an alternate course of action in the program.

4.3.2.3 Inserting

To insert an element in the list, the first task is to get a free node, assign the element, say *item*, to be inserted to the *info* field of the node. This is shown in the following steps:

(*a*) Allocate free node and hold its address in pointer variable *ptr*.

This task is done in C as shown:

```
ptr = malloc(sizeof(node));
```

Same task is done in C++ as shown:

```
ptr = new node;
```

(*b*) Assign *item* to the *info* part of the newly allocated node as

```
Set ptr->info = item
```

Figure 4.3: Visualization of common steps to inserting algorithms, allocating memory for new node and initializing it info par with *item*

The next step is to place new node at the appropriate position by adjusting the appropriate pointers. The insertion in the list can take place at the following positions:

- at the beginning of the list
- at the end of the list
- after a given element
- before a given element
- in a sorted list

4.3.2.3.1 Inserting at the Beginning

To insert an element at the beginning of the list, first we test whether the linked list is initially empty. If yes, then the element is inserted as the first and only element of the list by performing the following steps:

- Assign NULL value to the next pointer field of the new node.
- Assign address of the new node to *head*.

(*d*) Assign the value of *head* pointer to *next* part of the newly allocated node

```
Set ptr->next = head
```

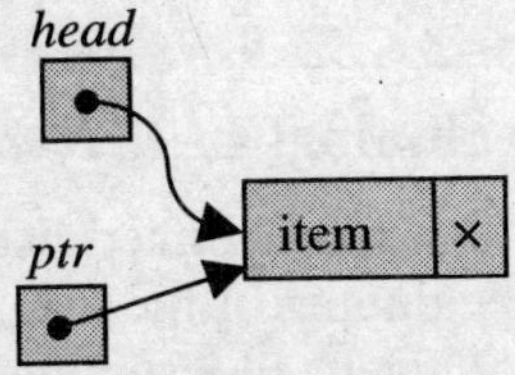

(*e*) Assign the value of *ptr* pointer to *head* pointer to attach the newly allocated node to the linked list

```
Set head = ptr
```

Figure 4.4: Visualization of inserting a new node in the beginning of linear list when the list is initially empty

However, if the list is initially not empty, then the element is inserted as the first element of the list by performing the following steps:

- Assign value of the *head* variable (the address of the first element of the existing list) to the next pointer field of the new node.
- Assign address of the new node to *head*.

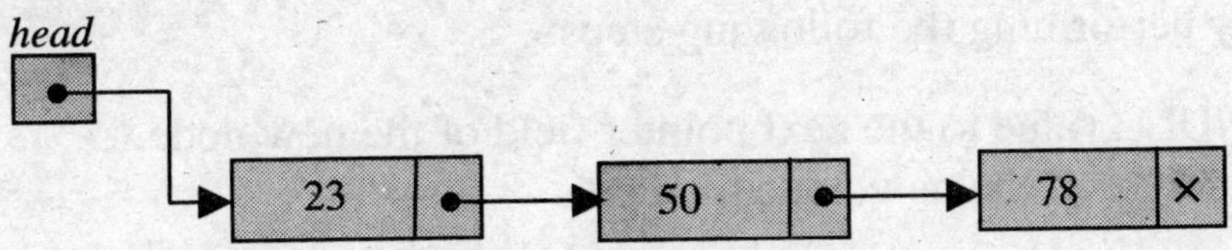

(*a*) Before insertion operations

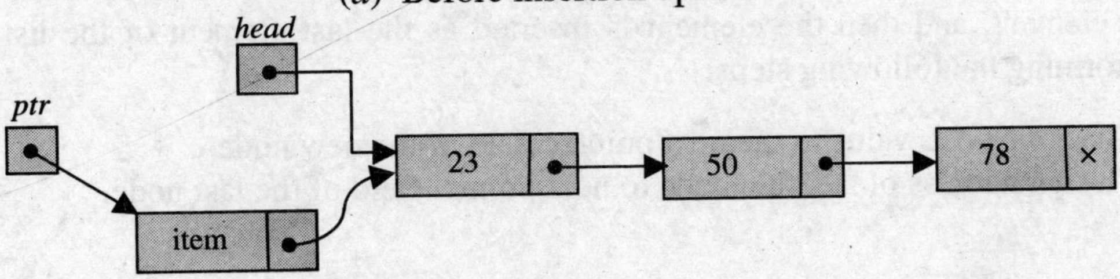

(*b*) Linked list after first step, `ptr->next = head`

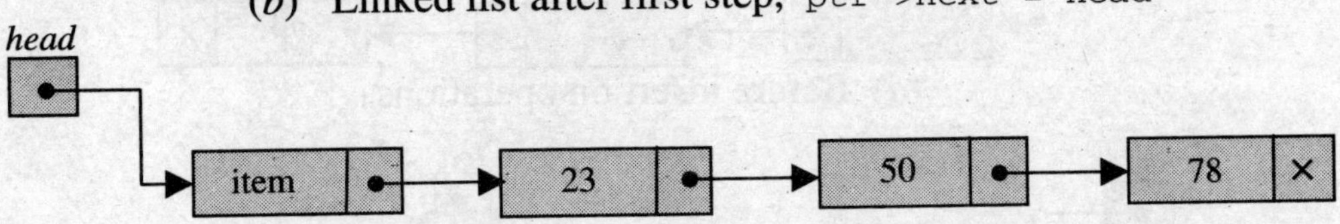

(*c*) Linked list after second and last step, `head = ptr`

Figure 4.5: Visualization of inserting a new node in the beginning of linear list when the list is non-empty

Algorithm 4.4

InsertAtBeginning(***LLIST, item*** **)**

Here *LLIST* is a linear linked list in memory. This algorithm inserts new element, *item*, in the beginning of the list, *i.e.*, as a first node. The variable *ptr* is used to hold the address of newly allocated node.

```
1. Set ptr = address of the new node
2. If ( ptr = NULL ) then
       Write: "Overflow"
       Return
   Endif
3. Set ptr->info = item
4. Set ptr->next = head
5. Set head = ptr
6. Return
```

4.3.2.3.2 Inserting at the End

To insert the element at the end of the list, first we test whether the linked list is initially empty. If yes, then the element is inserted as the first and only element of the list by performing the following steps:

- Assign NULL value to the next pointer field of the new node.
- Assign address of the new node to *head*.

However, if the list is initially not empty, then the list is traversed to reach the last element, and then the element is inserted as the last element of the list by performing the following steps:

- Assign NULL value to the next pointer field of the new node.
- Assign address of the new node to next pointer field of the last node.

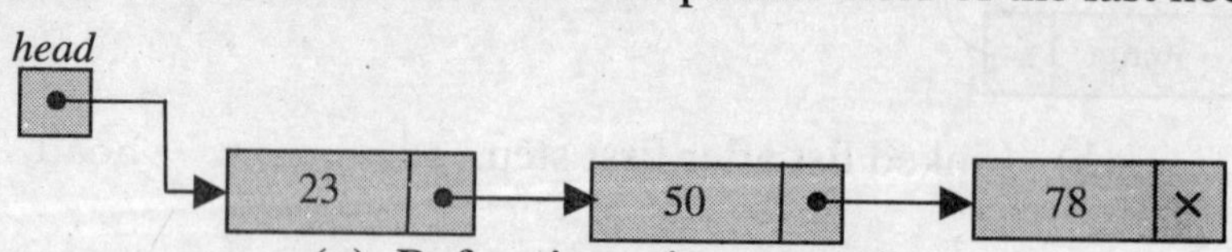

(*a*) Before insertion operations

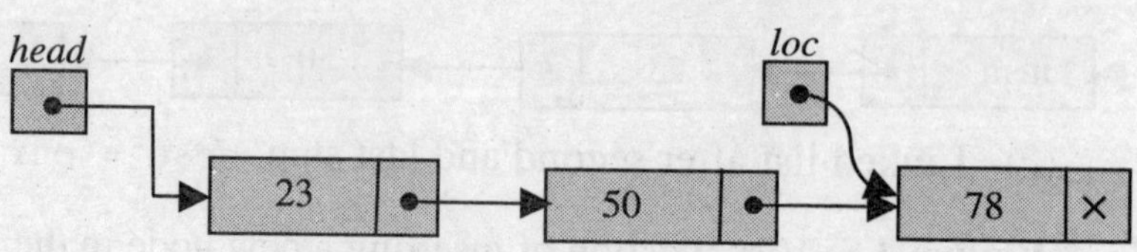

(*b*) After reaching to the last element

(*c*) After performing the first step, `ptr->next = NULL`

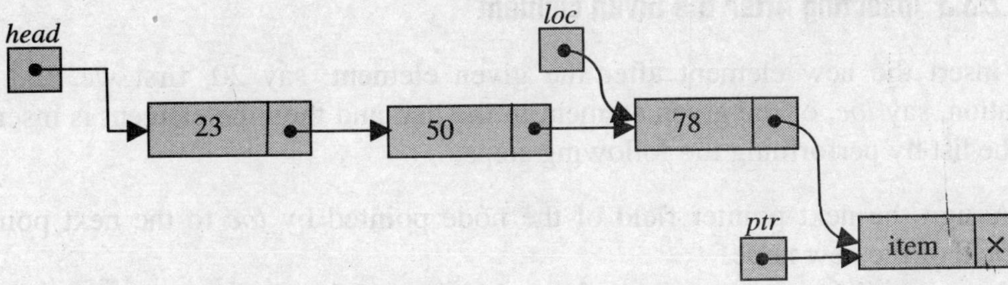

(*d*) After performing the second and last step, `loc->next = ptr`

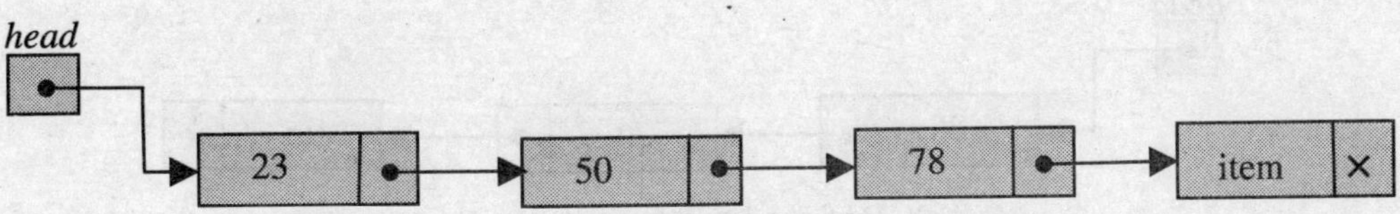

(*e*) Final list

Figure 4.6: Visualization of inserting a new node at the end of linear list when the list is non-empty

Algorithm 4.5

InsertAtEnd(***LLIST, item*** **)**

Here *LLIST* is a linear linked list in memory. This algorithm inserts new element, *item*, at the end of the list. However, if the list is initially empty, then it inserts as a first node. The variable *ptr* is used to hold the address of newly allocated node. Another variable, *loc*, is used to traverse the list to reach the last node of the list.

```
1. Set ptr = address of the new node
2. If ( ptr = NULL ) then
       Write: "Overflow"
       Return
   Endif
3. Set ptr->info = item
4. If ( head = NULL ) then
       Set head = ptr
       Return
   Endif
5. Set loc = head
```

```
6. Repeat step 7 While ( loc->next ≠ NULL )
7.     Set loc = loc->next
   Endwhile
8. Set loc->next = ptr
9. Return
```

4.3.2.3.3 Inserting After the Given Element

To insert the new element after the given element, say 20, first we find the location, say *loc*, of the given element in the list, and then the element is inserted in the list by performing the following steps:

- Assign the next pointer field of the node pointed by *loc* to the next pointer field of the new node.
- Assign address of new node to the next pointer field of node pointed by *loc*.

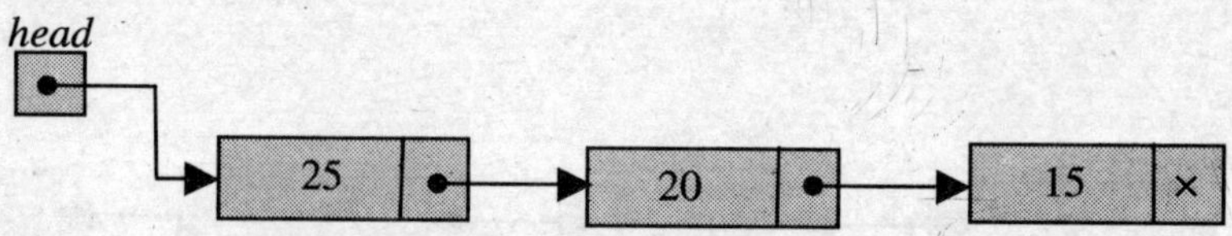

(*a*) Before insertion operations

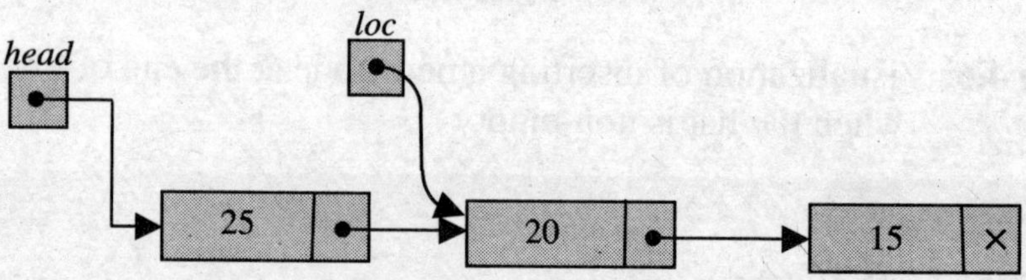

(*b*) After reaching the element with value 20, *i.e.*, after finding the location *loc* of the given element

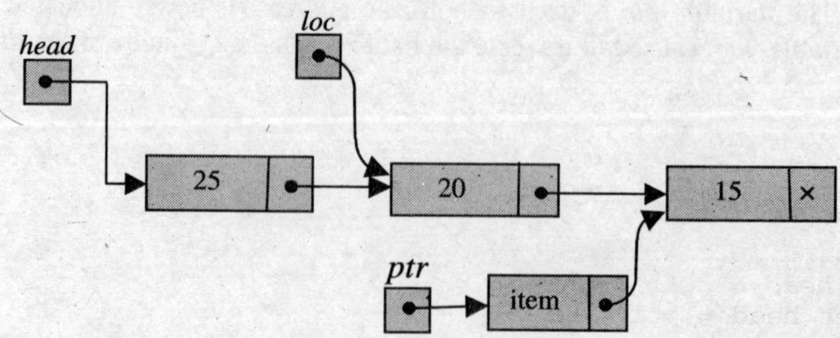

(*c*) After performing the first step, `ptr->next = loc->next`

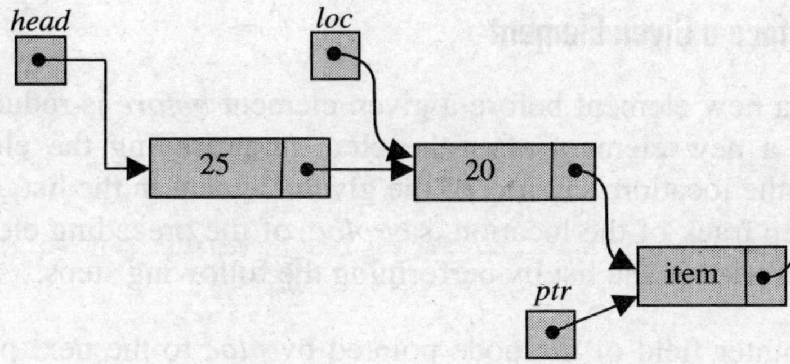

(*d*) After performing the second and last step, `loc->next = ptr`

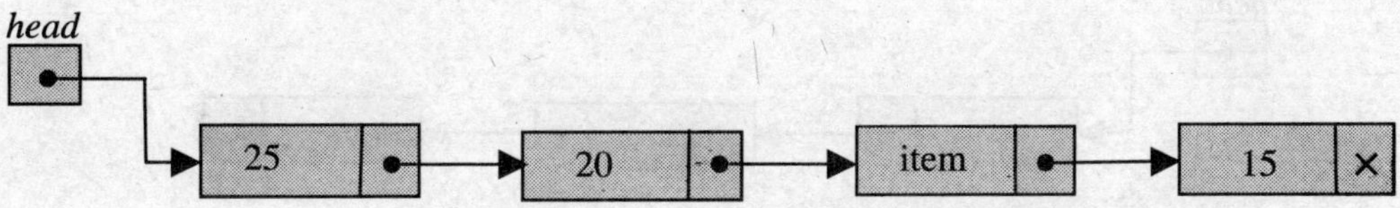

(*e*) Final list

Figure 4.6: Visualization of inserting a new element after a given element

Algorithm 4.6

InsertAfterGivenElement(*LLIST*, *item*, *after*)

Here *LLIST* is a linear linked list in memory. This algorithm inserts new element, *item*, after a given element, *after*, in the list. This algorithm first find the location of the node containing the given element *after* by calling sub algorithm 4.3. The variable *ptr* is used to hold the address of newly allocated node. Another variable, *loc*, is used to hold the address of the node containing element *after*.

```
1. Call SearchInUnsorted( LLIST, after, loc )
2. If ( loc = NULL ) then
      Write: "Element", after, "not found in list"
      Return
   Endif
3. Set ptr = address of the new node
4. Set ptr->info = item
5. Set ptr->next = loc->next
6. Set loc->next = ptr
7. Return
```

4.3.2.3.4 Inserting Before a Given Element

The task of inserting a new element before a given element *before* is reduced to the task of inserting a new element after the element preceding the element *before*. Here, we find the location, say *loc*, of the given element in the list, and at the same track we keep track of the location, say *ploc*, of the preceding element. Then the element is inserted in the list by performing the following steps:

- Assign the next pointer field of the node pointed by *ploc* to the next pointer field of the new node.
- Assign address of new node to next pointer field of the node pointed by *ploc*.

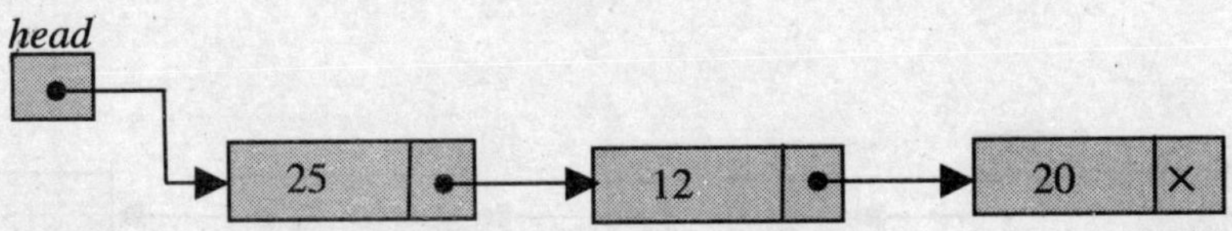

(*a*) Before insertion

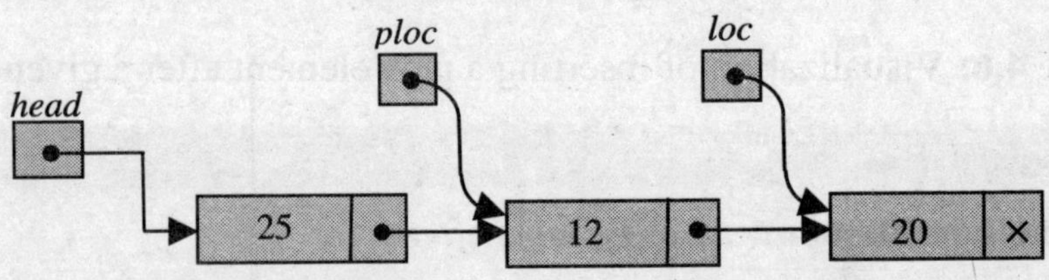

(*b*) After reaching the element with value 20, *i.e.*, after finding the location *loc* of the given element and location *ploc* its preceding element

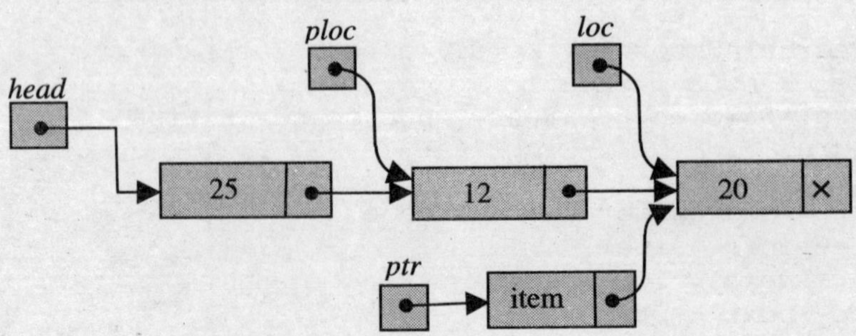

(*c*) After performing the first step, `ptr->next = ploc->next`

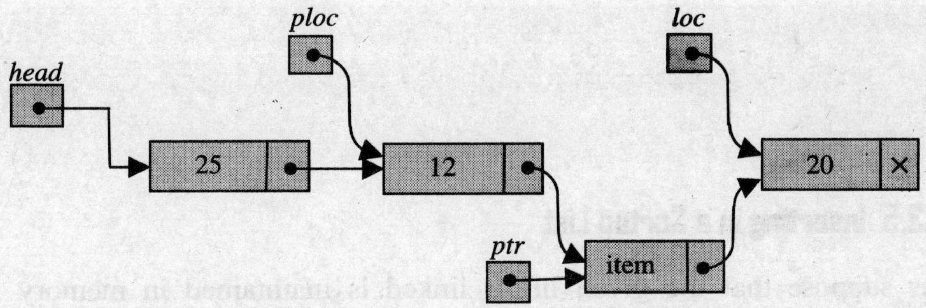

(*d*) After performing the second and last step, `ploc->next = ptr`

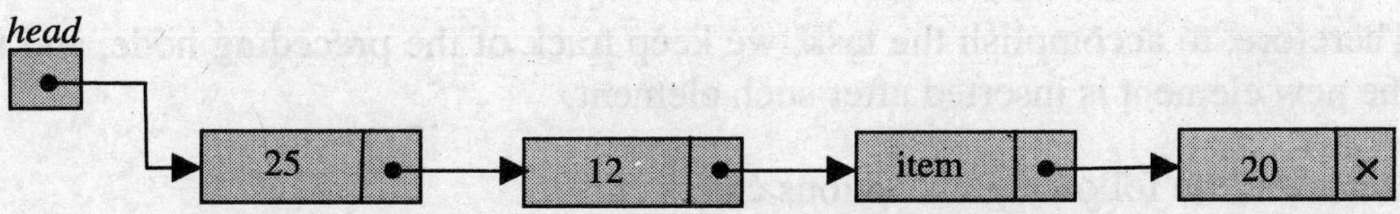

(*e*) Final list

Figure 4.7: Visualization of inserting a new element before a given element

Algorithm 4.7

InsertBeforeGivenElement(***LLIST*, *item*, *before*** **)**

Here *LLIST* is a linear linked list in memory. This algorithm inserts new element, *item*, before element, *before*, in the list. This algorithm first find the location. Say *loc*, of the node containing the given element *before* and location, say *ploc*, of the element preceding it. The variable *ptr* is used to hold the address of newly allocated

```
1. Set ploc = NULL, loc = head
2. Repeat step 3 While ( (loc≠NULL) and (loc->info≠item) )
3.    Set loc = loc->next
   Endwhile
4. If ( loc = NULL ) then
      Write: "Element", before, "not found in list"
      Return
   Endif
5. Set ptr = address of the new node
6. Set ptr->info = item
7. If ( ploc = NULL ) then       // insert as first element
      Set ptr->next = head
      Set head = ptr
```

```
    Else
        Set ptr->next = loc
        Set ploc->next = ptr
    Endif
 8. Return
```

4.3.2.3.5 Inserting in a Sorted List

Let us suppose that the given linear linked is maintained in memory in the ascending order. To insert new element *item*, the list is scanned from the beginning till we find a node with value greater than the given element. The new element is to be inserted before that element.

Therefore, to accomplish the task, we keep track of the preceding node, and then the new element is inserted after such element.

However, the following exceptions can occur

- New element is less than the first element, in that case new element is inserted in the beginning of the list.
- New element is greater than the last element, in that case new element is inserted in the end of the list.

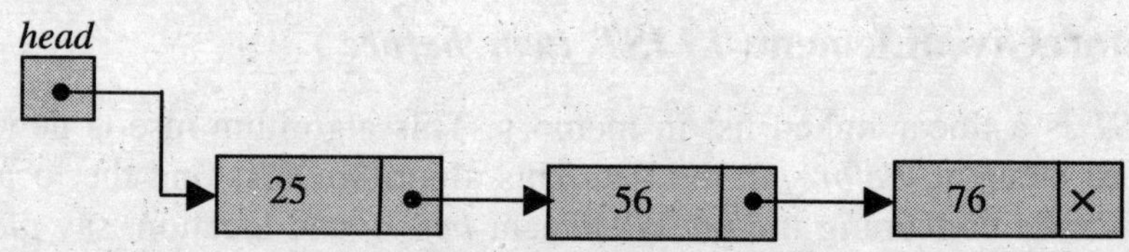

(*a*) Before insertion operations

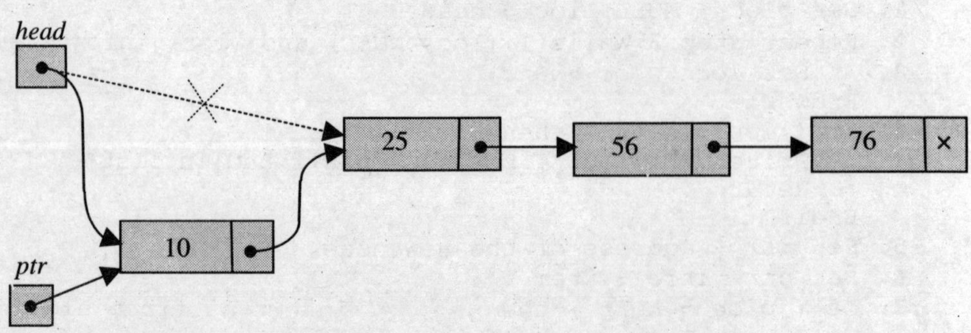

(*b*) New element 10, inserted in the beginning of the list since it is less than the first element of the list

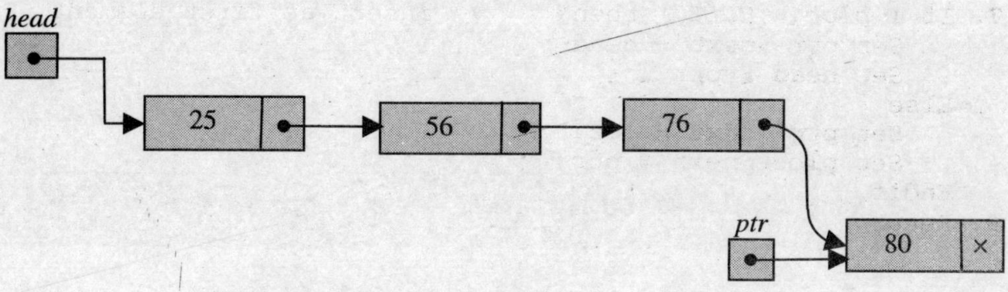

(*c*) New element 80, inserted in the end of the list since it is greater than the last element of the list

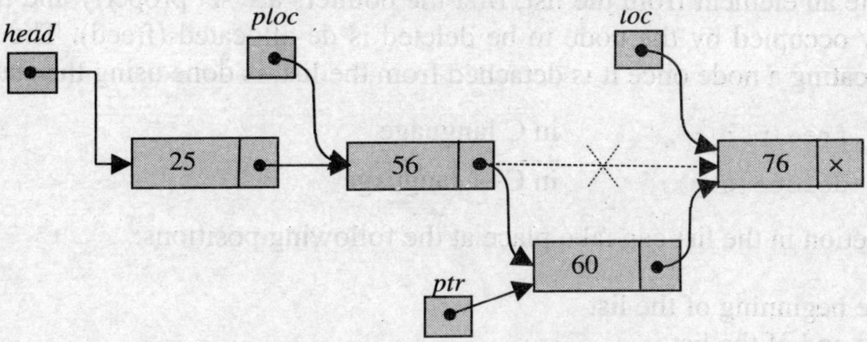

(*d*) New element 60, inserted after the element 56, as it is the preceding element to 76, the first element in the list greater than 60

Figure 4.8: Visualization of inserting a new element in a sorted list

Algorithm 4.8

InsertInSorted(***LLIST, item*** **)**

Here *LLIST* is a linear linked list maintained in ascending order in memory. This algorithm inserts new element, *item*, at its appropriate location so that the resulting list reaming in ascending order. This algorithm finds the location, say *loc*, of the first node having value greater than *item*. It also keep track of the location, say *ploc*, of the element preceding it. The variable *ptr* is used to hold the address of newly allocated node.

```
1. Set ptr = address of the new node
2. Set ptr->info = item
3. Set ploc = NULL, loc = head
4. Repeat steps 5 and 6 While ((loc≠NULL)and(loc->info<item))
5.    Set ploc = loc
6.    Set loc = loc->next
   Endwhile
```

```
7. If ( ploc = NULL ) then        // insert as first element
      Set ptr->next = head
      Set head = ptr
   Else
      Set ptr->next = loc
      Set ploc->next = ptr
   Endif
8. Return
```

4.3.2.4 Deleting

To delete an element from the list, first the pointers are set properly and then the memory occupied by the node to be deleted is de-allocated (freed). The task of de- allocating a node once it is detached from the list, is done using the statement

`free(ptr);`	in C language
`delete(ptr);`	in C++ language

The deletion in the list can take place at the following positions:

- at the beginning of the list
- at the end of the list
- after a given element
- before a given element
- from a sorted list

4.3.2.4.1 Deleting from the Beginning

An element from the beginning of the lists can be deleted by performing following steps:

- Assign the value of *head* (address of the first node of the list) to a temporary variable *ptr*,
- Assign the value of the next pointer field of the first node to *head*.
- Deallocate the memory occupied by the node pointed to by *ptr*.

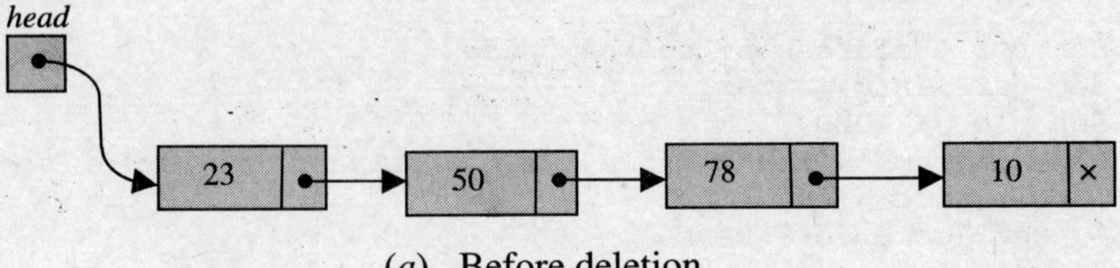

(*a*) Before deletion

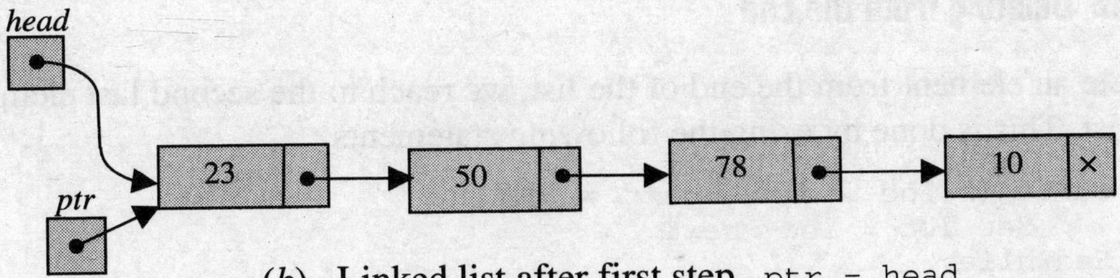

(*b*) Linked list after first step, `ptr = head`

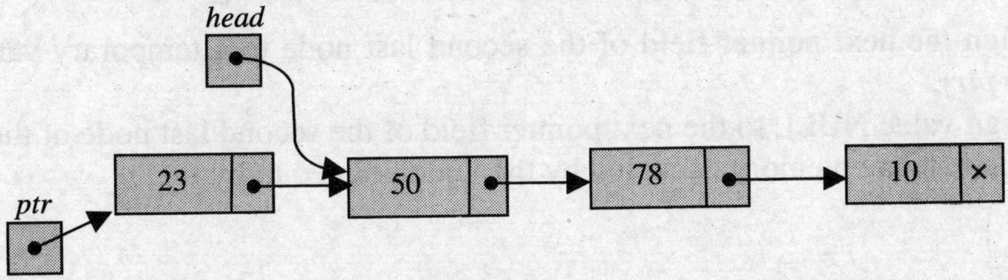

(*c*) Linked list after second first step, `head = head->next`

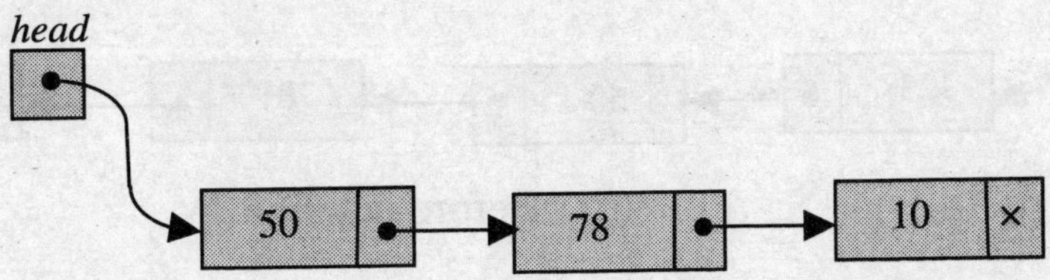

(*d*) Linked after third and final step, `free(ptr)`

Figure 4.9: Visualization of deleing a node from the beginning of a list,

Algorithm 4.9

DeleteFromBeginning(***LLIST*** **)**

Here *LLIST* is a linear linked list in memory. This algorithm deletes node from the beginning of the list. This algorithm first stores the address of the first node in a temporary variable *ptr* for removing the node from the memory later on, and then advances the *head* pointer to the second node.

```
1. If ( head = NULL ) then
      Write: "Underflow"
      Return
   Endif
2. Set ptr = head
3. Set head = head->next
4. Remove node with address ptr
5. Return
```

4.3.2.4.2 Deleting from the End

To delete an element from the end of the list, we reach to the second last element of the list. This is done by using the following statements

```
while ( (loc->next)->next ≠ NULL )
    Set loc = loc->next
Endwhile
```

Then the last element can be deleted by performing following steps:

- Assign the next pointer field of the second last node to a temporary variable (say *ptr*),
- Assign value NULL to the next pointer field of the second last node of the list.
- Deallocate the memory occupied by the node pointed to by *ptr*.

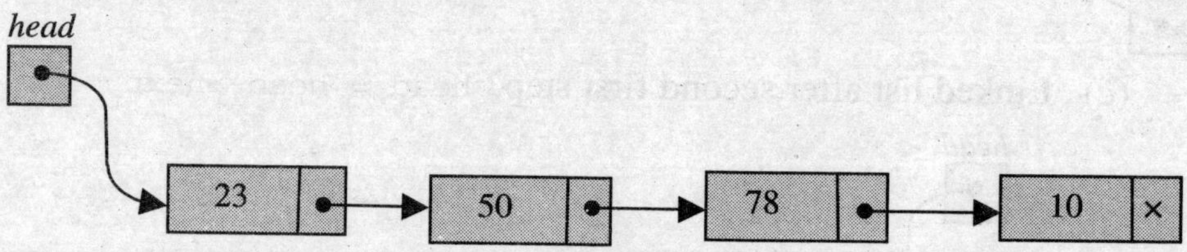

(*a*) Before deletion

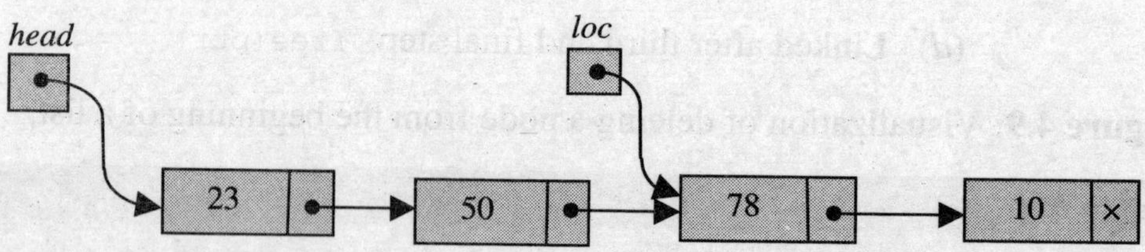

(*b*) After reaching to the second last element

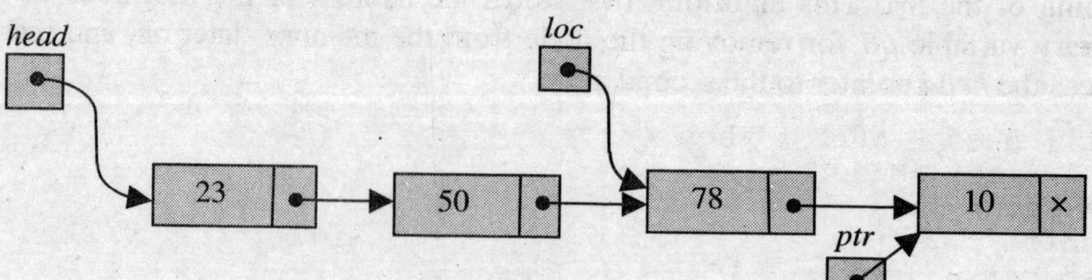

(*c*) After the first step for deletion, `ptr = loc->next`

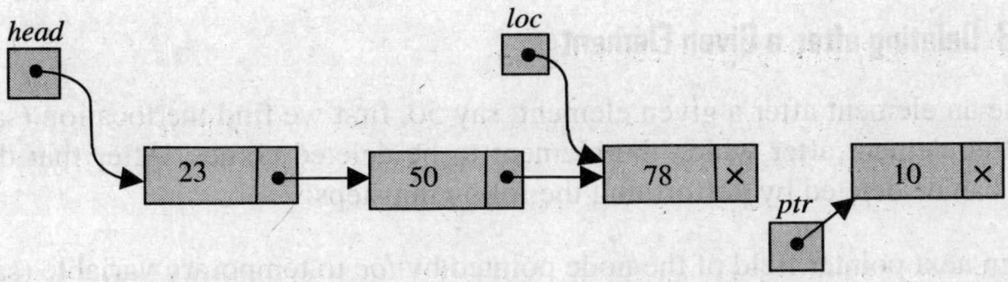

(*d*) After the second step for deletion, `loc->next = NULL`

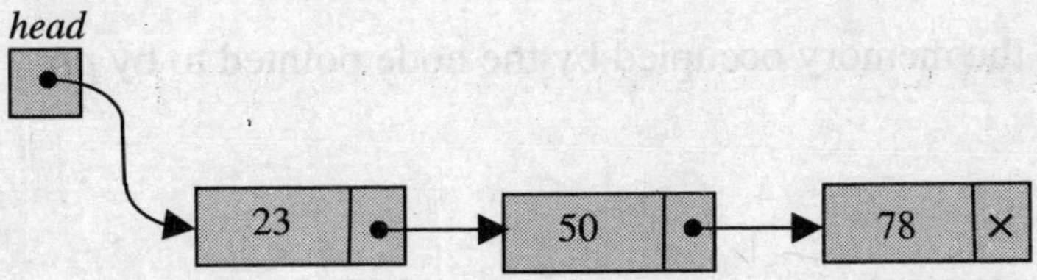

(*e*) Linked after third and final step, `free(ptr)`

Figure 4.10: Visualization of deleing a node from the end of a list

Algorithm 4.10

DeleteFromEnd(***LLIST*** **)**

Here *LLIST* is a linear linked list in memory. This algorithm deletes node from the end of the list. This algorithm first traverses the list, using variable *loc*, to reach the second last node of the list, and the stores the address of the last node in variable *ptr* for removing the node from the memory later on, and then sets the next pointer field of the second last node to *NULL*.

```
1. If ( head = NULL ) then
      Write: "Underflow"
      Return
   Endif
2. Set loc = head
3. Repeat step 4 While ( (loc->next)->next ≠ NULL )
4.    Set loc = loc->next
   Endwhile
5. Set ptr = loc->next
6. Set loc->next = NULL
7. Remove node with address ptr
8. Return
```

4.3.2.4.3 Deleting after a Given Element

To delete an element after a given element, say 50, first we find the location (say *loc*) of the element after which the element to be deleted comes. After that the element can be deleted by performing the following steps:

- Assign next pointer field of the node pointed by *loc* to temporary variable (say *ptr*),
- Assign the next pointer field of the node to be deleted to the node pointed to by *loc*
- Deallocate the memory occupied by the node pointed to by *ptr*.

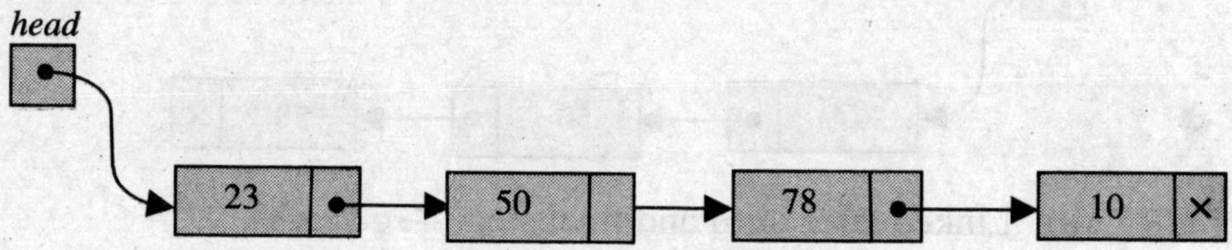

(*a*) Before deletion

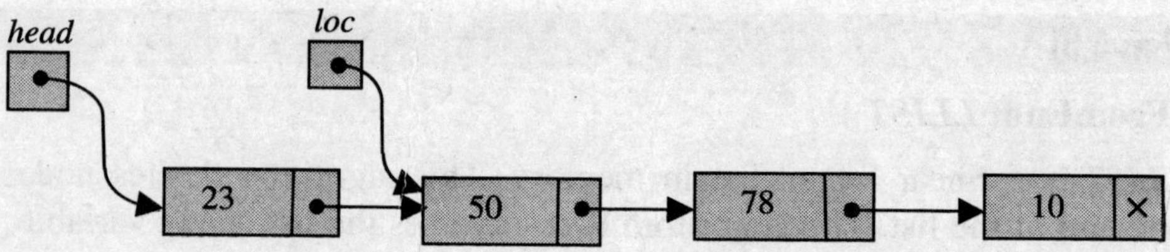

(*b*) After reaching to the given element 50

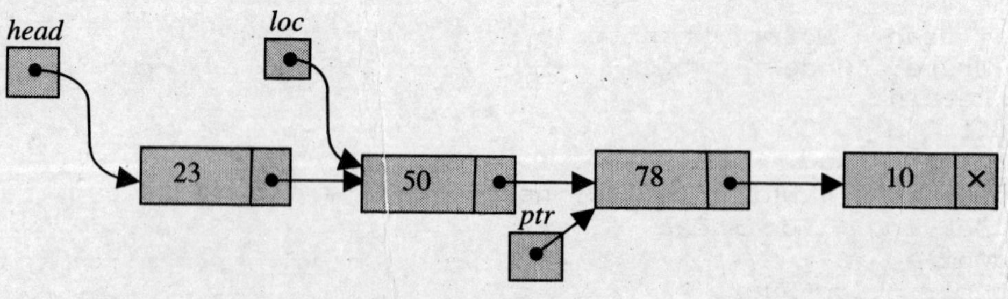

(*c*) After the first step for deletion, `ptr = loc->next`

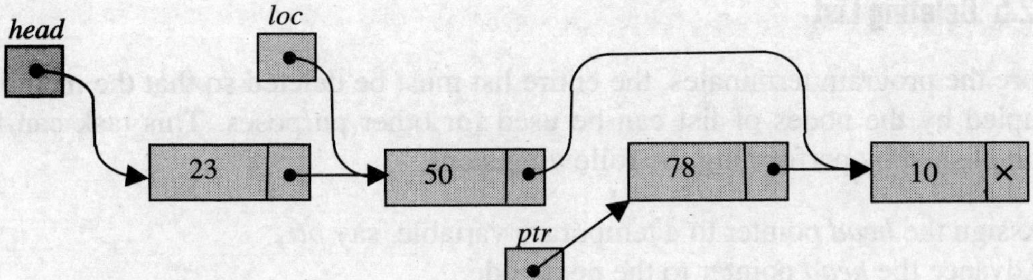

(*d*) After the second step for deletion, `loc->next = ptr->next`

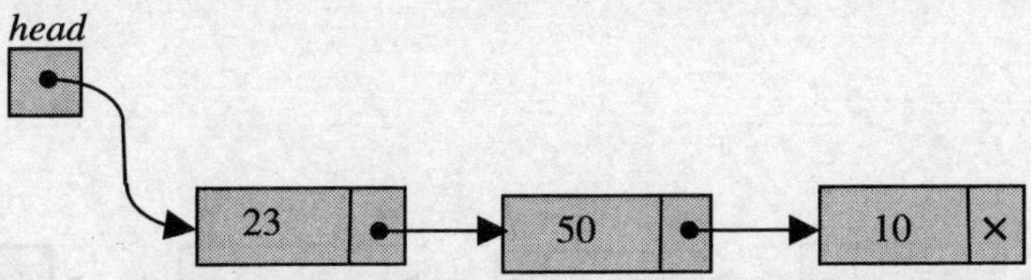

(*e*) Linked after third and final step, `free(ptr)`

Figure 4.11: Visualization of deleing a node after a given node of a list

Algorithm 4.11

DeleteAfterGivenElement(***LLIST*, *after*** **)**

Here *LLIST* is a linear linked list in memory. This algorithm deletes node after a node containing a given element, *after*, of the list. This algorithm first finds the location, *loc*, of the node containing the element *after* by calling using algorithm 4.2. The address of the node to be deleted is stored in variable *ptr* for removing the node from the memory later on.

```
1. If ( head = NULL ) then
     Write: "Underflow"
     Return
   Endif
2. Call SearchInUnsorted( LLIST, after, loc )
3. If ( loc = NULL ) then
     Write: "Element", after, "not found in list"
     Return
   Endif
4. Set ptr = loc->next
5. Set loc->next = ptr->next
6. Remove node with address ptr
7. Return
```

4.3.2.5 Deleting List

Before the program terminates, the entire list must be deleted so that the memory occupied by the nodes of list can be used for other purposes. This task can be accomplished by performing the following steps:

- Assign the *head* pointer to a temporary variable, say *ptr*,
- Advance the *head* pointer to the next node,
- Deallocate the memory occupied by the node pointed to by *ptr*.

The above steps are repeated till the entire list is deleted.

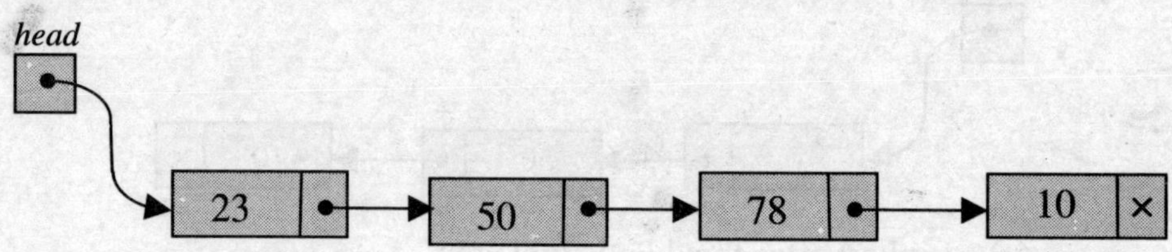

(*a*) Current Linked List

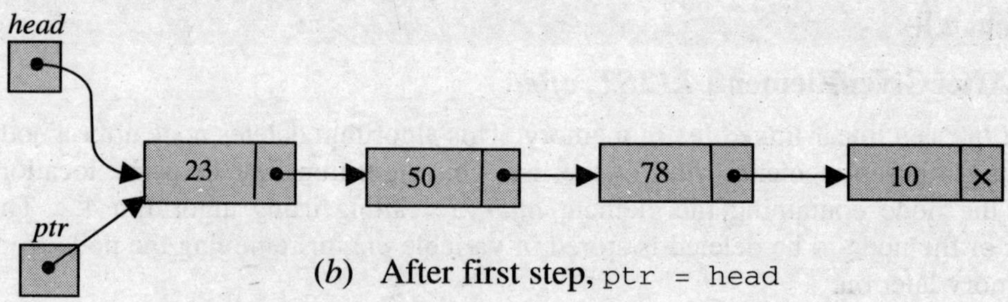

(*b*) After first step, `ptr = head`

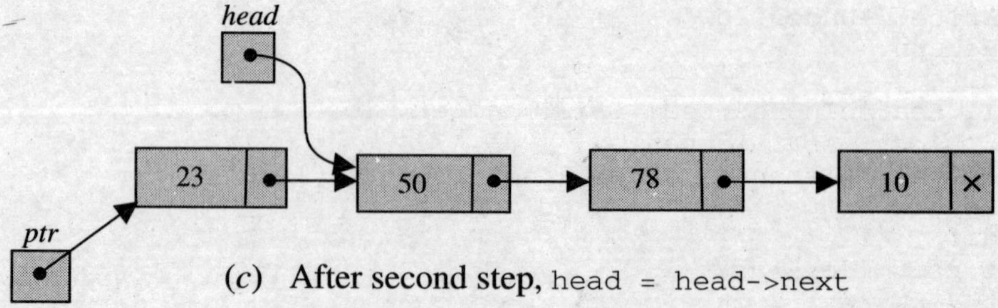

(*c*) After second step, `head = head->next`

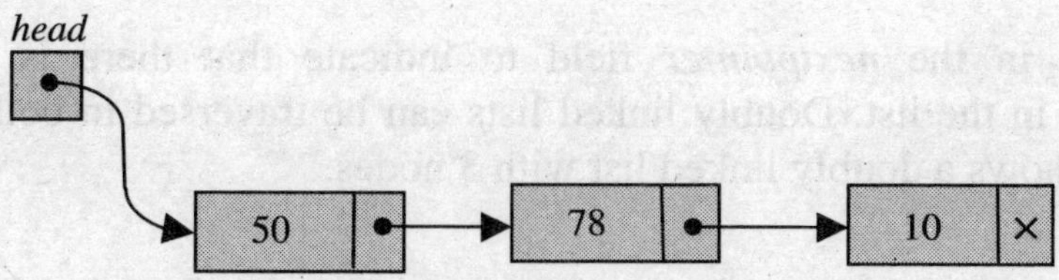

(*d*) After third step, `free(ptr)`

Figure 4.12: (*b*)-(*d*) Visualization of deleing the steps to delete the first element from the linked

Steps (*b*) to (*d*) for repeated for each element of the linked list (node) till all the nodes of the linked list are removed from memory.

Algorithm 4.12

DeleteList (***LLIST*** **)**

Here *LLIST* is a linear linked list in memory. This algorithm removes the entire list from memory.

```
1. Repeat steps 2 to 4 While ( head ≠ NULL )
2.      Set ptr = head
3.      Set head = head->next
4.      Remove node with address ptr
   Endwhile
5. Return
```

4.4 DOUBLY LINKED LIST

In a *doubly linked list*, also called *two-way list*, each node is divided into three parts:

- the first part, called *previouspointer field*, contains the address of the preceding element in the list,
- the second part contains the information of the element, and
- the third part, called *nextpointer field*, contains the address of the succeeding element in the in the list.

In addition, two pointer variables, for example *head* and *tail*, are used that contains the address of the first element and the address of the last element of the list, respectively. The first element contains NULL value in the *previouspointer* to indicate there is no element preceding it in the list, and the last element have

NULL value in the *nextpointer* field to indicate that there is no element succeeding it in the list. Doubly linked lists can be traversed in both directions. Figure 4.13 shows a doubly linked list with 3 nodes.

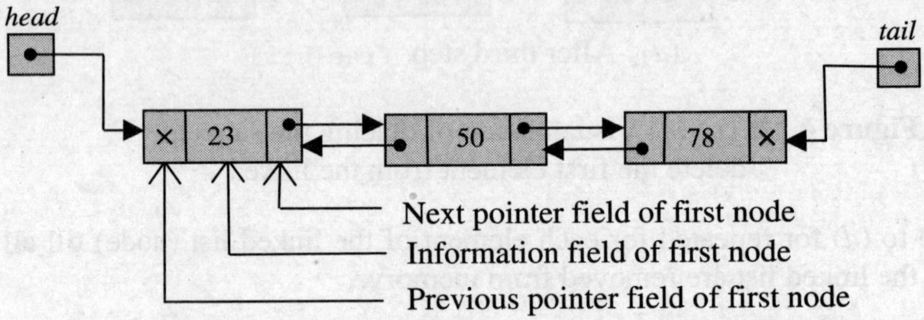

Figure 4.13: Doubly linked list with 3 nodes

4.4.1 Representation of Doubly Linked Lists

Let *DLIST* be a doubly linked list. Then in order to represent *DLIST* in memory, we will use a record (structure), called *node*, with three fields – first one we will call *info* that will be used to hold information part, the second we will call *next* that will be used to hold the next pointer field of the node and the third we will call *prev* that will be used to hold the previous pointer field of the node. In addition, we will also use a *head* variable that holds the address of the first node and *tail* that hold the address of the last node of the list.

A special value denoted by *NULL* in *next* field of the last node will be used to indicate that there is no element after it (end of the list). The *NULL* value will also be used in *prev* field of the first node to indicate that there is no node before it (beginning of the list).

4.4.2 Operations on Doubly Linked Lists

In this section, we will describe operations on doubly linked lists.

4.4.2.1 Traversing

The steps for the traversal of a doubly linked list are same as that of linear linked list. The only difference is that a doubly linked list can be traversed easily in both the direction — *forward as well as backward.*

To traverse the list in the forward direction use *head* pointer as the entry to the list and follow the *next* pointer field to move from node to node.

To traverse the list in the backward direction use *tail* pointer as the entry to the list and follow the *previous* pointer field to move from node to node.

The writing of algorithms for traversal in both the direction is left as an exercise for the students.

4.4.2.2 Searching

Like traversal, there is no difference in search operations as well. Again the difference is that searching can done in both the directions.

The writing of algorithms for, named *searchForward(DLIST, item, loc)* and *searchBackward(DLIST, item, loc*), search operation in both the direction is left as an exercise for the students.

4.4.2.3 Inserting

To insert an element in the list, the first task is to get a free node, assign the element to be inserted to the *info* field of the node, and then new node is placed at the appropriate position by adjusting the appropriate pointers. The insertion in the list can take place at the following positions:

- at the beginning
- at the end
- after a given element
- before a given element

Before, we describe these cases, we will consider a case of insertion when double linked list is initially empty. This task is accomplished using following steps:

- Get free node and store its address in pointer variable *ptr*.
- Assign *NULL* value to the *next* and *prev* fields of the new node.
- Assign *ptr* to *head* and *tail* pointer variables.

(*a*) Before insertion

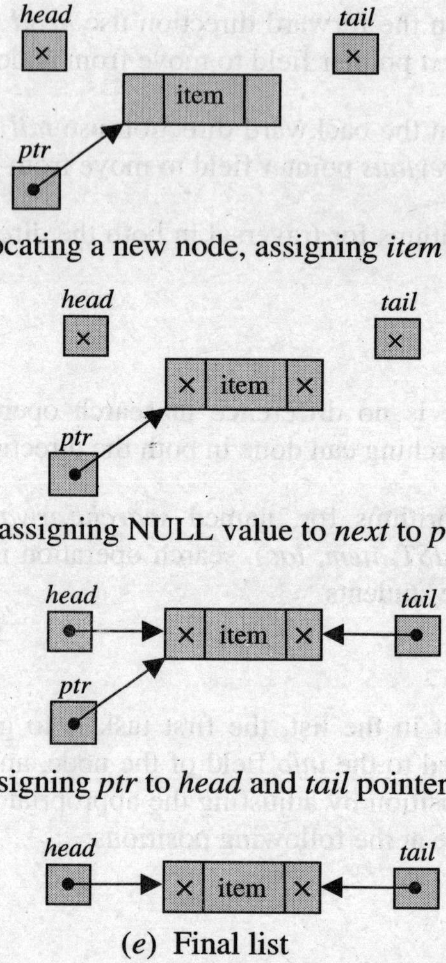

(*b*) After allocating a new node, assigning *item* to *info* part

(*c*) After assigning NULL value to *next* to *prev* part

(*d*) After assigning *ptr* to *head* and *tail* pointer variables

(*e*) Final list

Figure 4.14: Visualization of inserting a new element in an empty list

4.4.2.3.1 Inserting at the Beginning

An element is inserted as the first element of the list by performing the following steps:

- Assign *NULL* value to the previous pointer field of the new node.
- Assign value of the *head* variable (the address of the first element of the existing list) to the next pointer field of the new node.
- Assign address of the new node to previous pointer field of the node currently pointed by *head* variable, *i.e.*, first element of the existing list.
- Finally, assign the address of the new to node to *head* variable.

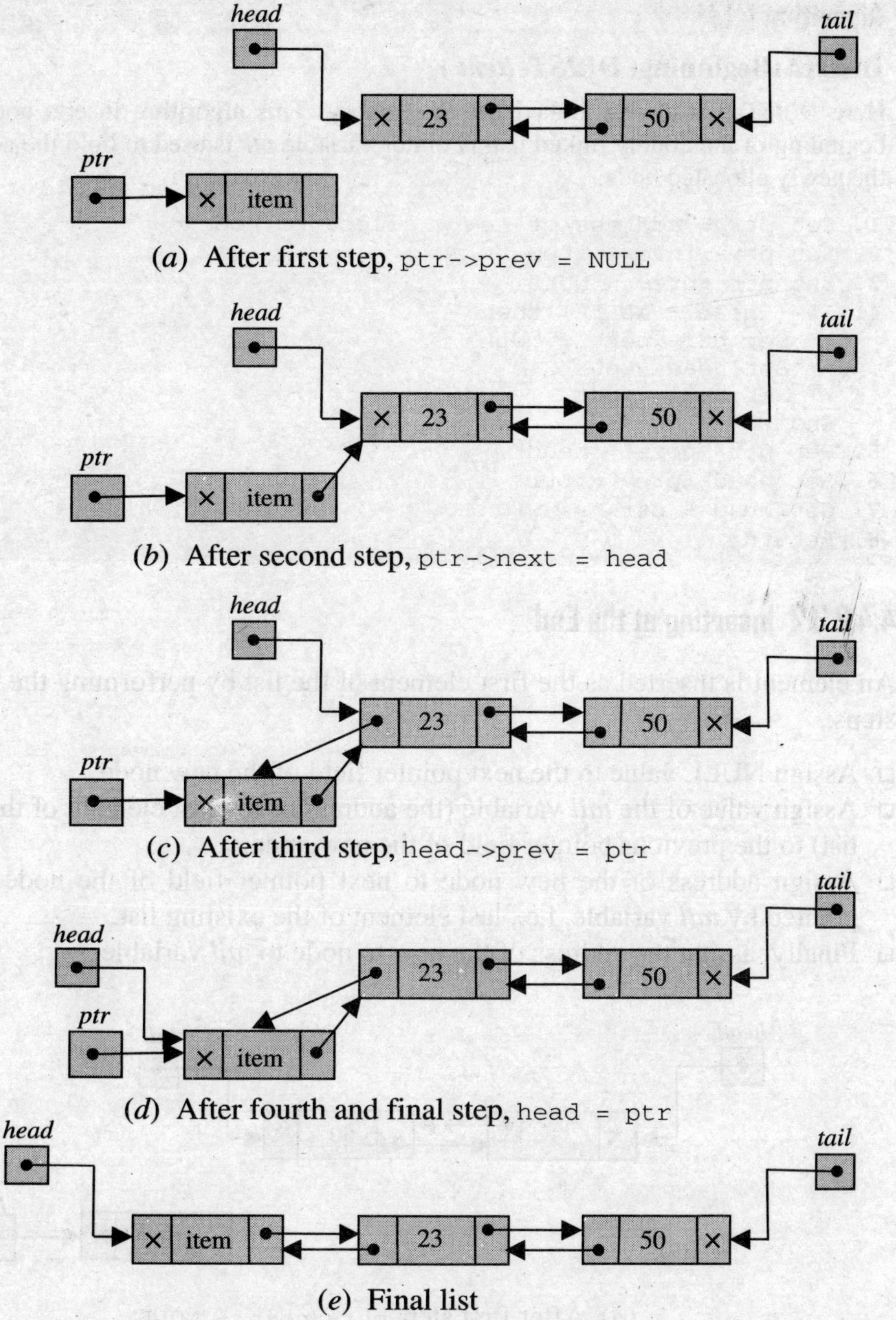

(*a*) After first step, `ptr->prev = NULL`

(*b*) After second step, `ptr->next = head`

(*c*) After third step, `head->prev = ptr`

(*d*) After fourth and final step, `head = ptr`

(*e*) Final list

Figure 4.15: Visualization of inserting a new element at beginning of doubly linked list

Algorithm 4.13

InsertAtBeginning(*DLIST*, *item*)

Here *DLIST* is a doubly linked list in memory. This algorithm inserts node in the beginning of the doubly linked lists. Pointer variable *ptr* is used to hold the address of the newly allocated node.

```
1. Set ptr = address of newly allocated node
2. Set ptr->info = item
3. Set ptr->prev = NULL
4. If ( head = NULL ) then
      Set ptr->next = NULL
      Set head = ptr
      Set tail = ptr
   Endif
5. Set ptr->next = head
6. Set head->prev = ptr
7. Set head = ptr
8. Return
```

4.4.2.3.2 Inserting at the End

An element is inserted as the first element of the list by performing the following steps:

- Assign NULL value to the next pointer field of the new node.
- Assign value of the *tail* variable (the address of the last element of the existing list) to the previous pointer field of the new node.
- Assign address of the new node to next pointer field of the node currently pointed by *tail* variable, i.e., last element of the existing list.
- Finally, assign the address of the new to node to *tail* variable.

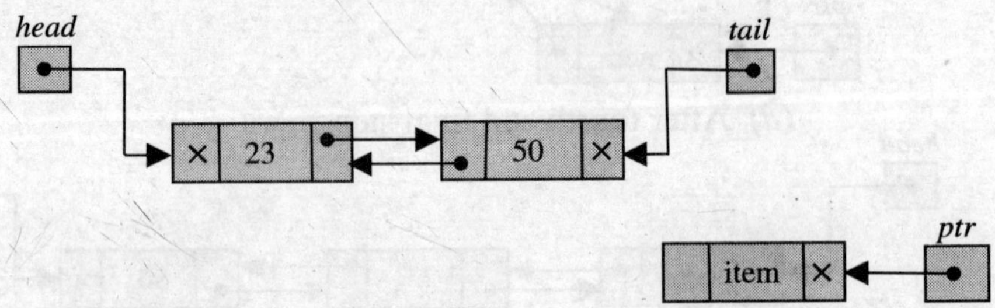

(*a*) After first step, `ptr->next = NULL`

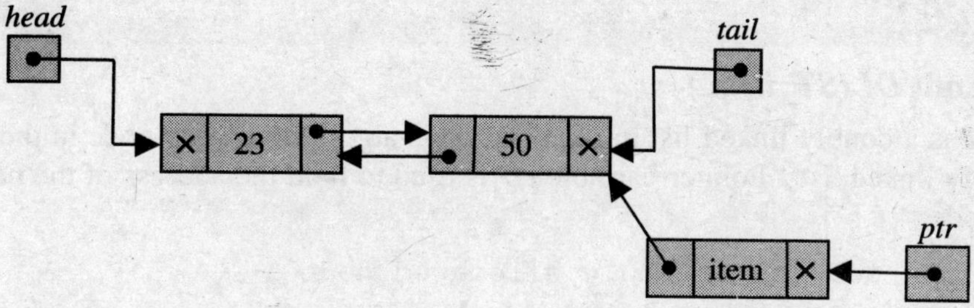

(*b*) After second step, `ptr->prev = tail`

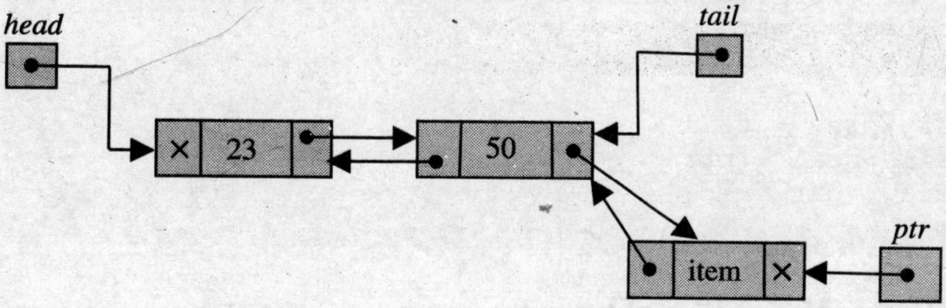

(*c*) After third step, `tail->next = ptr`

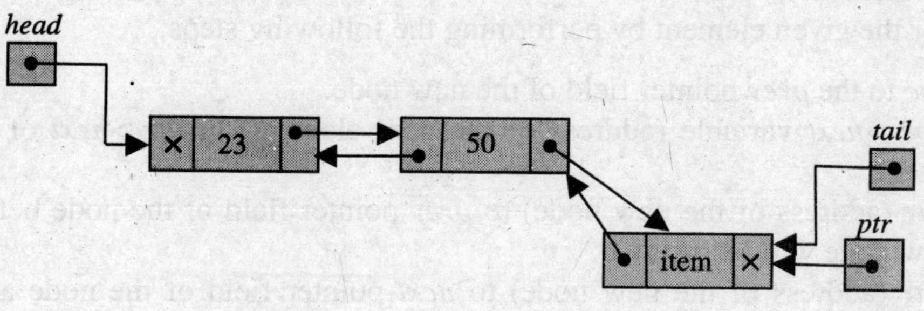

(*d*) After fourth and final step, `tail = ptr`

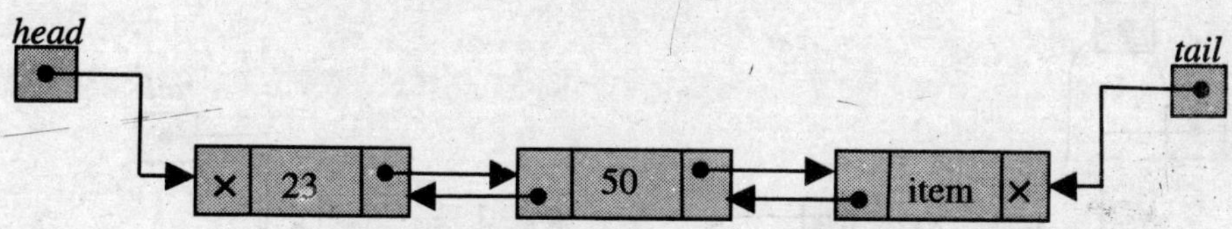

(*e*) Final list

Figure 4.16: Visualization of incerting a new element at end

Algorithm 4.14

InsertAtEnd(***DLIST, item*** **)**

Here *DLIST* is a doubly linked list in memory. This algorithm inserts node in the end of the doubly linked lists. Pointer variable *ptr* is used to hold the address of the newly allocated node.

```
1. Set ptr = address of newly allocated node
2. Set ptr-info = item
3. Set ptr->next = NULL
4. If ( head = NULL ) then
     Set ptr->prev = NULL
     Set head = ptr
     Set tail = ptr
   Endif
5. Set ptr->prev = tail
6. Set tail->next = ptr
7. Set tail = ptr
8. Return
```

4.4.2.3.3 Inserting After a Given Element

Once we find the location, say *loc*, of the given element (23), *i.e.*, first we reach out to the element after which new element is to be inserted. Then new element is inserted after the given element by performing the following steps:

- Assign *loc* to the *prev* pointer field of the new node.
- Assign *loc->next* variable (address of the next element) to *ptr->next* of the new element.
- Assign *ptr* (address of the new node) to *prev* pointer field of the node before which new node will be inserted.
- Assign *ptr* (address of the new node) to *next* pointer field of the node after which new node will be inserted.

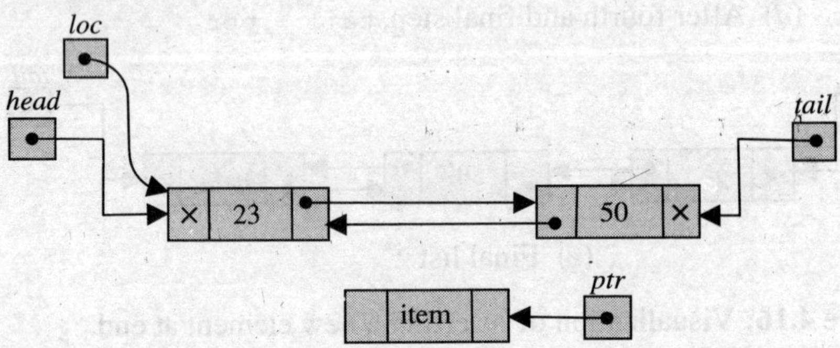

(*a*) After reaching out to the given element 23

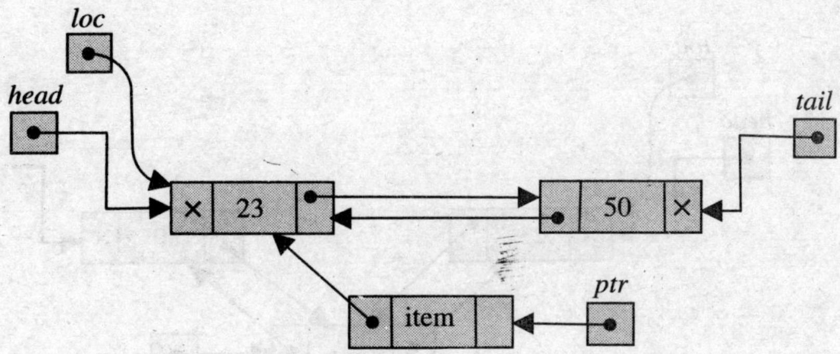

(*b*) After first step, `ptr->prev = loc`

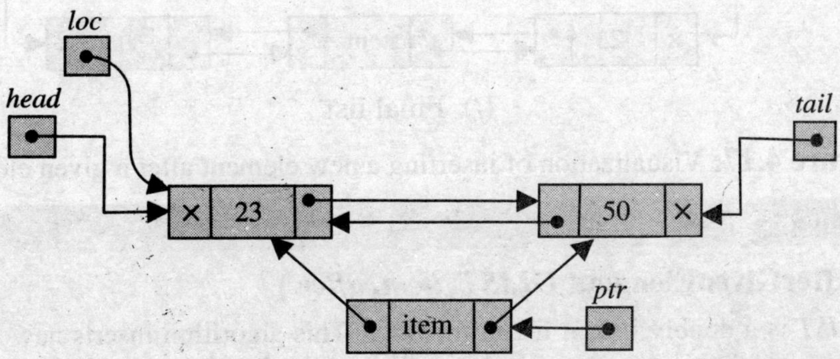

(*c*) After second step, `ptr->next = loc->next`

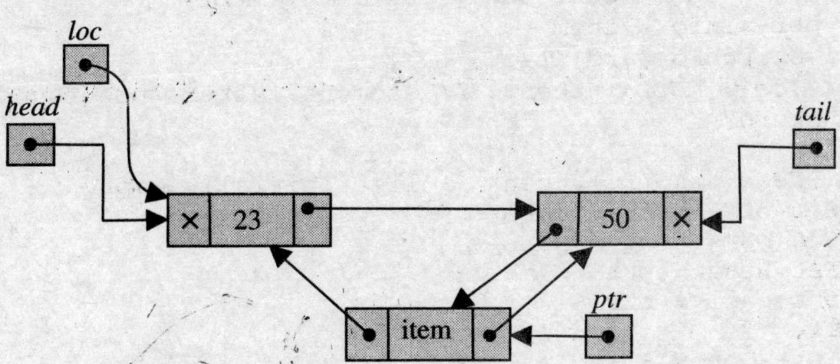

(*d*) After third step, `(loc->next)->prev = ptr`

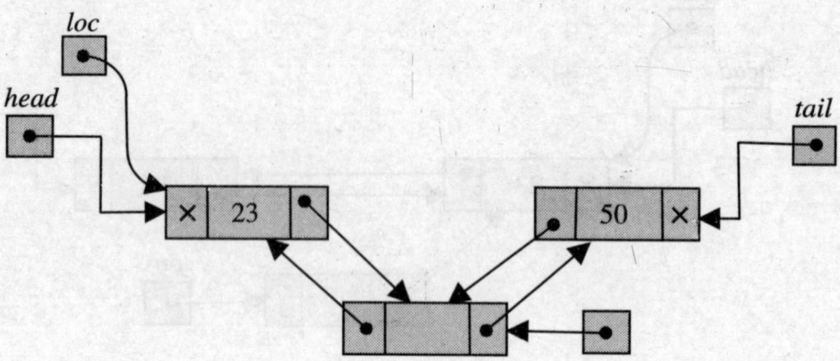

(*e*) After fourth and final step, `loc->next = ptr`

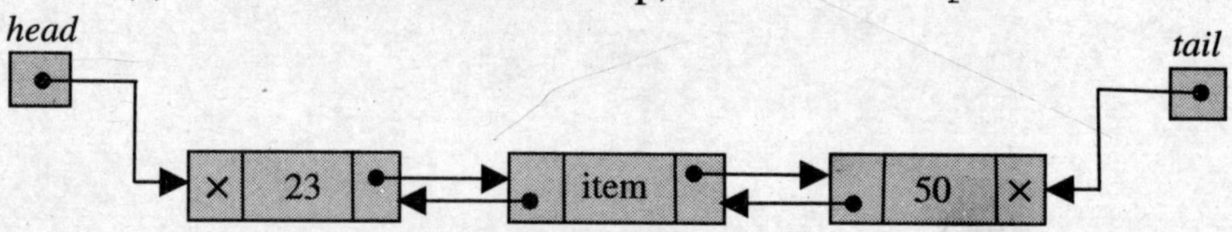

(*f*) Final list

Figure 4.17: Visualization of inserting a new element after a given element

Algorithm 4.15

InsertAfterGivenElement(***DLIST*, *item*, *after*** **)**

Here *DLIST* is a doubly linked list in memory. This algorithm inserts new node with value *item* after the node with value *after*. This algorithm first find the location *loc* of the given element *after*. Pointer variable *ptr* is used to hold the address of the newly allocated node.

```
1. Set ptr = address of newly allocated node
2. Set ptr->info = item
3. Call SearchForward(DLIST, after, loc)
4. If ( loc = NULL ) then   // element 'after' not found
      Return
   Endif
5. If ( head = NULL ) then  // list initially empty
      Set ptr->prev = NULL
      Set ptr->next = NULL
      Set head = ptr
      Set tail = ptr
   Endif
6. Set ptr->prev = loc
7. Set ptr->next = loc->next
8. Set (loc->next)->prev = ptr
9. Set loc->next = ptr
10. Return
```

4.4.2.3.4 Inserting Before a Given Element

Once we find the location, say *loc*, of the given element (50), *i.e.*, first we reach out to the element before which new element is to be inserted. Then new element is inserted before the given element by performing the following steps:

- Assign *loc* to the *next* pointer field of the new node.
- Assign *loc->prev* variable (address of the previous element) to *ptr->prev* of the new element.
- Assign *ptr* (address of the new node) to *next* pointer field of the node after which new node will be inserted.
- Assign *ptr* (address of the new node) to *prev* pointer field of the node before which new node will be inserted.

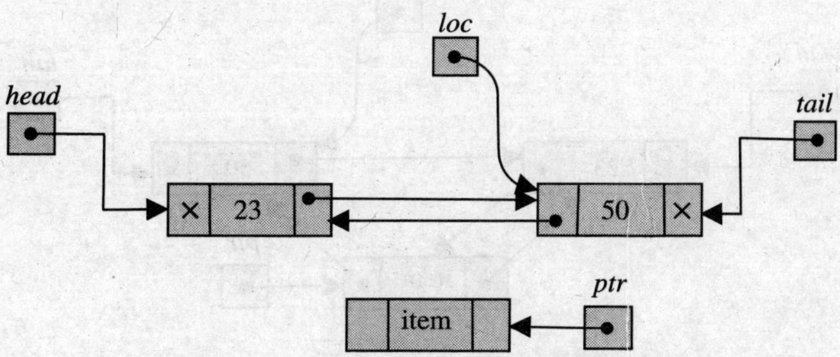

(*a*) After reaching out to the given element 50

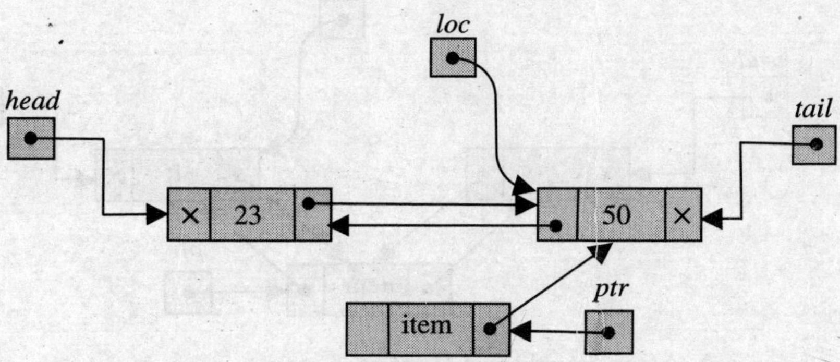

(*b*) **After first step,** `ptr->next = loc`

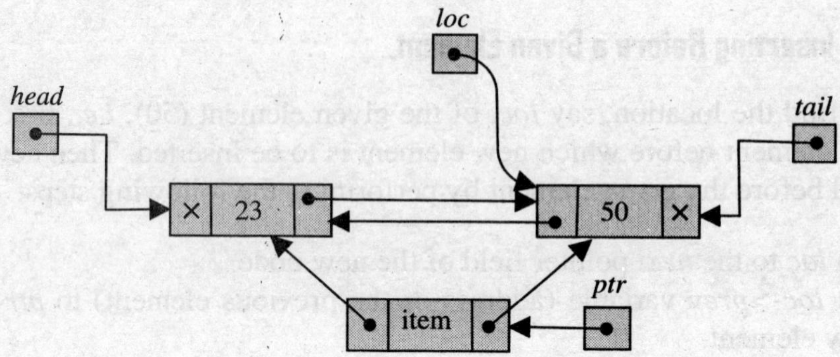

(*c*) After second step, `ptr->prev = loc->prev`

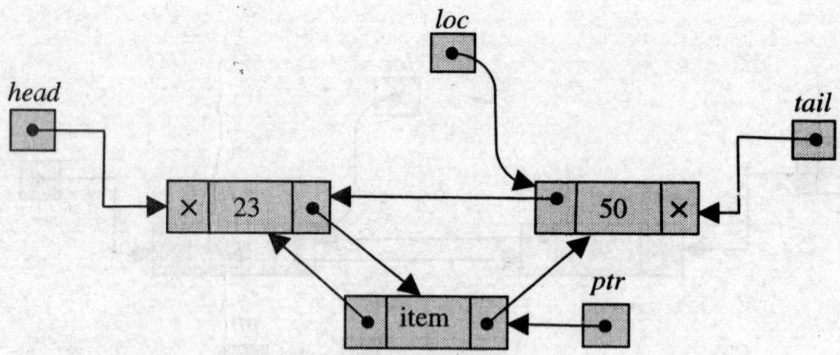

(*d*) After third step, `(loc->prev)->next = ptr`

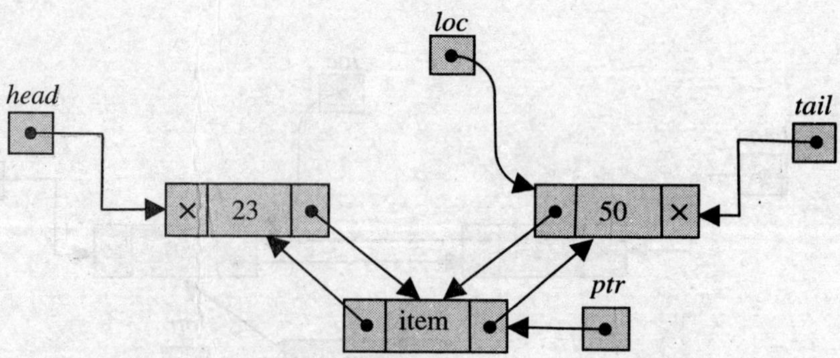

(*e*) After fourth and final step, `loc->prev = ptr`

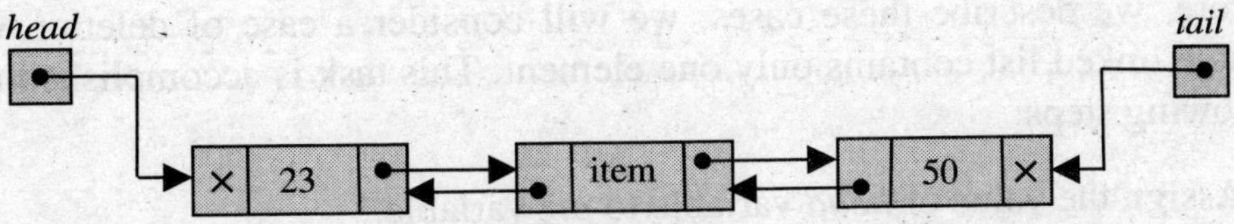

(*f*) Final list

Figure 4.18: Visualization of inserting a new element before a given element

Algorithm 4.16

InsertBeforeGivenElement(***DLIST*****,** ***item*****,** ***before*** **)**

Here *DLIST* is a doubly linked list in memory. This algorithm inserts new node with value *item* before the node with value *before*. This algorithm first find the location *loc* of the given element *before*. Pointer variable *ptr* is used to hold the address of the newly allocated node.

```
1. Set ptr = address of newly allocated node
2. Set ptr->info = item
3. Call SearchForward(DLIST, before, loc)
4. If ( loc = NULL ) then   // element 'before' not found
      Return
   Endif
5. If ( head = NULL ) then  // list initially empty
      Set ptr->prev = NULL
      Set ptr->next = NULL
      Set head = ptr
      Set tail = ptr
   Endif
6. Set ptr->next = loc
7. Set ptr->prev = loc->prev
8. Set (loc->prev)->next = ptr
9. Set loc->prev = ptr
10. Return
```

4.4.2.4 Deleting

To delete an element from the list, first the pointers are set properly and then the memory occupied by the node to be deleted is deallocated (freed).

The deletion in the list can take place at the following positions:

- at the beginning
- at the end
- after a given element
- before a given element

Before, we describe these cases, we will consider a case of deletion when the double linked list contains only one element. This task is accomplished using the following steps:

- ❑ Assign the value of *head* variable to *ptr* variable.
- ❑ Remove the node with address in *ptr*.
- ❑ Assign *NULL* value to *head* and *tail* pointer variables to indicate that doubly linked list is empty.

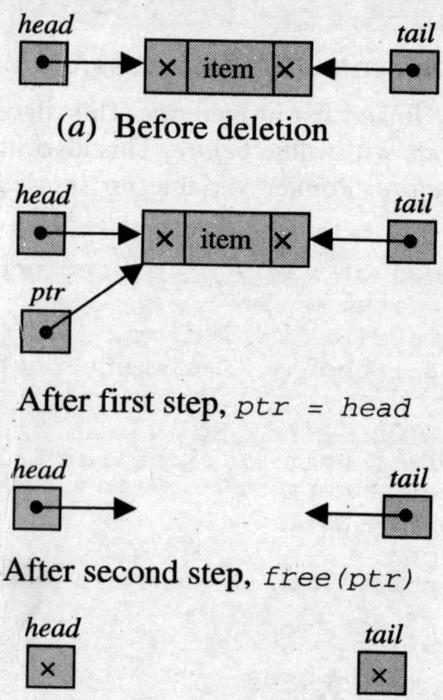

(*a*) Before deletion

(*b*) After first step, `ptr = head`

(*c*) After second step, `free(ptr)`

(*d*) After third and final step, `head =NULL, tail = NULL`

Figure 4.19: Visualization of deleting a element when doubly linked list contains only one element

4.4.2.4.1 Deleting from the Beginning

An element from the beginning of the lists can be deleted by performing following steps:

- ❑ Assign the value of *head* (address of the first element of the list) to a temporary variable (say *ptr*),

- Further, there are two cases:
  - o If there is only one element in the existing list, both *head* and *tail* variable are set to *NULL*.
  - o If there are more than one element in the list, then following steps given below:
    - ◊ Assign *NULL* value to the previous pointer field of the second node.
    - ◊ Assign address of the second node to *head*.
- Deallocate the memory occupied by the node pointed to by *ptr*.

We have already described the steps to delete a node when there is only one node in the doubly linked list. Here we will describe the steps when the doubly linked list contain two or more elements.

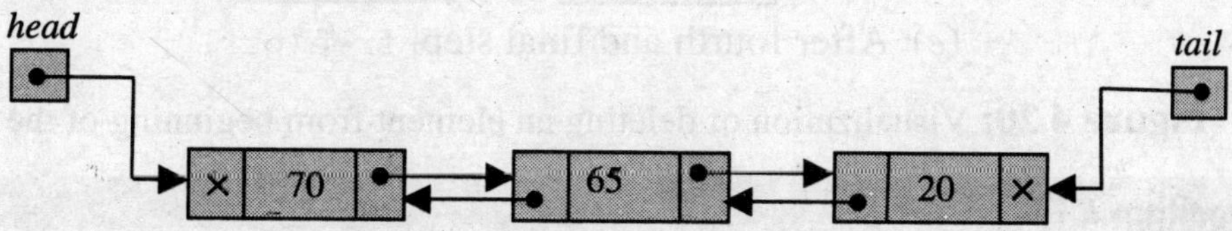

(*a*) Given list before deletion

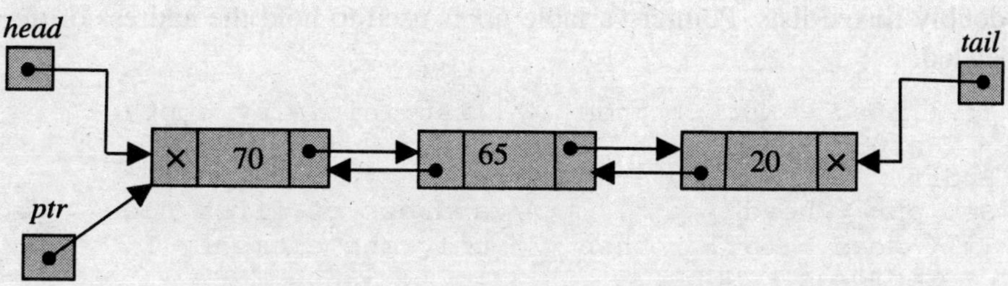

(*b*) After the first step, `ptr = head`

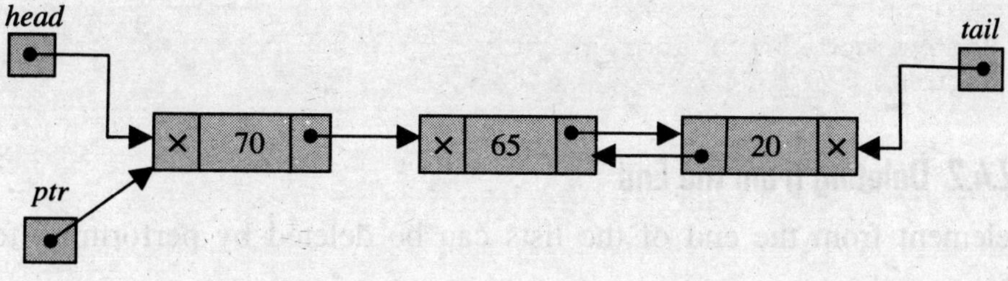

(*c*) After second step, `(head->next)->prev = NULL`

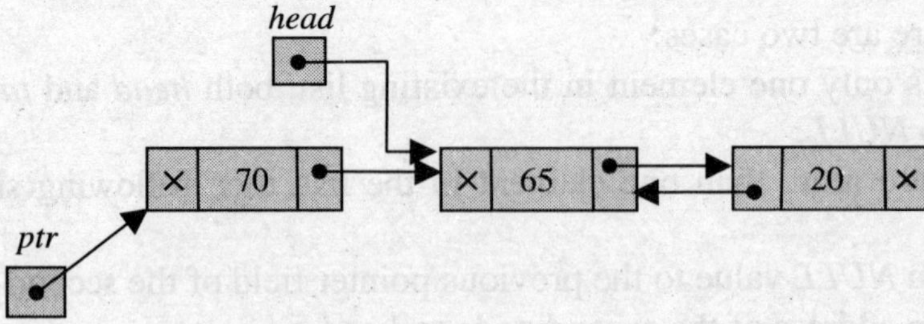

(*d*) After third step, `head = head->next`

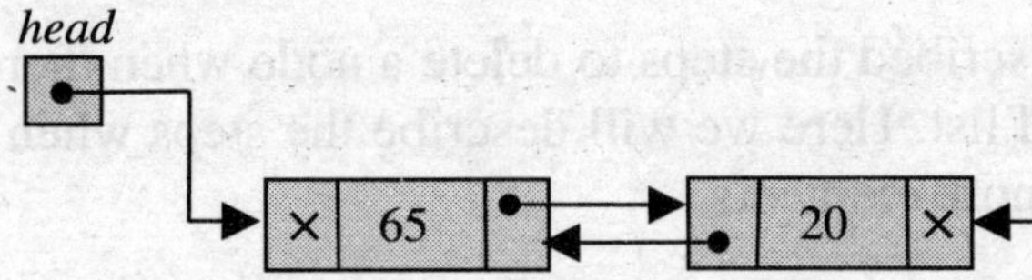

(*e*) After fourth and final step, `free(ptr)`

Figure 4.20: Visualization of deleting an element from beginning of the list

Algorithm 4.17

DeleteFromBeginning(***DLIST*** **)**

Here *DLIST* is a doubly linked list in memory. This algorithm deletes the first node of the doubly linked lists. Pointer variable *ptr* is used to hold the address of the node to be deleted.

```
1. If ( head = NULL ) then  // list initially empty
     Return
   Endif
2. Set ptr = head           // address of first node
3. If ( head = tail ) then  // only one element
     Set head = NULL
     Set tail = NULL
   Else
     Set head = head->next
   Endif
4. Remove node with address ptr
5. Return
```

4.4.2.4.2 Deleting from the End

An element from the end of the lists can be deleted by performing following steps:

- Assign the value of *tail* (address of the last element of the list) to a temporary variable (say *ptr*),

- Further, there are two cases:
  - o If there is only one element in the existing list, both *head* and *tail* variable are set to NULL.
  - o If there are more than one element in the list, then following steps given below:
    - ◊ Assign NULL value to the next pointer field of the second last node.
    - ◊ Assign address of the second last node to *tail*.
- Deallocate the memory occupied by the node pointed to by *ptr*.

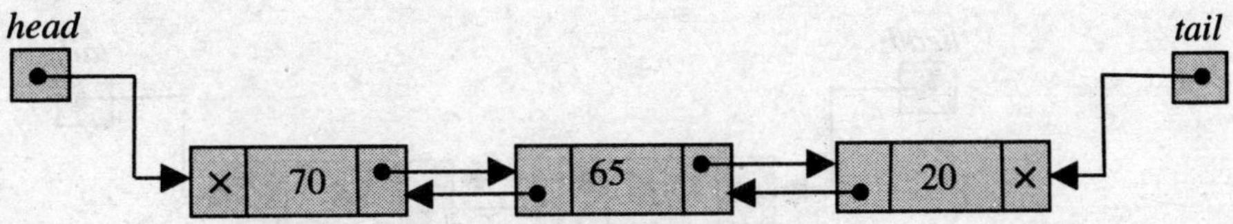

(*a*) Given list before deletion

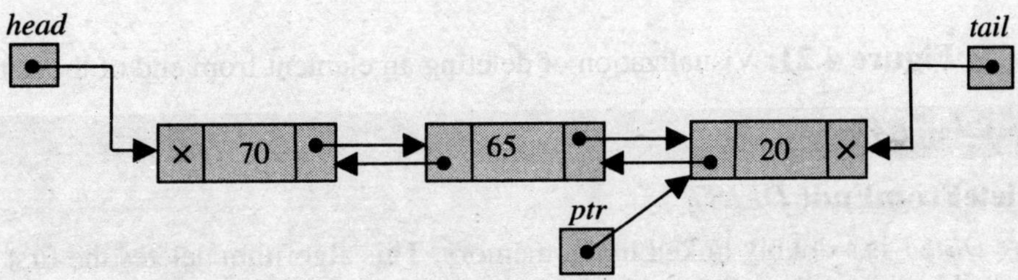

(*b*) After the first step, `ptr = tail`

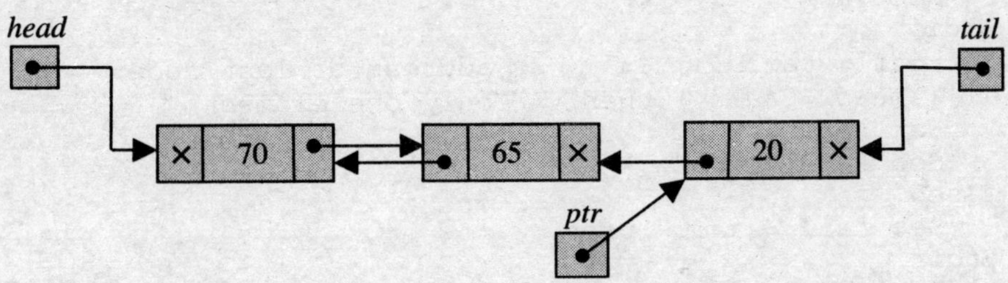

(*c*) After second step, `(tail->prev)->next = NULL`

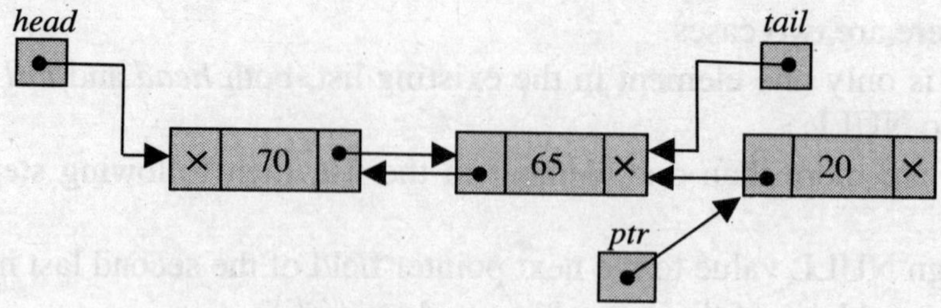

(*d*) After third step, `tail = tail->prev`

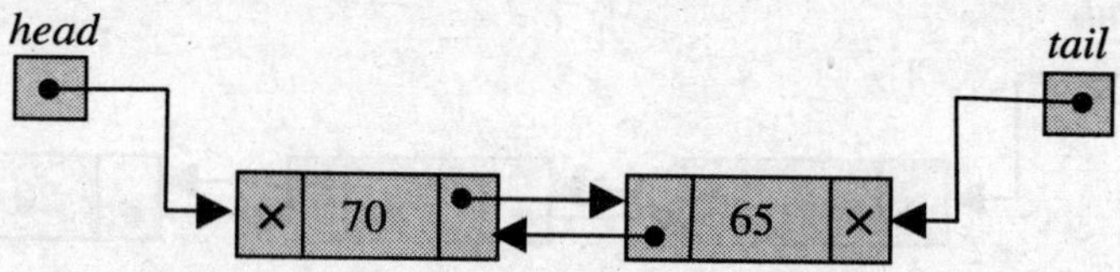

(*e*) After fourth and final step, `free(ptr)`

Figure 4.21: Visualization of deleting an element from end of the list

Algorithm 4.18

DeleteFromEnd(***DLIST*** **)**

Here *DLIST* is a doubly linked list in memory. This algorithm deletes the first node of the doubly linked lists. Pointer variable *ptr* is used to hold the address of the node to be deleted.

```
1. If ( head = NULL ) then  // list initially empty
      Return
   Endif
2. Set ptr = tail            // address of last node
3. If ( head = tail ) then  // only one element
      Set head = NULL
      Set tail = NULL
   Else
      Set tail = tail->prev
   Endif
4. Remove node with address ptr
5. Return
```

4.4.2.4.3 Deleting after a Given Element

An element after a given element can be deleted by performing following steps:

- Find the location, say *loc*, of the given element 70 in our example case, *i.e.*, reach to the element after which to delete.
- Assign the value of *loc->next* to a temporary variable (say *ptr*),
- Assign the value of *ptr->next* to a *loc->next*,
- Assign the value of *loc* to a (*ptr->next*)->prev,

However, if the node that is going to be deleted happens to be the last node, then the above last two steps are replaced by the following steps:

- Assign *NULL* value to the *loc->next*.
- Assign *loc* to the *tail*.

- Finally, deallocate the memory occupied by the node pointed to by *ptr*.

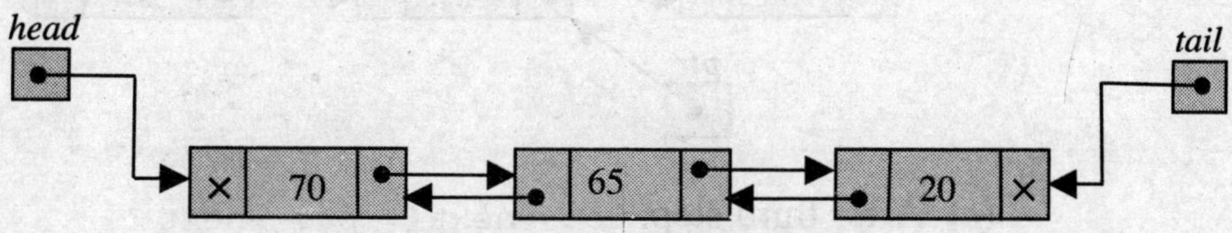

(*a*) Given list before deletion

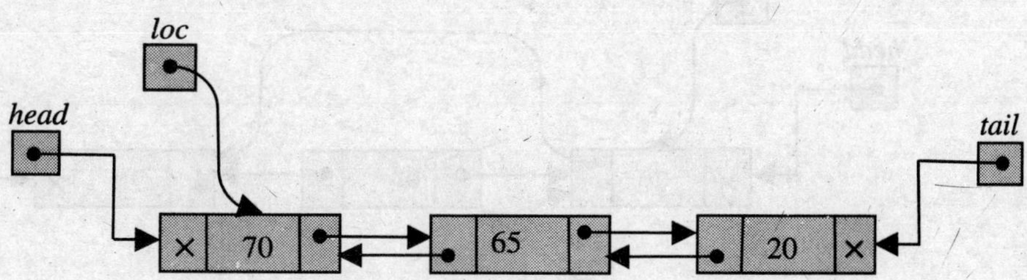

(*b*) After reaching out to the given element, say 70

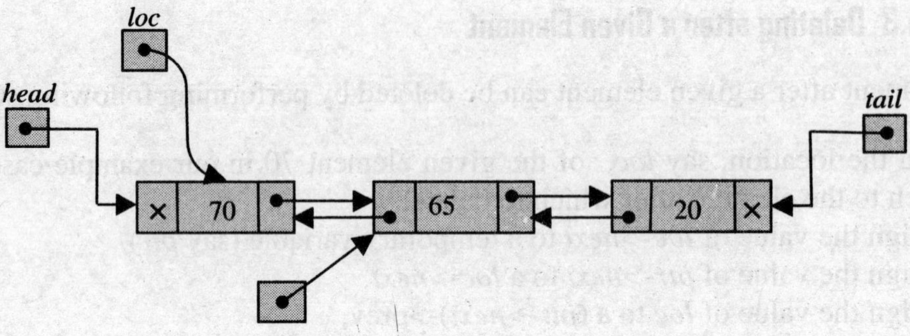

(*c*) **After first step,** `ptr = loc->next`

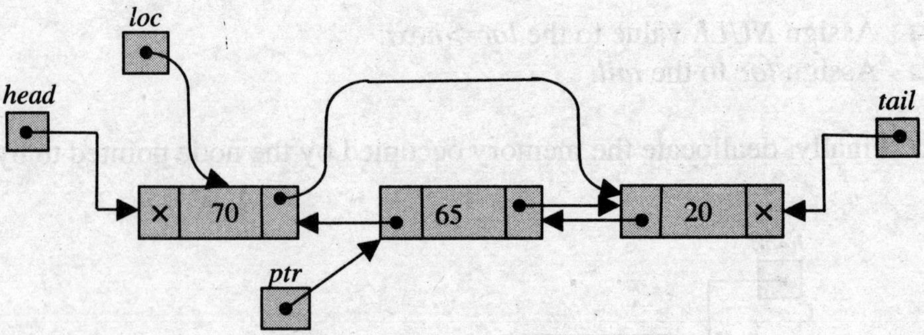

(*c*) **After third step,** `loc->next = ptr->next`

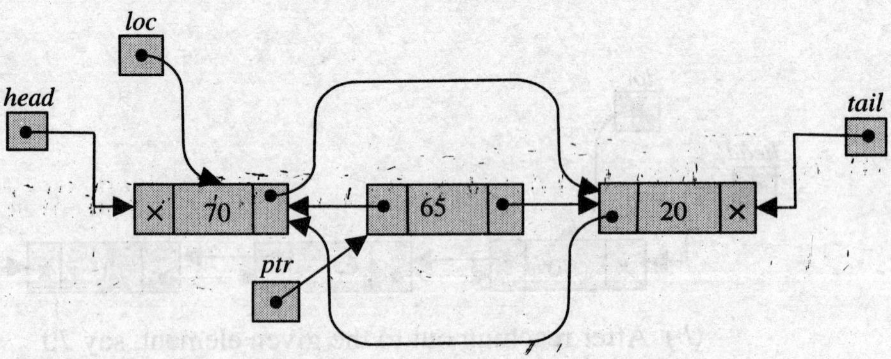

(*d*) **After third step,** `(ptr->next)->prev = loc`

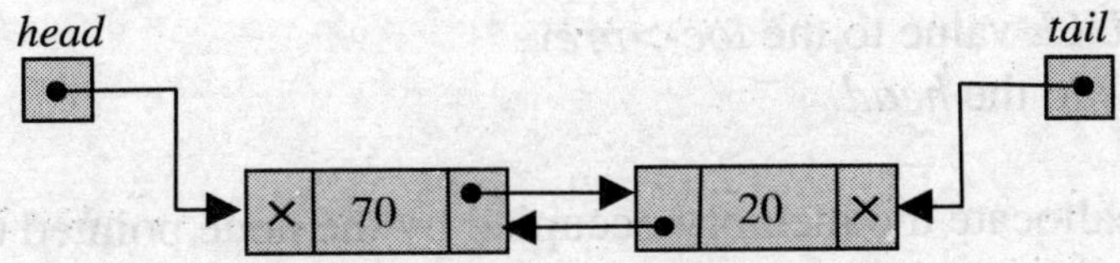

(*e*) After fourth and final step, `free(ptr)`

Figure 4.22: Visualization of deleting an element after a given element

Algorithm 4.19

DeleteAfterGivenElement(***DLIST, after*** **)**

Here *DLIST* is a doubly linked list in memory. This algorithm deletes the node after the given node with value *after* of the doubly linked lists. Pointer variable *loc* is used to hold the location of the node after which to delete. Pointer variable *ptr* is used to hold the address of the node to be deleted.

```
1. Call Search( DLLIST, after, loc )
2. If ( loc = NULL ) then    // element 'after' not found
      Return
   Endif
3. Set ptr = loc->next
4. If ( (loc->next)->next = NULL ) then    // last element
      Set loc->next = NULL
      Set tail = loc
   Else
      Set loc->next = ptr->next
      Set (ptr->next)->prev = loc
   Endif
5. Remove node with address ptr
6. Return
```

4.4.2.4.4 Deleting before a Given Element

An element before a given element can be deleted by performing following steps:

- Find the location, say *loc*, of the given element 20 in our example case, *i.e.*, reach to the element before which to delete.
- Assign the value of *loc->prev* to a temporary variable (say *ptr*),
- Assign the value of *ptr->prev* to a *loc->prev*,
- Assign the value of *loc* to a *(ptr->prev)->next*,

However, if the node that is going to be deleted happens to be the first node, then the above last two steps are replaced by the following steps:

- Assign *NULL* value to the *loc->prev*.
- Assign *loc* to the *head*.

- Finally, deallocate the memory occupied by the node pointed to by *ptr*.

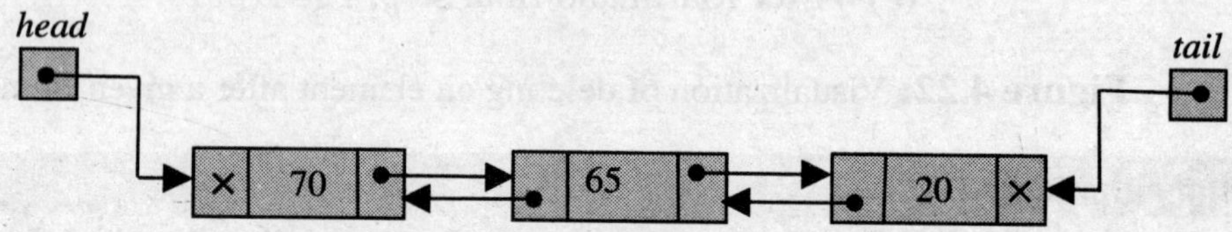

(*a*) Given list before deletion

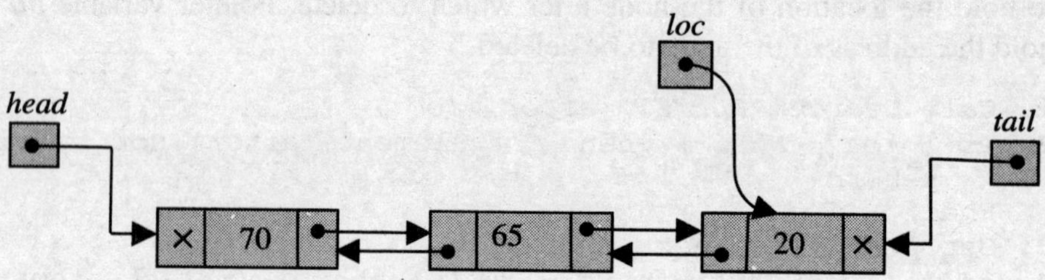

(*b*) After reaching out to the given element, say 20

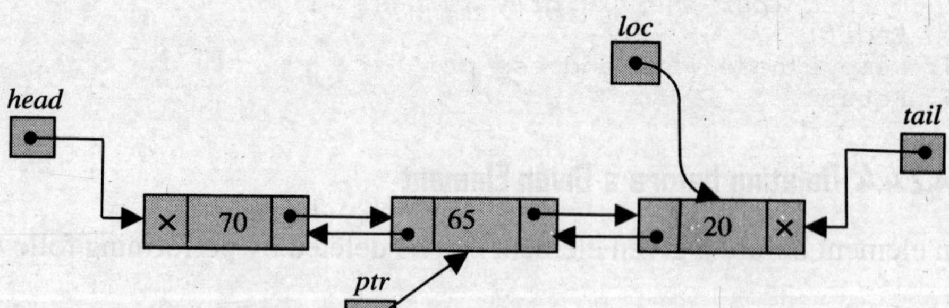

(*c*) After first step, `ptr = loc->prev`

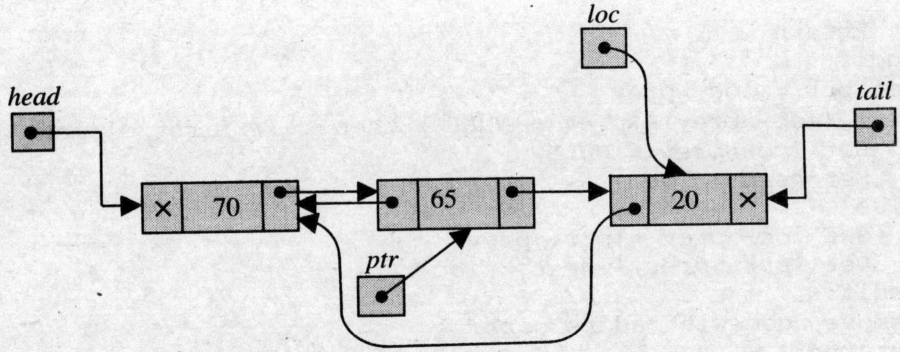

(*c*) **After third step,** `loc->prev = ptr->prev`

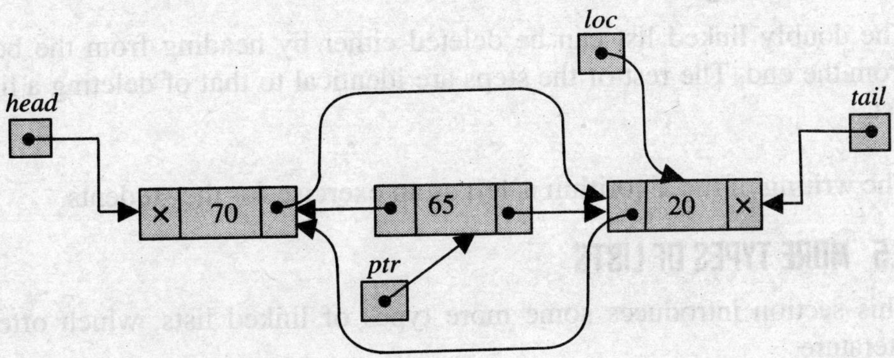

(*d*) **After third step,** `(ptr->prev)->next = loc`

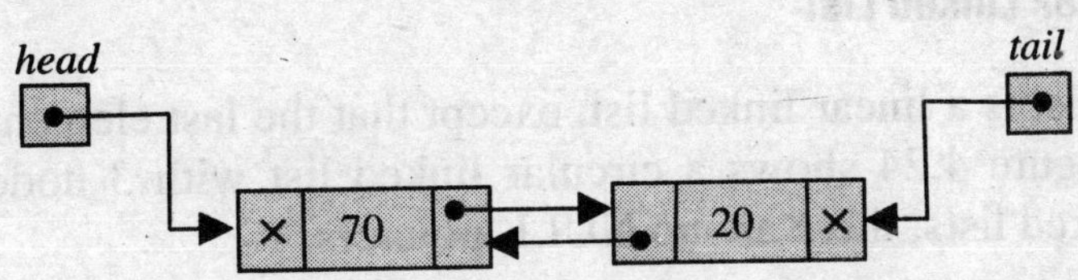

(*e*) **After fourth and final step,** `free(ptr)`

Figure 4.23: Visualization of deleting an element after a given element

Algorithm 4.20

DeleteBeforeGivenElement(***DLIST, before*** **)**

Here *DLIST* is a doubly linked list in memory. This algorithm deletes the node before the given node with value *before* of the doubly linked lists. Pointer variable *loc* is used to hold the location of the node before which to delete. Pointer variable *ptr* is used to hold the address of the node to be deleted.

```
1. Call Search( DLLIST, before, loc )
2. If ( loc = NULL ) then   // element 'after' not found
```

```
        Return
    Endif
3. Set ptr = loc->prev
4. If ( (loc->prev)->prev = NULL ) then    // first element
        Set loc->prev = NULL
        Set head = loc
   Else
        Set loc->prev = ptr->prev
        Set (ptr->prev)->next = loc
   Endif
5. Remove node with address ptr
6. Return
```

4.4.2.5 Deleting List

The doubly linked list can be deleted either by heading from the beginning or from the end. The rest of the steps are identical to that of deleting a linear linked list.

The writing of the algorithm is left as an exercise for the students.

4.5 MORE TYPES OF LISTS

This section introduces some more types of linked lists, which often occur in literature.

4.5.1 Circular Linked List

A circular list is a linear linked list, except that the last element points to the first element. Figure 4.24 shows a circular linked list with 3 nodes. For non-empty circular linked lists, there are no NULL pointers.

The memory declarations for representing circular linked lists are the same as for linear linked lists.

All operations performed on linear linked lists can be easily extended for circular linked lists with following exceptions:

1. While inserting new node at the end of the lists, its next pointer field is made to point to the first node.
2. While testing for end of the lists, we compare the next pointer field with the address of the first node.

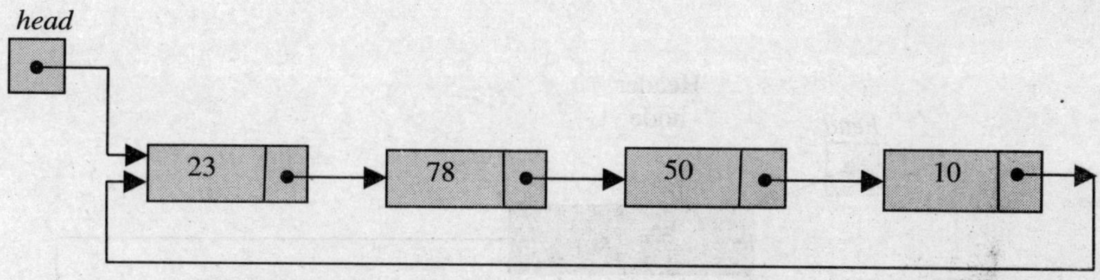

Figure 4.24: Circular linked list with 4 nodes

4.5.2 Header Linked Lists

A header list is linked list, which always contains a special node, called *header node*, at the beginning of the linked list. This header node usually contains vital information about the linked list such as the number of nodes in the lists, whether the list is sorted or not.

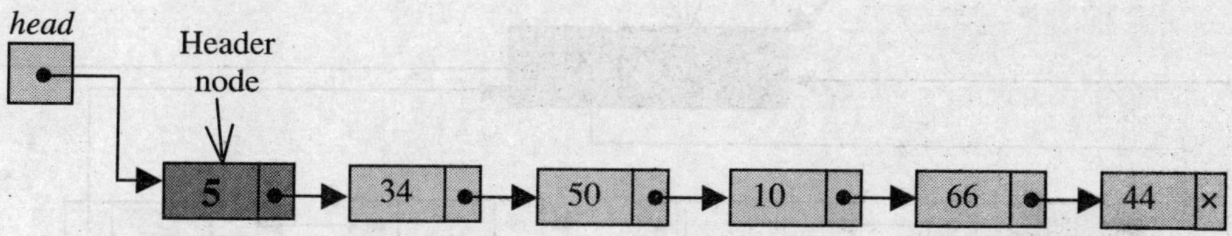

Figure 4.25: Header linear linked list, also known as grounded header list

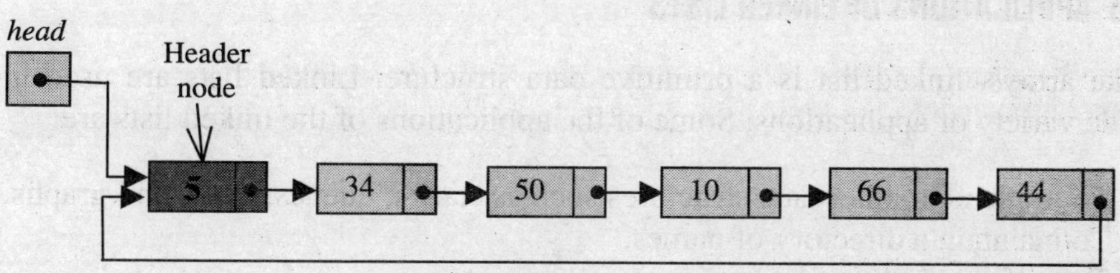

Figure 4.26: Circular header list

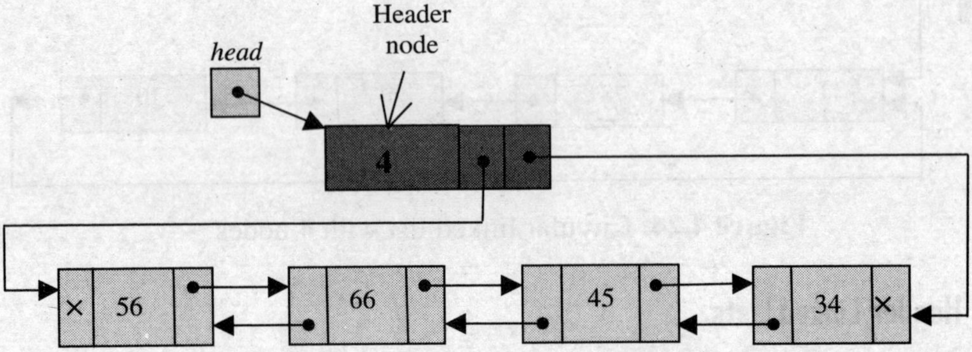

Figure 4.27: Two-way header list

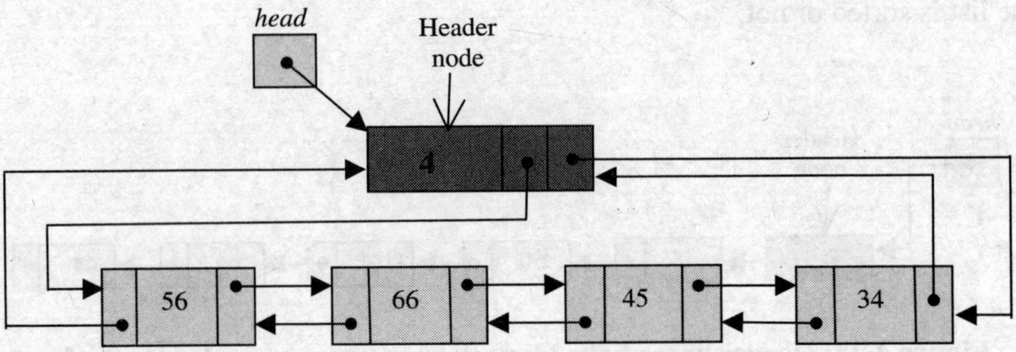

Figure 4.28: Two-way circular header list

4.6 APPLICATIONS OF LINKED LISTS

Like arrays, linked list is a primitive data structure. Linked lists are used in a wide variety of applications. Some of the applications of the linked lists are:

- To implement other data structures such as stacks, queues, trees, and graphs.
- To maintain a directory of names.
- To perform arithmetic operations on long integers.
- To manipulate polynomials.
- To represent sparse matrices.

4.7 COMPARATIVE VIEW OF LINKED LISTS AND ARRAY

Arrays and linked lists are the fundamental data structures. The rest of the data structures, such as *stacks*, *queues*, *trees* and *graphs*, are built on the top (using) of these data structures.

But, these data structures (arrays and linked lists) have their own inherit advantages and disadvantages. The following table gives a comparative view these data structures so that based on the demand of the software under construction, you can take an informative decision to choose array or linked lists to represent your complex data structure.

Table 4.1: Comparative view of arrays and linked lists

Arrays	Linked Lists
Its elements are stored in contiguous memory locations.	Its elements are not stored in contiguous memory locations.
System keeps track of address of the first element only, and the other elements accessed by computing their addresses at execution time using formula for address calculation.	System keeps track of address of the first element only, and the other elements are accessed following the chain of pointers.
It involves no overhead as for memory requirements are concerned.	It involves the overhead of memory for the storage pointers.
Time taken to access any element is same irrespective of its position in the linear array.	Time taken to access an element depends the position of the element in the linear linked list.
Elements can be accessed randomly.	Elements can be accessed in sequence only.
Addition and deletion operations are time consuming since on average half the elements are to moved down or up.	Addition and deletion operations are implemented efficiently by just adjusting few pointers and without disturbing other elements.
If the elements of a linear array are sorted, a given element can be searched quickly using binary search technique.	Even if the elements of a linear linked list are sorted, binary search technique can not be applied as there is no way to compute the address of the middle element.

SUMMARY

In this chapter, we have learnt about the

- variety of lists in general.
- representation of linear linked list in memory.
- algorithms for various operations that are performed on linear linked lists.
- representation of doubly linked list in memory.
- algorithms for various operations that are performed on doubly linked lists.
- other variations of linked lists.
- applications of linked lists.

REVIEW EXERCISES

1. How does a linear linked list compare with a linear array?
2. Is it possible in C language to implement a heterogeneous list? If, yes how?
3. What advantages does a doubly linked list have over linear linked lists?
4. How a linked list can be used to represent a polynomial of following type
   $$9x^3y^2 - 8x^2y^2 + 10xy + 3y^2$$
5. What is the advantage of a header node in a linked list?
6. What will be the complexity of the operation to remove an element from the end of the linear linked list?
7. What will be the complexity of the operation to add an element in the beginning of the linear linked list?
8. You are given a linear linked list sorted on ascending order. Can we apply binary search technique to search an element? Argue.
9. While implementing a linked list, do the programmers needs to implement a list of free nodes? Comment.
10. In a circular linked lists, how the end-of-list condition will be tested?
11. How many pointers need to be modified in the following operations?
    (*a*) Insert an element in the beginning of a linear linked list
    (*b*) Insert an element in the beginning of a doubly linked list
    (*c*) Insert an element in the middle of a doubly linked list
    (*d*) Delete an element from the end of a doubly linked list
    (*e*) Delete an element from the middle of a doubly linked list
    (*f*) Delete an element from the middle of a linear linked list

PROGRAMMING EXERCISES

1. Formulate an algorithm that removes all duplicate elements from a linear linked list.
2. Formulate an algorithm to traverse a circular linked list.
3. Formulate an algorithm that returns value 1 if the linear linked list is sorted in the ascending order otherwise it returns value 0.
4. Formulate an algorithm that makes copies of the given linear linked list.
5. Formulate an algorithm that counts number of elements in a linear linked list.
6. Formulate an algorithm that merges two sorted linear linked lists.
7. Formulate an algorithm that creates a new linear linked list by selecting alternate elements of a given linear linked list.
8. Formulate an algorithm that sorts a linear linked list of integer values in the descending order.
9. Formulate an algorithm to concatenate two sorted linked list.
10. Given a linear linked list whose elements are of type integer. Formulate an algorithm that copies the even integer numbers in one list and the odd integer numbers in another list.
11. For a given a linear linked, formulate an algorithm that:
    (*a*) returns the location of the successor of a given element.
    (*b*) returns the location of the predecessor of a given element
    (*c*) deletes the alternate elements from the list

11. Formulate an algorithm to remove all occurrences of a given element from a linear linked list.
12. Formulate an algorithm to remove last occurrence of a given element from a linear linked list.
13. Formulate an algorithm to remove first occurrence of a given element from a linear linked list.
14. Formulate an recursive algorithm to reverse a linear linked list.
15. Repeat all of the above programming exercises for doubly linked list.
16. Write a menu driven program to demonstrate the implementation of all the discussed operations on linear linked lists.
17. Write a menu driven program to demonstrate the implementation of all the discussed operations on doubly linked lists.

❑ ❑ ❑

Chapter 5

Stacks

Learning Objectives

After reading this chapter, students will be able to

- explain the concept of stack
- explain the way stacks are represented in memory using linear array
- write algorithms for performing operations on array based stacks
- explain the way stacks are represented in memory using linear linked list
- write algorithms for performing operations on linked list based stacks
- demonstrate the applications of stacks

5.1 INTRODUCTION

A *stack* is one of the most commonly used data structures. A *stack*, also called a Last-In-First-Out (LIFO) system, is a linear list in which insertions and deletions can take place only at one end, called the *top*. This structure operates in much the same way as stack of books, floppy disks or trays, as shown in Figure 5.1. If we want to place another item on the stack, it can be placed only at the top. Similarly, if we want to remove an item from stack of trays, it can only be removed from the top.

Therefore, we can say that the insertion and deletion operations in stack terminology are known as *push* and *pop* operations.

(*a*) (*b*) (*c*)

Figure 5.1: (*a*) Stack of books (*b*) Stack of floppy disks (*c*) Stack of trays

From the point of view of the subject of data structures, a stack can be viewed as shown in Figure 5.2.

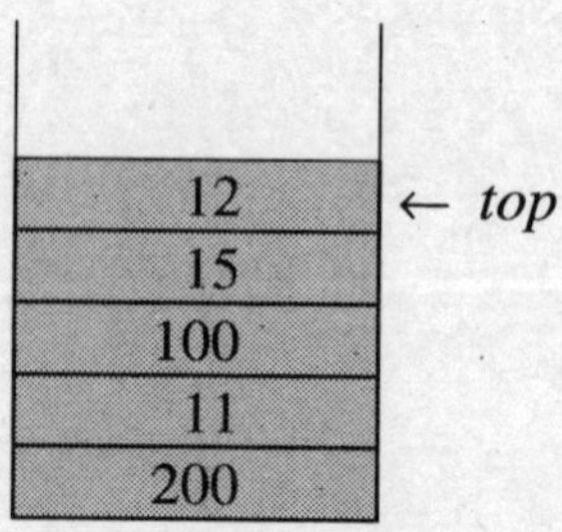

stack

Figure 5.2: A stack with 6 elements

Example 5.1:

Following figure illustrates a stack, which can accommodate maximum of 10 elements.

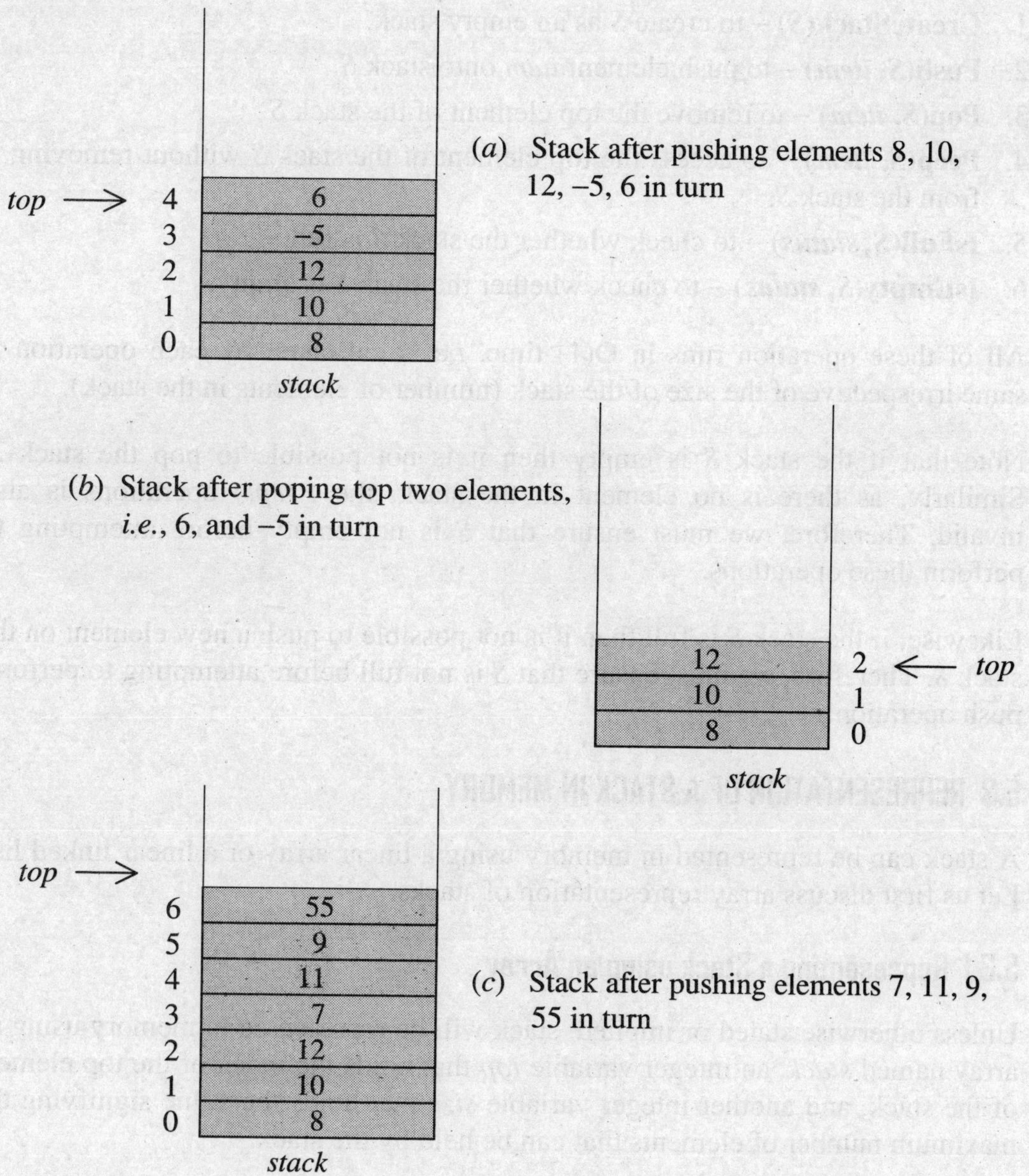

(*a*) Stack after pushing elements 8, 10, 12, –5, 6 in turn

(*b*) Stack after poping top two elements, *i.e.*, 6, and –5 in turn

(*c*) Stack after pushing elements 7, 11, 9, 55 in turn

Figure 5.2: Illustration of a stack whose elements are integer values

5.2 OPERATIONS ON STACKS

The following operations are performed on stacks.

1. **CreateStack(*S*)** – to create *S* as an empty stack.
2. **Push(*S*, *item*)** – to push element *item* onto stack *S*.
3. **Pop(*S*, *item*)** – to remove the top element of the stack *S*.
4. **Peep(*S*, *item*)** – to access the top element of the stack *S* without removing it from the stack *S*.
5. **IsFull(*S*, *status*)** – to check whether the stack *S* is full.
6. **IsEmpty(*S*, *status*)** – to check whether the stack *S* is empty.

All of these operation runs in O(1) time, *i.e.*, time taken by each operation is same irrespective of the size of the stack (number of elements in the stack).

Note that if the stack *S* is empty then it is not possible to pop the stack *S*. Similarly, as there is no element in the stack, the *Peep()* operations is also invalid. Therefore, we must ensure that *S* is not empty before attempting to perform these operations.

Likewise, if the stack *S* is full then it is not possible to push a new element on the stack *S*. Therefore, we must ensure that *S* is not full before attempting to perform push operation.

5.3 REPRESENTATION OF A STACK IN MEMORY

A stack can be represented in memory using a linear array or a linear linked list. Let us first discuss array representation of stacks.

5.3.1 Representing a Stack using an Array

Unless otherwise stated or implied, stack will be represented in memory using an array named *stack*, an integer variable *top* that holds the index of the top element of the stack, and another integer variable *size* that holds the value signifying the maximum number of elements that can be held by the stack.

With these declarations, stack of Figure 5.2 will be represented in computer memory as

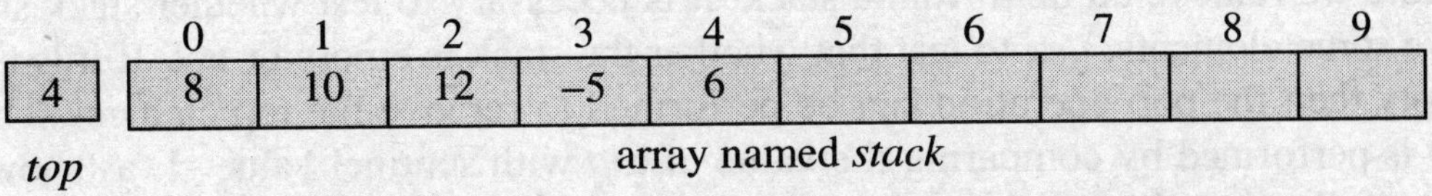

(*a*) Representation of stack of Figure 5.2(*a*) in memory

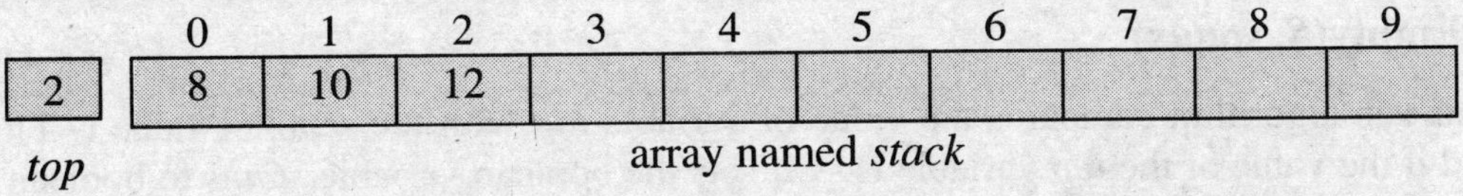

(*b*) Representation of stack of Figure 5.2(*a*) in memory

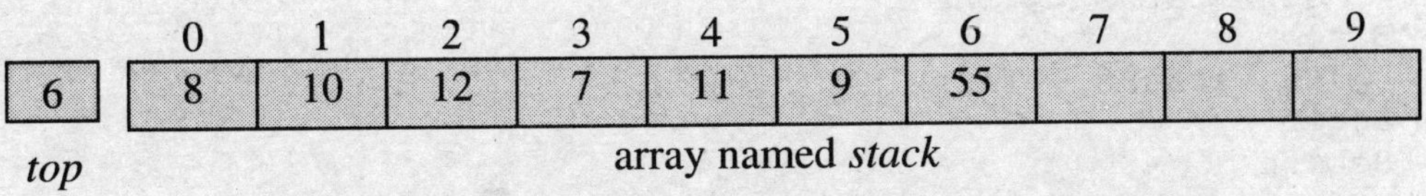

(*c*) Representation of stack of Figure 5.2(*a*) in memory

Figure 5.3: Array representation of stack of Figure 5.2

5.3.1.1 Creating Empty Stack

Before we can use a stack, it is to be initialized. As the index of array elements can take any value in the range 0 to (*size*-1), the purpose of initializing the stack is served by assigning value -1 (sentinel value) to the *top* variable. This simple task can be accomplished by the following algorithm.

Algorithm 5.1

CreateStack(*S*)

This sub algorithm assigns value -1 to variable *top* to put the stack in the initial state, *i.e.*, empty.

```
1. Set top = -1
2. Return
```

5.3.1.2 Testing Stack for Underflow

Before we remove an item from a stack, it is necessary to test whether stack still have some elements, *i.e.*, to test that whether the stack is empty or not. If it is not empty then the pop operation can be performed to remove the top element. This test is performed by comparing the value of *top* with sentinel value -1, as shown in the following algorithm.

Algorithm 5.2

IsEmpty(*S*, *status*)

This sub algorithm compares the value of variable *top* with the sentinel value (- 1), and if the value of the *top* variable is -1 it sets the boolean variable *status* to boolean value *true* else to boolean value *false*.

```
1. If ( top = -1 ) then
      Set status = true
   Else
      Set status = false
   Endif
2. Return
```

5.3.1.3 Testing Stack for Overflow

Before we insert new item onto the stack, it is necessary to test whether stack still have some space to accommodate the incoming element i.e. to test that whether the stack is full or not. If it is not full then the *push* operation can be performed to insert the element at top of the stack. This test is performed by comparing the value of the variable *top* with value of variable (*size*-1), the largest index value that the *top* can take as shown in the following algorithm.

Algorithm 5.3

IsFull(*S*, *status*)

This sub algorithm compares the value of variable *top* with (*size*-1), and if the value of the *top* variable is equal to (*size*-1), it sets the boolean variable *status* to boolean value *true* else to boolean value *false*.

```
1. If ( top = (size-1) ) then
      Set status = true
   Else
      Set status = false
   Endif
2. Return
```

5.3.1.4 Push Operation

Before the push operation, if the stack is empty, then the value of the *top* will be -1 (sentinel value) and if the stack is not empty then the value of the *top* will be the index of the element currently on the top. Therefore, before we place value onto the stack, the value of the *top* is incremented so that it points to the new top of stack, where incoming element is placed.

Algorithm 5.4

Push(*S*, *item*)

This sub algorithm calls sub algorithm *IsFull* to see whether the stack is full, and if the answer is yes, it flags "overflow" condition and returns. However, if the stack is not full, it pushes (adds) new element *item* onto the top of the stack.

```
1. Call IsFull(S, status)
2. If ( status = true ) then
      Write: "Overflow"
      Return
   Endif
3. Set top = top + 1
4. Set S[top] = item
5. Return
```

5.3.1.5 Pop Operation

The element on the top of stack is assigned to a variable (formal argument), and after assigning the top element to a local variable, the variable *top* is decremented so that it points to the new top.

Algorithm 5.5

Pop(*S*, *item*)

This sub algorithm calls sub algorithm *IsEmpty* to see whether the stack is empty, and if the answer is yes, it flags "underflow" conditions and exits. However, if the stack is not empty, it pops (removes) element from the top of the stack and assigns it to variable *item*.

```
1. Call IsEmpty(S, status)
2. If ( status = true ) then
      Write: "Underflow"
      Return
   Endif
3. Set item = S[top]
```

```
4. Set top = top - 1
5. Return
```

5.3.1.6 Accessing Top Element

There may be instances where we want to access the top element of the stack without removing it from the stack, *i.e.*, without popping it.

Algorithm 5.6

Peep(*S*, *item*)

This algorithm calls algorithm *IsEmpty* to see whether the stack is empty, and if the answer is yes, it flags "underflow" conditions and exits. However, if the stack is not empty, it peeps (access top element without removing it) element from the top of the stack and assigns it to variable *item*.

```
1. Call IsEmpty(S, status)
2. If ( status = true )
       Write: "Underflow"
       Return
   Endif
3. Set item = S[top]
4. Return
```

5.3.2 Representing a Stack Using a Linked List

A stack represented using a linked list is also known as *linked stack*. The array-based representation of stacks suffers from following limitations

- Size of the stack must be known in advance.
- We may come across situations when an attempt to push an element causes overflow. However, stack, as an abstract data structure can not be full. Hence, abstractly, it is always possible to push an element onto stack. Therefore, representing stack as an array prohibits the growth of stack beyond the finite number of elements.

The linked list representation allows a stack to grow to a limit of the computer's available (free) memory.

In linked representation, stack is represented using linear linked list. The *info* fields of the nodes hold the elements of the stack while the *next* fields hold the pointers to the neighbouring elements of the stack. The pointer variable *top* (instead of *start/head* consistent with the stack terminology) is used to hold the address (pointer) of the first element.

Note that the first element of the linear linked list is the element at the top of the stack and the last element of the linear linked list is the element at the bottom of the stack.

Therefore, the push operation is implemented by inserting new element at the beginning of the list, and the pop operation is implemented by removing the element from the beginning of the list.

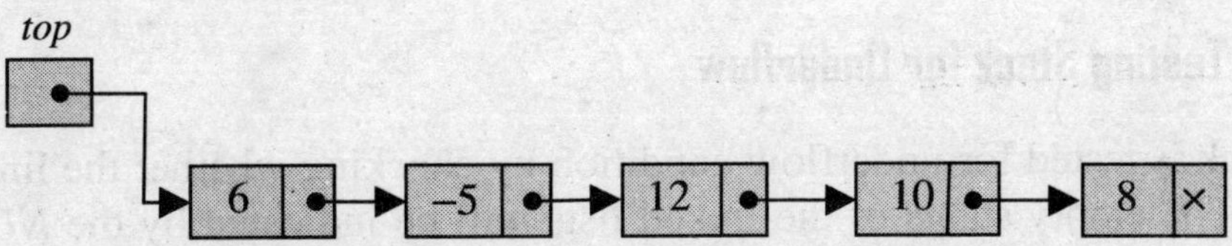

(*a*) Representation of stack of Figure 5.2(*a*) in memory

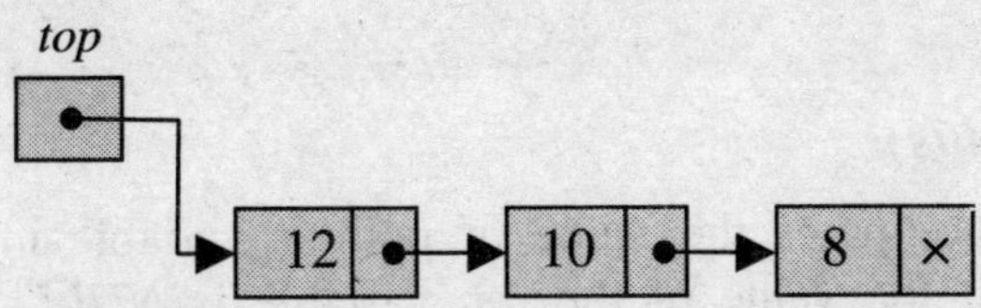

(*b*) Representation of stack of Figure 5.2(*b*) in memory

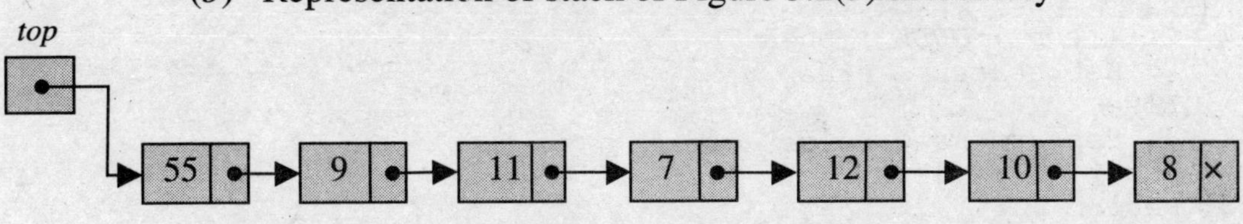

(*c*) Representation of stack of Figure 5.2(*c*) in memory

Figure 5.4: Linked representation of stack of Figure 5.2

With this representation, we will develop algorithms for various operations to be performed on a stack represented using linear linked list.

5.3.2.1 Creating Empty Stack

Before we can use a stack, it is to be initialized. To initialize a stack, we will create an empty linear linked list. The empty linear linked list is created by setting pointer variable *top* to value *NULL* (sentinel value).

Algorithm 5.7

CreateStack(*S*)

This sub algorithm assigns value *NULL* to pointer variable *top* to put the stack in the initial state, *i.e.*, empty.

```
1. Set top = NULL
2. Return
```

5.3.2.2 Testing Stack for Underflow

The stack is tested for underflow condition by checking whether the linked list is empty. The empty status of the linked lists will be indicated by the *NULL* value of pointer variable *top*.

Algorithm 5.8

IsEmpty(*stack, status*)

This sub algorithm compares the value of pointer variable *top* with the sentinel value (*NULL*), and if the value of the *top* variable is *NULL*, it sets the boolean variable *status* to boolean value *true* else to boolean value *false*.

```
1. If ( top = NULL ) then
      Set status = true
   Else
      Set status = false
   Endif
2. Return
```

5.3.2.3 Testing Stack for Overflow

Since a stack represented using a linked list can grow to a limit of a computer's available (free) memory, therefore, overflow condition rarely occurs. Therefore, this operation is usually is not implemented when stack is implemented using linked lists.

5.3.2.4 Push Operation

To push a new element onto the stack, the element is inserted in the beginning of the linked list.

Algorithm 5.9

Push(*S*, *item*)

This sub algorithm pushes (adds) new element to the stack by inserting the given element in the beginning of the linear linked list. The local pointer variable *ptr* is used to hold the address of the newly allocated.

```
1. Set ptr = address of the newly allocated node
2. If ( ptr = NULL ) then
       Write: "Overflow"
       Return
   Endif
3. Set ptr->info = item
4. Set ptr->next = top
5. Set top = ptr
6. Return
```

5.3.2.5 Pop Operation

To pop an element from the stack, the element is removed from the beginning of the linked list. This task is accomplished as shown in the following algorithm.

Algorithm 5.11

Pop(*S*, *item*)

This sub algorithm pops (removes) top element to the stack by removing element from the beginning of the linear linked list. The local pointer variable *ptr* is used to hold the address of the first node, before releasing it.

```
1. If ( top = NULL ) then
     Write: "Underflow"
     Return
   Endif
2. Set item = ptr->info
3. Set ptr = top
4. Set top = top->next
5. Remove node with address ptr
6. Return
```

5.3.2.6 Accessing Top Element

The top element is accessed as shown in the following algorithm.

Algorithm 5.12

Peep(*S*, *item*)

This sub algorithm accesses top element without removing it, from the stack and assigns it to variable *item*.

```
1. If ( top = NULL ) then
      Write: "Underflow"
      Return
   Endif
2. Set item = ptr->ptr
3. Return
```

5.3.2.7 Dispose a Stack

Because stack is implemented using linked lists, therefore it is programmer's job to write the code to release the memory occupied by the stack.

Algorithm 5.13

DisposeStack(stack)

This algorithm removes the entire linked stack from memory. It makes use of local pointer variable *ptr* to hold the address of the node before removing that node from the linked stack.

```
1. Repeat steps 2 to 4 While ( top ≠ NULL )
2.     Set ptr = top
3.     Set top = top->next
4.     Remove node with address ptr
   Endwhile
5. Return
```

This dispose operations is $O(n)$ time.

5.4 ARITHMEIC EXPRESSIONS

In this section, we will consider various aspects of arithmetic expressions that include notations used for writing arithmetic expressions, converting expression from one notation to another, and evaluating them.

5.4.1 Notations for Arithmetic Expressions

Let us first consider various types of notations used for writing arithmetic expressions. In our discussion, we will consider the following set of operations.

Table 5.1: List of Operators

Symbol Used	Operation Performed	Precedence
* (asterisk)	Multiplication	Highest
/ (slash)	Division	Highest
% (percentage)	Modulus (Remainder)	Highest
+ (plus)	Addition	Lowest
– (hyphen)	Subtraction	Lowest

For simplicity, we will assume that a given expression contains no unary operation. We also assume that the operations on the same level of precedence are performed from left to right.

Since in lab work, the readers will be implementing the above operations using either C or C++ language and these languages doesn't provide arithmetic operator for exponentiation operation, and therefore, the exponentiation operator is not considered in our discussion as well.

5.4.1.1 Infix Notation

In this notation, the operator symbol is placed between its two operands. For example

- to add A to B we can write as A + B or B + A
- to subtract D from C we write as C – D, but we can't write D – C as this operation is not commutative

In this notation, we must distinguish between

(A + B) / C   and   A + (B / C)

5.4.1.2 Polish (Prefix) Notation

In this notation, named after the Polish mathematician ***Jan Lukasiewicz***, the operator symbol is placed before its two operands. For example,

- to add A to B we can write as +AB or +BA
- to subtract D from C we have to write as –CD not as –DC

In order to translate an arithmetic expression in infix notation to polish notation, we do step by step using brackets ([]) to indicate the partial translation.

Consider the following expression in infix notation:

(A – B / C) * (A * K – L)

partial translations may look like:

(A – [/BC]) * ([*AK] – L)

[–A/BC] * [–*AKL]

*–A/BC–*AKL

The fundamental property of polish notation is that the order in which the operations are to perform is completely determined by the positions of the operators and operands in the expression. Accordingly one never needs parenthesis when writing expressions in polish notation.

This notation is also called *prefix* notation.

5.4.1.3 Reverse Polish (Postfix) Notation

In this notation the operator symbol is placed after its two operands. For example,

- to add A to B we can write as AB+ or BA+
- to subtract D from C we have to write as CD– not as DC–

In order to translate an arithmetic expression in infix notation to reverse polish notation, we do step by step using brackets ([]) to indicate the partial translation.

Consider the following expression in infix notation:

(A – B / C) * (A * K – L)

the partial translations may look like:

(A – [BC/]) * ([AK/] – L)

[ABC/–] * [AK/L–]

ABC/–AK/L–*

Like polish notation, here too one never needs the use of parenthesis when writing expressions in reverse polish notation.

This notation is frequently called *postfix* (or *suffix*) notation.

5.4.2 Evaluating Arithmetic Expressions

Evaluation of arithmetic expressions involves following steps:

- Converting arithmetic expression from infix notation to postfix notation, and
- Evaluating the expression in postfix notation

We will consider these steps separately. Note that in each of these steps, stack is used.

5.4.2.1 Infix-to Postfix Conversion

Let q be an arithmetic expression written in infix notation. Besides operands and operators, it may also contain left and right parenthesis. We assume the given expressions contain only operators listed in Table 5.1, and operations of the same precedence are evaluated from left to right.

For simplicity, we will assume that the given expression contain only single letter variables and single digit operands.

Algorithm 5.14

InfixToPostfix(*q*, *p*)

Here q is the arithmetic expression in-infix notation. This algorithm translates this expression into its equivalent postfix expression p. To accomplish this task, it uses a stack S with element of character type.

```
1. Create Empty Stack S
   // Scan expression q from left-to-right for each element
2. Repeat steps 3 to 6 While ( not endof expression q )
3.    If ( ch is left parenthesis ) then
          Push ch onto stack S
      Endif
4.    If ( ch is right parenthesis ) then
         (a) Repeat steps 4b While ((S is not empty) and
                   (element at top of S is not left parenthesis))
         (b)     Pop stack S and append poped character to p
             Endwhile
         (c) If ( S is empty ) then
                Print : "Error: Incorrect expression"
                Return
             Endif
         (d) Remove left parenthesis from stack S
                [ don't add the left parenthesis to p ]
      Endif
5.    If ( ch is operand ) then
          Append ch to P
      Endif
6.    If ( ch is operator ) then
         (a) Repeat step 6b while (( element at top of stack is
             operator and its precedence ≥ ch ) and (stack
             is not empty) )
         (b)     Pop stack and append poped element to p
             Endwhile
         (c) Push ch onto stack S
      Endif
   Endwhile
7. Repeat step 8 While ((stack is not empty) and (element at top
         of stack is not left parenthesis ) do
8.       Pop stack and append poped element to p
   Endwhile
9. If ( element at top of stack is left parenthesis ) then
      Print: "Error: Incorrect expression"
   Endif
10. Return
```

Things will be clearer after going through following working example.

Example 5.2:

Consider the following infix expression q:

$$(7-5)*(9/2)$$

The progress of the algorithm to translate q to postfix expression p is shown in Table 5.2.

Table 5.2: Conversion from Infix to Postfix Notation

Character Scanned	Stack	Expression *p*
(	(	
7	(	7
–	(, –	7
5	(, –	7, 5
)	Empty	7, 5, –
*	*	7, 5, –
(	*, (	7, 5, –
9	*, (	7, 5, –, 9
/	*, (, /	7, 5, –, 9
2	*, (, /	7, 5, –, 9, 2
)	*	7, 5, –, 9, 2, /
End of expression	Empty	7, 5, –, 9, 2, /, *

5.4.2.2 Evaluating Expression in Postfix Notation

Algorithm 5.3

EvaluatePostfixExpression(***p, result*** **)**

Here *p* is the arithmetic expression in postfix notation. This algorithm evaluates this expression and returns the value of the expression through variable *result*.

```
1. Create Empty Stack S
2. Repeat steps 3 to 7 While ( not end-of expression p )
3.    If ( element is operand ) then
         Push element onto stack
      Endif
4.    If ( element is operator, say ⊗ ) then
         (a) Pop two elements and let first as operand y and
             the second as operand x
         (b) Evaluate x ⊗ y, let its value be z
         (c) Push z onto stack
      Endif
   Endwhile
5. Pop stack and assign this value to parameter result
6. Exit
```

Things will be clearer after going through next working example.

Example 5.3:

Consider the following postfix expression *p*:

7, 5, –, 9, 2, /, *

The progress of the algorithm 5.3 to evaluate postfix expression *p* is shown in the following table.

Table 5.3: Evaluation of Postfix Expression

Character Scanned	Stack
7	7
5	7, 5
–	2
9	2, 9
2	2, 9, 2
/	2, 4.5
*	9
End of expression	9

The final number in stack, *i.e.*, 9, is the value of postfix expression *p*.

5.5 QUICKSORT - APPLICATION OF STACKS

Quicksort is a sorting algorithm that the idea of *divide and conquer*. This algorithm uses the first element, called *pivot*, and partitions the array into two halves in such a way that the elements in the left sub array are less than the pivot and the elements in the right sub array are greater than the pivot. Then these two subarrays are sorted separately. This procedure is recursive in nature with the base criteria – the number of elements in the array are not more than 1.

Suppose variable *beg* and *end* represents the index of the first and last element of the array respectively, the quick sort can be defined recursively as

```
If ( beg < end ) then
   Find the location of the pivot such that it partitions the
   array into two halves
   Quicksort the left half
   Quicksort the right half
Endif
```

The main task in quick sort is to find the element that partitions the array into two halves and to place it at its proper location in the array. Usually, the procedure places the first element in the array at its final location. This task is performed as stated below.

To begin with, set the index of the first element of the array to *loc* and *left* variables, and index of the last element of the array to *right* variable. Then proceed as follows:

1. Beginning with the element pointed to by *right*, the array is scanned from right to left, comparing each element on the way with the element pointed to by *loc*, till either
   (a) Element smaller than the element pointed to by *loc* is found. In this case, the elements are interchanged and procedure continues with step 2.
   (b) If the value of the *right* variable becomes equal to the value of *loc*, the procedure terminates here. This condition indicates that the element is placed in its final position *loc*.
2. Beginning with the element pointed to by *left*, the array is scanned from left to right, comparing each element on the way with the element pointed to by *loc*, till either
   (a) Element greater than the element pointed to by *loc* is found. In this case, the elements are interchanged and procedure continues with step 1.
   (b) If the value of the *left* variable becomes equal to the value of *loc*, the procedure terminates here. This condition indicates that the element is placed in its final position *loc*.

As this procedure terminates, first element, the pivot, of original the array will be placed at *loc*, its final location in the sorted array. Elements to left of it will be less than it and elements to its right will be greater than it.

Example 5.4:

To illustrate the above procedure, consider the array

25 10 30 15 20 28

Solution:

Here the pivot element is 25.

To begin with set *loc* = 0, *left* = 0, *right* = 5 as

a[0]	*a*[1]	*a*[2]	*a*[3]	*a*[4]	*a*[5]
25	10	30	15	20	28
↑					↑
loc *left*					*right*

Start scanning elements from right. Since *a*[*loc*] < *a*[*right*], we decrease the value of variable *right* to get

a[0]	*a*[1]	*a*[2]	*a*[3]	*a*[4]	*a*[5]
25	10	30	15	20	28
↑				↑	
loc *left*				*right*	

Now, *a*[*loc*] > *a*[*right*], interchange these elements to get

a[0]	*a*[1]	*a*[2]	*a*[3]	*a*[4]	*a*[5]
20	10	30	15	25	28
↑				↑	
left				*loc* *right*	

Now start scanning elements from left. Since *a*[*loc*] > *a*[*left*], we increase the value of variable *left* to get

a[0]	*a*[1]	*a*[2]	*a*[3]	*a*[4]	*a*[5]
20	10	30	15	25	28
	↑			↑	
	left			*loc* *right*	

Since again *a*[*loc*] > *a*[*left*], we increase the value of variable *left* to get

a[0]	*a*[1]	*a*[2]	*a*[3]	*a*[4]	*a*[5]
20	10	30	15	25	28
		↑		↑	
		left		*loc* *right*	

Now *a*[*loc*] < *a*[*left*], interchange these elements to get

a[0]	*a*[1]	*a*[2]	*a*[3]	*a*[4]	*a*[5]
20	10	25	15	30	28
		↑		↑	
		loc		*right*	
		left			

Now again start scanning elements from right. Since *a*[*loc*] < *a*[*right*], we decrease the value of variable *right* to get

a[0]	*a*[1]	*a*[2]	*a*[3]	*a*[4]	*a*[5]
20	10	25	15	30	28
		↑	↑		
		loc	*right*		
		left			

Now, *a*[*loc*] > *a*[*right*], interchange these elements to get

a[0]	*a*[1]	*a*[2]	*a*[3]	*a*[4]	*a*[5]
20	10	15	25	30	28
		↑	↑		
		left	*loc*		
			right		

Now again start scanning elements from left. Since *a*[*loc*] > *a*[*left*], we increase the value of variable *left* to get

a[0]	*a*[1]	*a*[2]	*a*[3]	*a*[4]	*a*[5]
20	10	15	25	30	28
			↑		
			loc		
			left		
			right		

Since *left* becomes equal to *loc*, thus indicating the termination of the procedure.

The element 25 is placed in its final position and it divides the array into two sub arrays as

20 10 15 and 30 28

Left sub array (20 10 15) Right sub array (30 28)

As you can see, the elements in the left sub array are smaller than 25, and elements in the right sub array are greater than 25.

This means that element 25 is correctly placed in its final position and it partitions the remaining elements in two sub arrays where elements in the left sub array are less than it and elements in the right sub array are greater it..

The above partitioning step is repeated with each sub array containing 2 or more elements. Since, we can work on one sub array at a time, we must be able to keep track of the second sub array. This task is accomplished either using stack explicitly (iterative implementation) or implicitly (recursive implementation). Both the implementations are given in this section.

The complete sorting process is visualized in Figure 5.5.

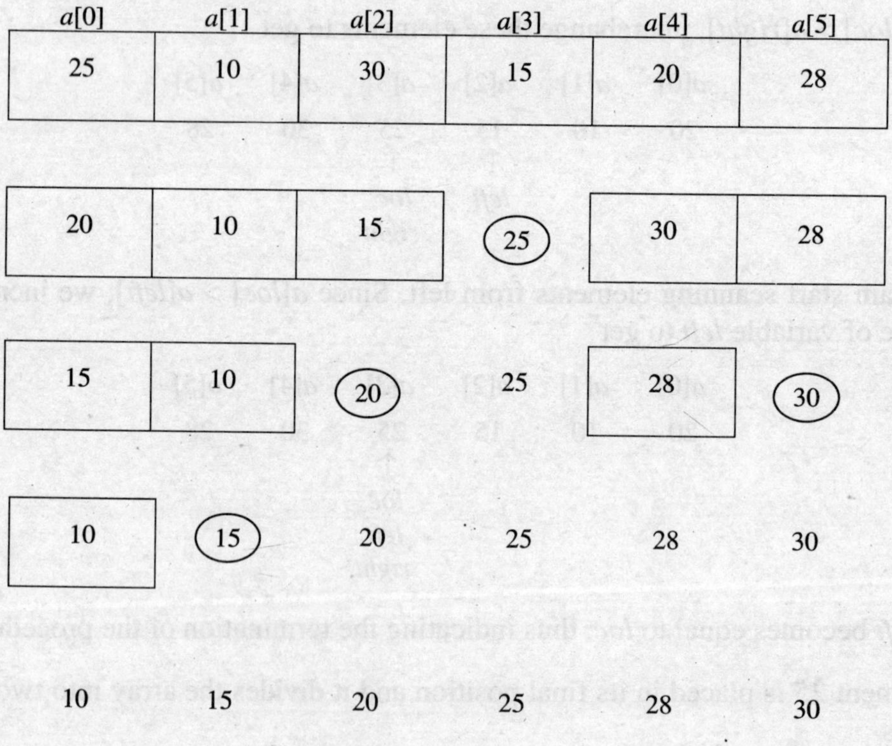

Figure 5.5: Illustration of successive steps of Quick sort, here circled element is the partitioning element (also called *pivot* element)

Algorithm 8.8

PartitionArray(***a, beg, end, loc*** **)**

Here *a* is a linear array in memory, and *beg* and *end* represents the lower bound and upper bound of the sub array in question. It partition the array into two halves by placing the partitioning element at index *loc*, which is its final position.

```
1.   Set left = beg, right = end, loc = beg
2.   Set done = false
3.   Repeat steps 4 to 10 While ( not done )
4.       Repeat step 5 While (a[loc]≤a[right]) and (loc≠right))
5.          Set right = right − 1
         Endwhile
6.       If ( loc = right ) then
            Set done = true
         Else if ( a[loc] > a[right] ) then
            Interchange a[loc] and a[right]
            Set loc = right
         Endif
7.       If ( not done ) then do step 8
8.          Repeat step 9 While (a[loc]≥a[left]) and (loc≠left))
9.             Set left = left + 1
            Endwhile
10.         If ( loc = left ) then
               Set done = true
            Else if ( a[loc] < a[left] ) then
               Interchange a[loc] and a[left]
               Set loc = left
            Endif
         Endif
     Endwhile
11.  Return
```

The QuickSort algorithm in iterative form takes the following shape

Algorithm 8.9

QuickSortIterative(***a, n*** **)**

Here *a* is a linear array of size *n* (>1) in memory. This algorithm sorts this array in ascending order using quick sort method, handling the left sub array first and then the right sub array. The variable *loc* is used to hold the index of splitting element. To keep track of the sub arrays it uses stack, of integers, explicitly.

```
1.  CreateStack(STK)
2.  Call Push(STK, 0)        // push lower index of starting array
3.  Call Push(STK, n-1)      // push upper index of starting array
```

```
4.   Repeat steps 5 to 11 While ( STK is not empty )
5.       Call POP(STK, ub)      // pop upper index into up
6.       Call POP(STK, lb)      // pop upper index into lb
7.       Call PartitionArray( a, lb, ub, loc )
8.       Call Push(STK, loc+1)  // push lower index of right subarray
9.       Call Push(STK, ub)     // push upper index of right subarray
10.      Call Push(STK, lb)     // push lower index of left subarray
11.      Call Push(STK, loc-1)  // push upper index of left subarray
     Endwhile
12.  Exit
```

Iterative procedure *quickSortIterative()* can be called from the calling function by the call statement as *quickSortIterative(a, n)*, where *a* in an array of size *n*.

SUMMARY

In this chapter, we have learnt about the

- basics of a stack data structure.
- different operations performed on a stack.
- representation of a stack using linear array.
- representation of a stack using linear linked list.
- applications of stacks.
- different notation used to represent mathematical expressions.
- quick sort method to sort an array.

REVIEW EXERCISES

1. What is a stack? Is stack a linear or non-linear data structure?
2. Stack is a special type of list? Comment.
3. How does an array based stack compares with linked stack?
4. Why an operation to check stack overflow is not implemented on linked stacks?
5. How *peep()* operation differs from *pop()* operation?
6. While representing a stack using linked lists, we have implemented additional operation *dispose()* to remove the stack from memory. Why such operation is not implemented for stack represented using an array.

7. Consider the following stack of characters

   STK: A B C F

   Describe the stack when the following operations are performed in that sequence. Note that top of the stack refers to the rightmost element.

   (*a*) Pop(STK, ITEM) (*b*) Push(STK, K)
   (*c*) Push(STK, L) (*d*) Push(STK, R)
   (*e*) Pop(STK, ITEM) (*f*) Pop(STK, ITEM)

9. Translate following mathematical expressions into its equivalent postfix expressions by inspection and by using the algorithm:

   (*a*) (A – B) * (D / E)
   (*b*) (A + B / D) / (E – F) + G
   (*c*) A * B – (C + D) / (E – F) + G / H

10. Convert following arithmetic expression infix notation to postfix notation using stack, and show the status of the stack after every step.

    A + ((B – C) / D) * F / G – H

11. Evaluate the following postfix expression "2 3 + 4 * 5 /" by showing the status of the stack in the visual form.

12. Given the following arithmetic expression in infix notation as

    12 / (7 – 3) + 2 * (3 + 8) – 7

    Translate this expression into postfix notation and then evaluate it.

13. How iterative implementation of quick sort method will process following list of numbers?

    23 12 11 45 30 8 55 22 66

14. Show how the string DATA STRUCTURE will be processed during partitioning phase of the quick sort?

PROGRAMMING EXERCISES

1. Write a menu driven program to implement a stack when it is represented using a linear array.
2. Write a menu driven program to implement a stack when it is represented using a linear linked list.

3. Write a program to convert an arithmetic expression from infix notation to postfix notation.
4. Write a program to evaluate an arithmetic expression given in postfix notation.
5. Write a program to sort a list of numbers in the descending order using quick sort method. The program should make use of stack.

❑ ❑ ❑

Chapter 6

Queues

Learning Objectives

After reading this chapter, students will be able to

- explain the concept of queue
- explain the way queues are represented in memory using linear array
- distinguish between linear and circular queue
- write algorithms for performing operations on array based queues
- explain the way queues are represented in memory using linear linked list
- write algorithms for performing operations on linked list based queues
- explain the concept of deque
- explain the concept of priority queue
- explain the ways a priority queue can be represented
- explain the applications of queues

6.1 INTRODUCTION

All of us are familiar with queues. In simple terms, a queue is a line of persons waiting for their turn at some service counter/window. A service counter can be a ticketing window of a cinema hall, a ticketing window of a bus stand or railway station, a service counter of a bank, a service counter of a gas agency, a fees deposit counter in a college, etc. Depending on the type of service provided by the service counter and the number of persons interested in this service, there could be queues of varying lengths. The service at the service counter is provided on the First-Come First-Serve (FCFS) basis, *i.e.*, in order of their arrival in the queue.

(*a*) (*b*) (*c*)

Figure 6.1: Queues at different occasions

From the point of view of the subject of data structures, a queue, named *Q*, can be viewed as shown in Figure 6.2.

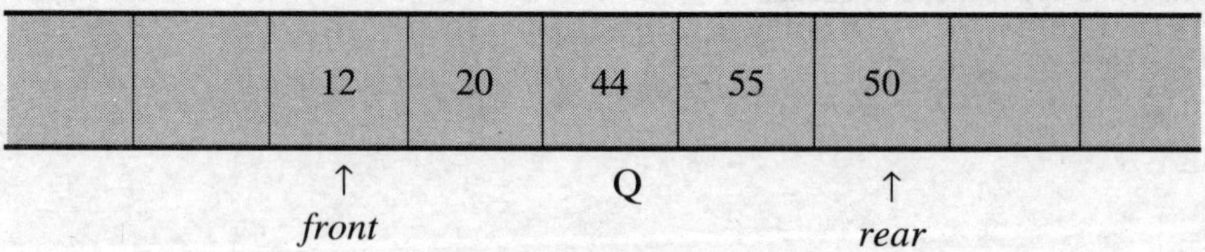

Figure 6.2: Queue with 5 elements

This chapter describes a queue, its representation in computer memory, and the implementation of different operations that can be performed on them. It also describes a deque and a priority queue in brief.

6.2 QUEUE DEFINED

In the context of data structures, a *queue* is a linear list in which insertions can take place at one end of the list, called the *rear* of the list, and deletions can take place only at other end, called the *front* of the list. The behaviour of a queue is like a First-In-First-Out (FIFO) system. Figure 6.4 shows a queue as black box in which elements enters from one side and leaves from other side.

In queue terminology, the insertion and deletion operations are known as *enqueue* and *dequeue* operations.

Example 6.1:

Following figure illustrates a queue, which can accommodate maximum of 10 elements.

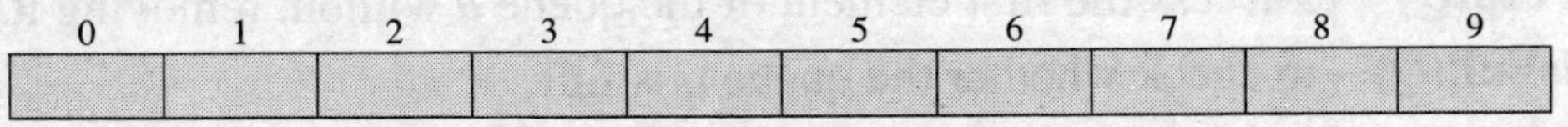

(*a*) An empty queue

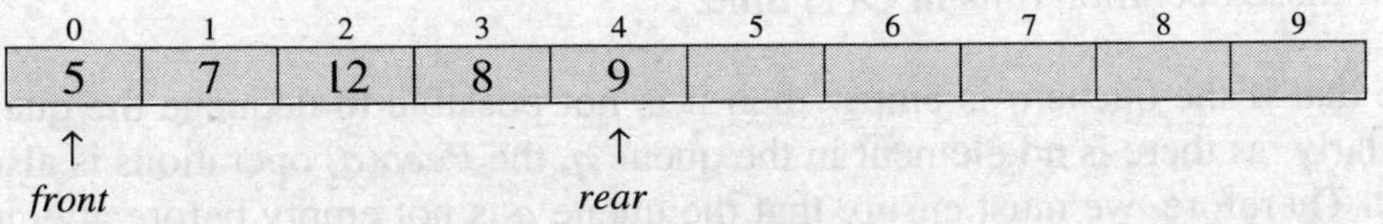

(*b*) Queue after enqueuing elements 5, 7, 12, 8, and 9 in order

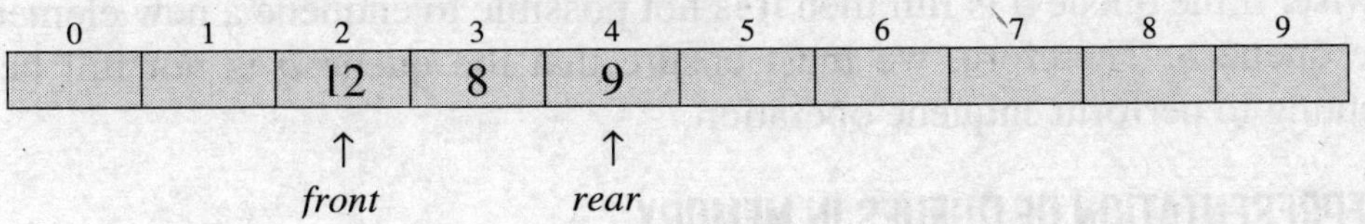

(*c*) Queue after dequeuing elements 5, 7 from queue

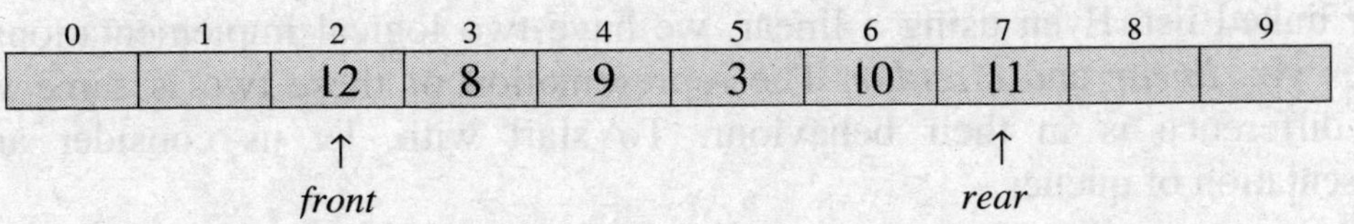

(*d*) Queue after enqueuing elements 3, 10, 11 in a queue

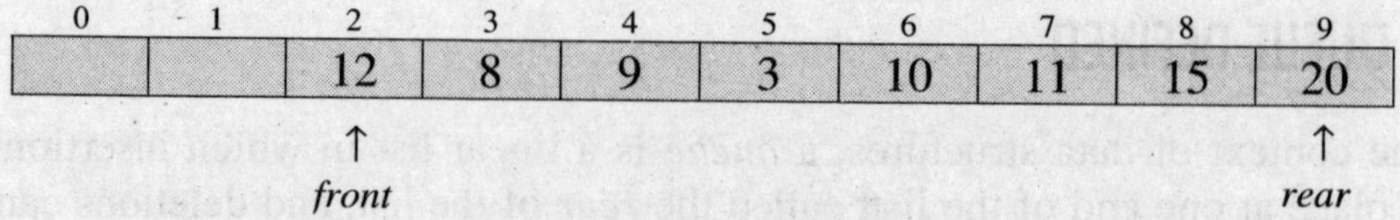

(*e*) Queue after enqueuing elements 15 and 20 in a queue

Figure 6.3: Illustration of a queue whose elements are integer values

6.3 OPERATIONS ON QUEUES

The following operations, for full functionality, are performed on queues:

1. **CreateQueue(*Q*)** – to create *q* as an empty queue.
2. **Enque(*Q*, *item*)** – to insert (add) element *item* in a queue *q*.
3. **Dequeue(*Q*)** – to remove element of queue *q*.
4. **Peep(*Q*)** – to access the first element of the queue *q* without removing it.
5. **IsFull(*Q*)** – to check whether the queue *q* is full.
6. **IsEmpty(*Q*)** – to check whether the queue *q* is empty.

All of these operation runs in O(1) time.

Note that if the queue *q* is empty then it is not possible to dequeue the queue *q*. Similarly, as there is no element in the queue *q*, the *Peep(q)* operations is also not valid. Therefore, we must ensure that the queue *q* is not empty before attempting to perform these operations.

Likewise, if the queue *q* is full then it is not possible to enqueue a new element in to the queue *q*. Therefore, we must ensure that the queue *q* is not full before attempting to perform enqueue operation.

6.4 REPRESENTATION OF QUEUES IN MEMORY

Queues, like stacks, can also be represented in memory using a linear array or a linear linked list. Even using a linear, we have two logical implementations of queues viz. *linear* and *circular*. The representation of these two is same with only difference is in their behaviour. To start with, let us consider array representation of queues.

6.4.1 Representing a Queue Using an Array

A queue is represented by a linear array, say *queue*, and two integer variables *front* and *rear*. Here variable *front* holds the index of the first element of the queue, and variable *rear* holds the index of the last element of the queue.

Let us suppose that the elements of the *queue* are of integer type, and the queue can store maximum of 10 such elements, *i.e.*, size of queue is 10. With these declarations, queue of Figure 6.4 will be represented in computer memory as shown in Figure 6.5.

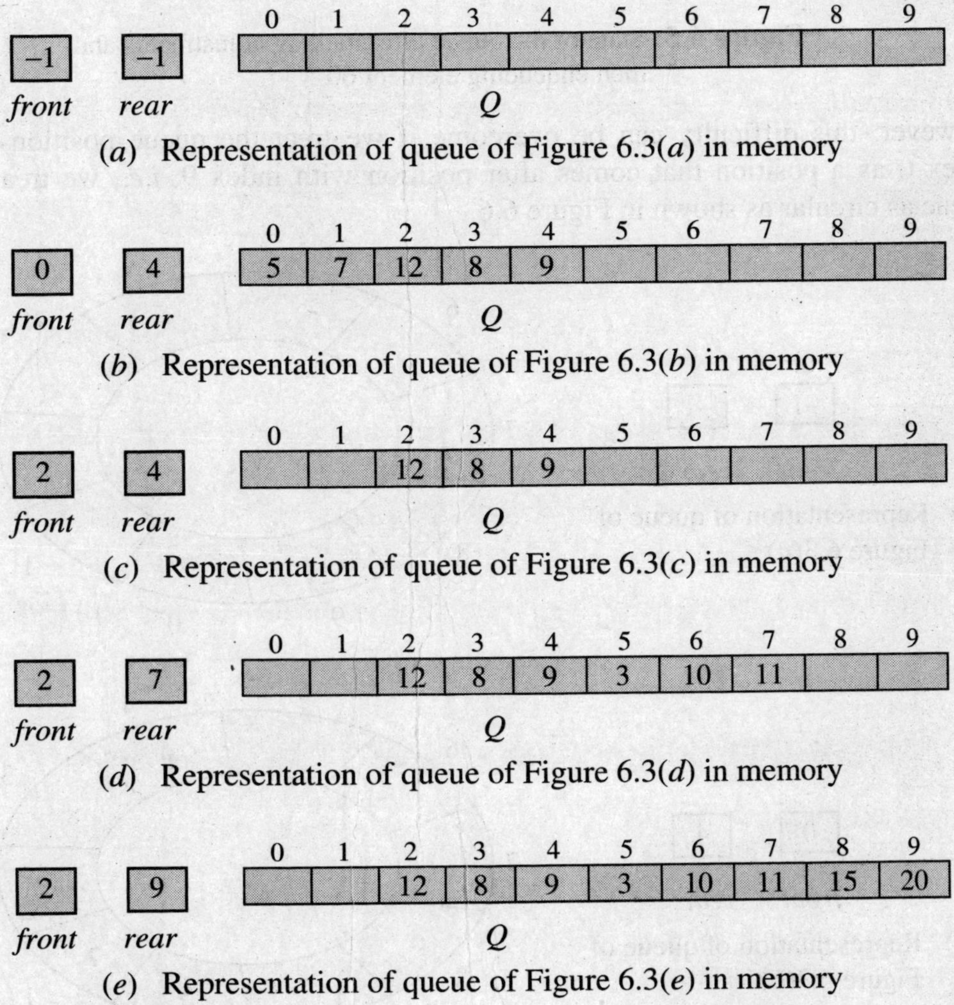

Figure 6.4: Array representation of linear queue of Figure 6.3

You must have observed, as shown in Figure 6.4(*e*), that it is not possible to enqueue more elements as such, though two positions in the linear queue are vacant. To overcome this problem, the elements of the queue are moved forward, so that the vacant positions are shifted towards the rear end of the linear queue. After shifting, *front* and *rear* are adjusted properly, and then the element is enqueued in the linear queue as usual. For example, we want to enqueue one more element, say 60, after making adjustments, queue will look as shown in Figure 6.5.

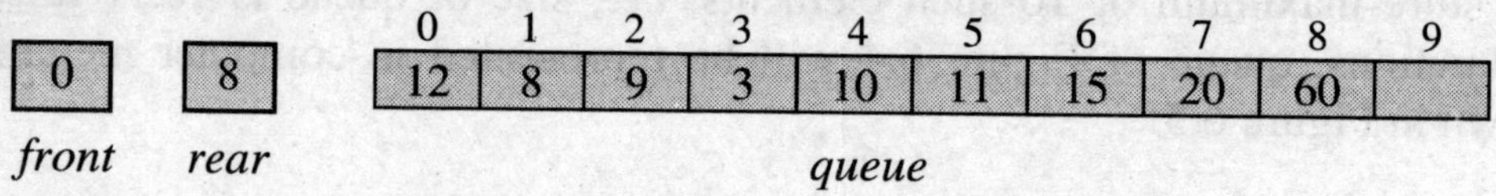

Figure 6.5: State of the queue after making adjustments and then enqueueing element 60

However, this difficulty can be overcome if we treat the queue position with index 0 as a position that comes after position with index 9, *i.e.*, we treat the queue as circular as shown in Figure 6.6.

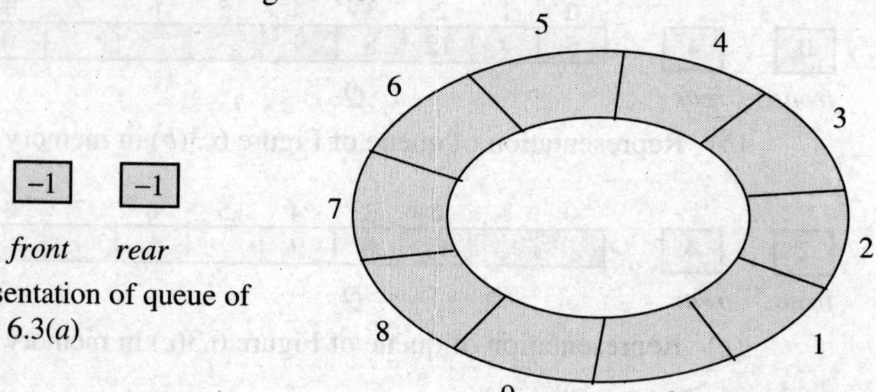

(*a*) Representation of queue of Figure 6.3(*a*)

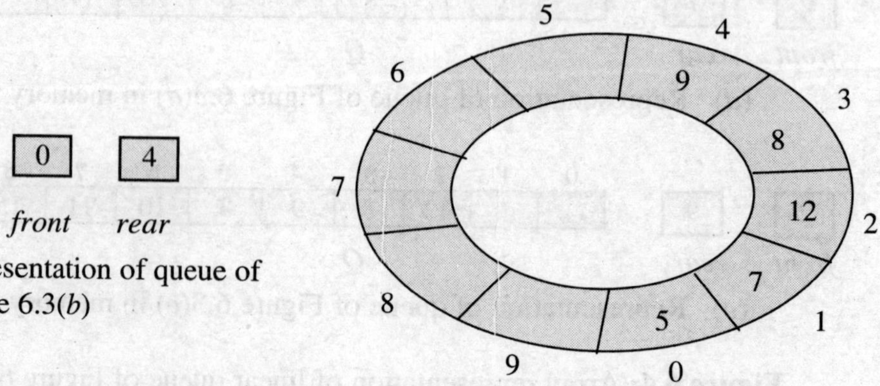

(*b*) Representation of queue of Figure 6.3(*b*)

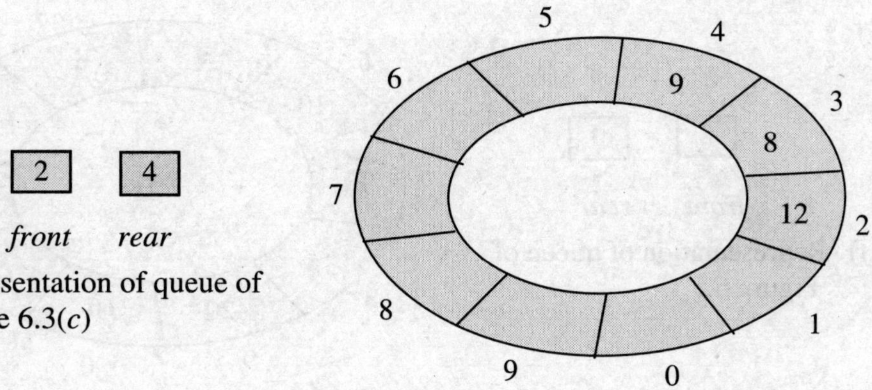

(*c*) Representation of queue of Figure 6.3(*c*)

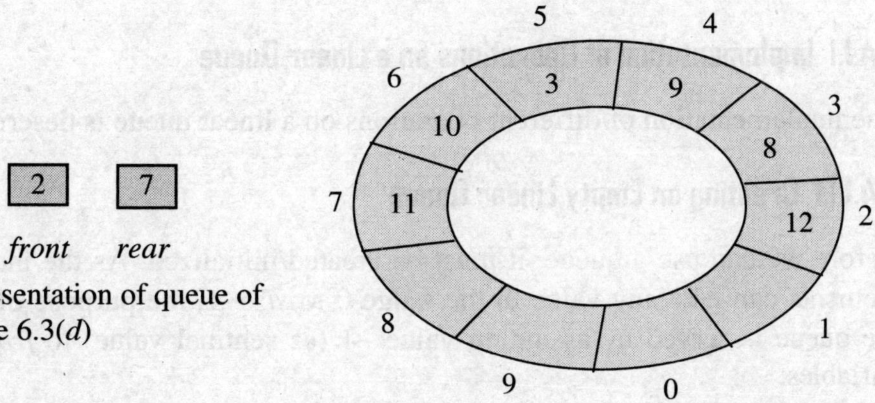

(*d*) Representation of queue of Figure 6.3(*d*)

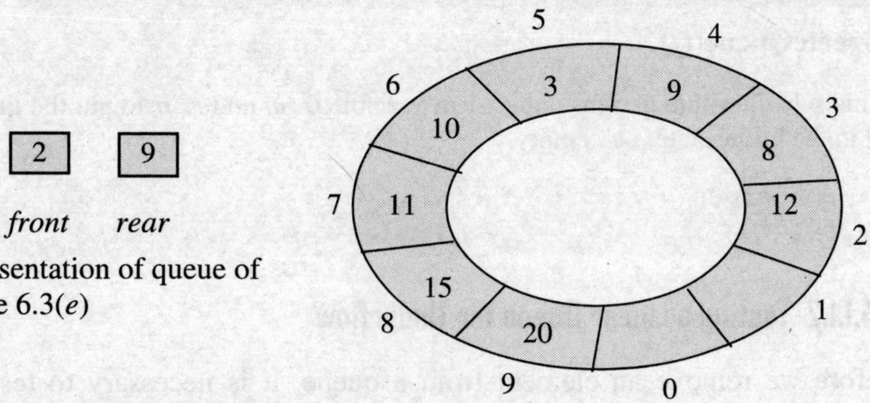

(*e*) Representation of queue of Figure 6.3(*e*)

Now to enqueue one more element, say 60, the *rear* is reset to 0, and the elements is inserted at that index as shown overleaf.

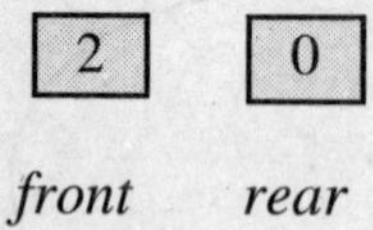

(*f*) Representation of queue of Figure 6.5

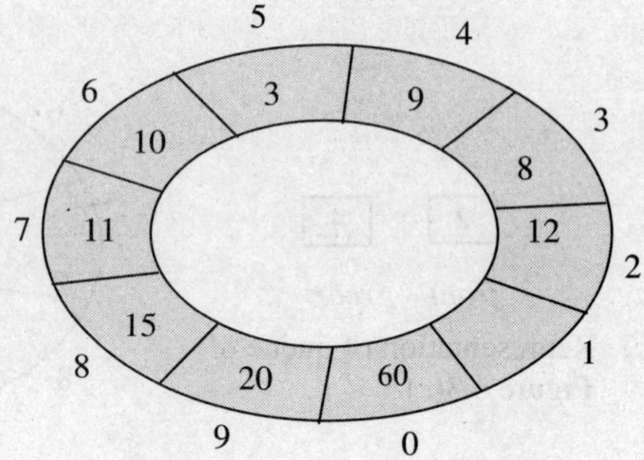

Figure 6.6: (*a*) – (*f*) Illustration of Operations on Circular Queues

6.4.1.1 Implementation of Operations on a Linear Queue

The implementation of different operations on a linear queue is described below.

6.4.1.1.1 Creating an Empty Linear Queue

Before we can use a queue, it must be created/initialized. As the index of array elements can take any value in the range 0 to *size*–1, the purpose of initializing the queue is served by assigning value –1 (as sentinel value) to *front* and *rear* variables.

Algorithm 6.1

CreateQueue(*Q*)

This sub algorithm assigns value -1 to variable *front* and *rear* to put the linear queue *Q* in the initial state, *i.e.*, empty.

```
1. Set front = rear = -1
2. Return
```

6.4.1.1.2 Testing a Linear Queue for Underflow

Before we remove an element from a queue, it is necessary to test whether a queue still have some elements, *i.e.*, to test that whether the queue is empty or not. If it is not empty then the dequeue operation can be performed to remove the front element. This test is performed by comparing the value of *front* with sentinel value −1, as shown below.

Algorithm 6.2

IsEmpty(*Q*, *status*)

This sub algorithm compares the value of variable *front* with the sentinel value (-1), and if the value of the *front* variable is -1 it sets the boolean variable *status* to boolean value *true* else to boolean value *false*.

```
1. If ( front = -1 ) then
      Set status = true
   Else
      Set status = false
2. Exit.
```

6.4.1.1.3 Testing a Linear Queue for Overflow

Before we insert new element in a queue, it is necessary to test whether queue still have some space to accommodate the incoming element i.e. to test that whether the queue is full or not. If it is not full then the *enqueue* operation can be performed to insert the element at rear end of the queue. This test is performed by test condition

```
( front = 0 ) and ( rear = size – 1 )
```

i.e., front element is at position with index 0 and the last element is at position with index *size*−1, which indicates that no position in linear queue is vacant.

Algorithm 6.3

IsFull(*Q*, *status*)

This sub algorithm compares the value of variables *front* with 0 and the value of *rear* with (*size*-1), and if the value of the *front* variable is equal to 0 and that *rear* variable is equal to (*size*-1), it sets the boolean variable *status* to boolean value *true* else to boolean value *false*.

```
1. If (front = 0 and rear = size-1 ) then
      Set status = true
   Else
      Set status = false
2. Return
```

6.4.1.1.4 Enqueue Operation on Linear Queue

Even if a linear queue is not full, there is another problem that may arise during enqueue operation. That problem is that, the value of the *rear* variable is equal to *size*–1, though the value of the *front* variable is not equal to 0. This possibility implies that the incoming element cannot be enqueued unless the elements are moved forward, and variables *front* and *rear* are adjusted accordingly, which is, of course, a time consuming process.

There are two conditions, which can occur, even if queue is not full. These are

- If a linear queue is empty, then the value of the *front* and *rear* variables will be -1 (sentinel value), then both *front* and *rear* are set to 0.
- If a linear queue is not empty, then there are further two possibilities:
  - ◊ If the value of the *rear* variable is less than *size*–1, then the *rear* variable is incremented.
  - ◊ If the value of the *rear* variable is equal to *size*–1, then the elements of the linear queue are moved forward, and the *front* and *rear* variables are adjusted accordingly.

Algorithm 6.4

Enqueue(*Q*, *item*)

This sub algorithm calls sub algorithm *IsFull* to see whether the *Q* is full, and if the answer is yes, it flags "overflow" condition and returns. However, if the *Q* is not full, it enqueues (adds/inserts) new element *item* at the rear of linear queue *Q*.

```
1. Call IsFull(Q, status)
2. If ( status = true ) then
       Write: "Overflow"
       Return
   Endif
3. If ( front = -1 ) then
       Set front = rear = 0
   Else if ( rear = size - 1 )
       For i = front to rear in steps of +1
            Set Q[i-front] = Q[i]
       Endfor
```

```
      Set rear = rear - front + 1
      Set front = 0
   Else
      Set rear = rear + 1
   Endif
4. Set Q[rear] = item
5. Return
```

6.4.1.1.5 Dequeue Operation on a Linear Queue

The front element of a linear queue is assigned to a local variable, which later on will be returned via the *return* statement. After assigning the front element of a linear queue to a local variable, the value of the *front* variable is modified so that it points to the new front. There are two possibilities:

- If there was only one element in a linear queue, then after dequeue operation queue will become empty. This state of a linear queue is reflected by setting *front* and *rear* variables to –1, the sentinel value.
- Otherwise the value of the *front* variable is incremented.

Algorithm 6.5

Dequeue(*Q*, *item*)

This sub algorithm calls sub algorithm *IsEmpty* to see whether the *Q* is empty, and if the answer is yes, it flags "underflow" condition and returns. However, if the *Q* is not empty, it dequeue (removes/deletes) element from front of linear queue *Q*, and assigns to local variable *item*.

```
1. Call IsEmpty(Q, status)
2. If ( status = true ) then
      Write: "Underflow"
      Return
   Endif
3. Set item = Q[front]
4. If ( front = rear ) then
      Set front = rear = -1
   Else
      Set front = front + 1
   Endif
5. Return
```

6.4.1.1.6 Accessing Front Element

In dequeue operation, the front element is removed from the queue. However, there are some situations (usually when queue used as a data structure to solve other problems), when to we need to see which element is at the front of the queue, but don't want to remove at this moment.

Algorithm 6.5

Peep(*Q*, *item*)

This sub algorithm calls sub algorithm *IsEmpty* to see whether the *Q* is empty, and if the answer is yes, it flags "underflow" condition and returns. However, if the *Q* is not empty, it assigns the front element of linear queue *Q* to local variable *item*.

```
1. Call IsEmpty(Q, status)
2. If ( status = true ) then
      Write: "Underflow"
      Return
   Endif
3. Set item = Q[front]
4. Return
```

6.4.1.2 Limitations of a Linear Queue

The only limitation of linear queue is that—

If the last position of the queue is occupied, it is not possible to enqueue any more elements even though some positions are vacant towards the front positions of the queue.

However, this limitation can be overcome by moving the elements forward, such that the first element of the queue goes to position with index 0, and the rest of the elements move accordingly. And finally the *front* and *rear* variables are adjusted appropriately.

But this operation may be very time consuming if the length of the linear queue is very long. As mentioned earlier, this limitation can be overcome if we treat that the queue position with index 0 comes immediately after the last queue position with index (*size*–1). The resulting queue is known as *circular queue*.

6.4.1.3 Implementation of Operations on a Circular Queue

The operations of initialization, testing for underflow for circular queue is similar to that of a linear queue. However, other operations are slightly different. These are described below.

6.4.1.3.1 Testing a Circular Queue for Overflow

Before we insert new element in a circular queue, it is necessary to test whether a circular queue still have some space to accommodate the incoming element i.e. to test that whether a circular queue is full or not. If it is not full then the enqueue operation can be performed to insert the element at rear of a circular queue. This test is performed by test conditions

- `( front = 0 ) and ( rear = SIZE−1)`
- `front = rear + 1`

If any one of these two conditions is satisfied, it means circular queue is full.

Algorithm 6.6

IsFull(*Q*, *status*)

This sub algorithm sets the boolean variable *status* to boolean value *true* if circular *Q* is empty else to boolean value *false*.

```
1. If (((front=0)and(rear=size-1))or(front=rear+1))then
      Set status = true
   Else
      Set status = false
2. Return
```

6.4.1.3.2 Enqueue Operation on a Circular Queue

Before the enqueue operation, there are three conditions, which can occur, even if a circular queue is not full. These are

- If the queue is empty, then the value of the *front* and *rear* will be −1 (sentinel value), then both *front* and *rear* are set to 0.
- If the queue is not empty then the value of the *rear* will be the index of the last element of the queue, then the *rear* variable is incremented.
- If the queue is not full and the value of *rear* variable is equal to SIZE−1, then *rear* variable is set to 0.

Algorithm 6.7

Enqueue(*Q*, *item*)

This sub algorithm calls sub algorithm *IsFull* to see whether the *Q* is full, and if the answer is yes, it flags "overflow" condition and returns. However, if the *Q* is not full, it enqueues (adds/inserts) new element *item* at the rear of circular queue *Q*.

```
1. Call IsFull(Q, status)
2. If ( status = true ) then
      Write: "Overflow"
      Return
   Endif
3. If ( front = -1 ) then
      Set front = rear = 0
   Else if ( rear = size-1 ) then
      Set rear = 0
   Else if ( rear = size-1 ) then
      Set rear = rear + 1
   Endif
4. Set Q[rear] = item
5. Return
```

6.4.1.3.3 Dequeue Operation on a Circular Queue

The front element of a circular queue is assigned to a local variable, which later on will be returned via the *return* statement. After assigning the front element of a circular queue, the value of the *front* variable is modified so that it points to the new front.

There are two possibilities:

- If there was only one element in a circular queue, then after dequeue operation the circular queue will become empty. This state of a circular queue is reflected by setting *front* and *rear* variables to –1, the sentinel value.
- If value of the front variable is equal to *size*–1, then set *front* variable to 0.

If none of the above conditions hold, then the *front* variable is incremented.

Algorithm 6.8

Dequeue(*Q*, *item*)

This sub algorithm calls sub algorithm *IsEmpty* to see whether the *Q* is empty, and if the answer is yes, it flags "underflow" condition and returns. However, if the *Q* is not empty, it dequeue (removes/deletes) element from front of circular *Q*, and assigns to local variable *item*.

```
1. Call IsEmpty(Q, status)
2. If ( status = true ) then
      Write: "Underflow"
      Return
   Endif
3. Set item = Q[front]
4. If ( front = rear ) then
      Set front = rear = -1
   Else if ( front = size-1 ) then
      Set front = 0
   Else
      Set front = front + 1
   Endif
5. Return
```

6.4.2 Representing a Queue using a Linked List

A queue represented using a linked list is also known as a *linked queue*. The array-based representation of queues suffers from following limitations

- Size of the queue must be known in advance.
- We may come across situations when an attempt to enqueue an element causes overflow. However, queue, as an abstract data structure cannot be full. Hence, abstractly, it is always possible to enqueue an element in a queue. Therefore, implementing queue as an array prohibits the growth of queue beyond the finite number of elements.

The linked list representation allows a queue to grow to a limit of the computer's memory.

Here we have defined two data type named *node* and *queue*. The *node* type, a self-referential structure, whose first element *info* hold the element of the queue and the second element *next* holds the address of the element after it in the queue. The second type is *queue*, a structure, whose first element *front* holds the address of the first element of the queue, and the second element *rear* holds the address of the last element of the queue. The last line declares a variable *q* of type *queue*.

With these declarations, we will write functions for various operations to be performed on a queue represented using linked list.

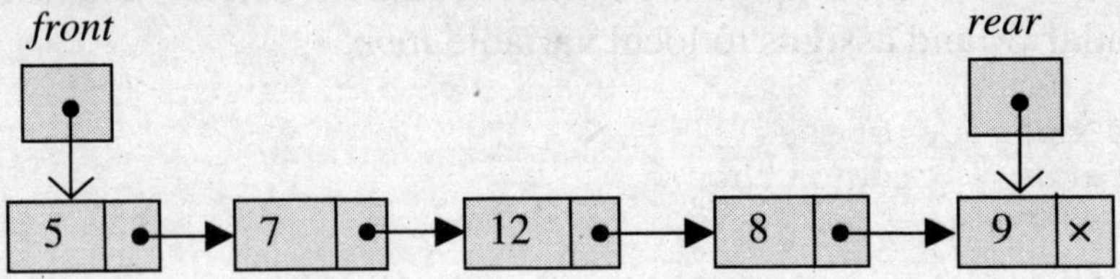

(*a*) Representation of queue Q of Figure 6.3(*a*) in memory

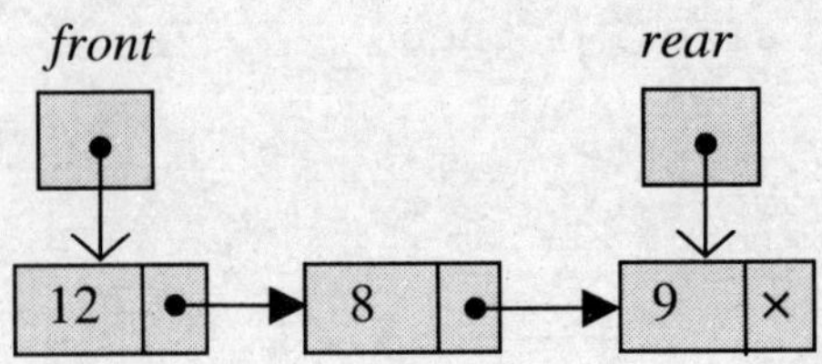

(*b*) Representation of queue of Figure 6.3(*b*) in memory

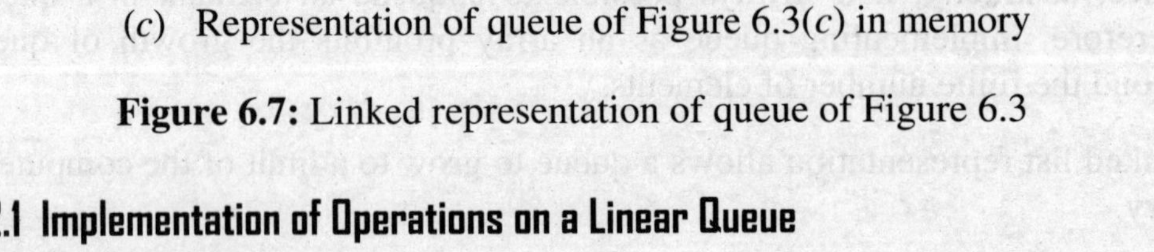

(*c*) Representation of queue of Figure 6.3(*c*) in memory

Figure 6.7: Linked representation of queue of Figure 6.3

6.4.2.1 Implementation of Operations on a Linear Queue

The implementation of different operations on a queue represented using linear linked list is described in this section.

6.4.2.1.1 Creating an Empty Queue

Before we can use a queue, it is to be created/initialized. To initialize a queue, we will create an empty linked list. Setting pointer variables *front* and *rear* to NULL value creates an empty linear linked.

Algorithm 6.8

CreateQueue(*Q*)

This sub algorithm assigns value NULL to pointer variables *front* and *rear* to put the linear queue *Q* in the initial state, *i.e.*, empty.

```
1. Set front = rear = NULL
2. Return
```

6.4.2.1.2 Testing Queue for Underflow

The queue is tested for underflow condition by checking whether the linked list is empty. The empty status of the linked lists will be indicated by the NULL value of pointer variable *front*.

Algorithm 6.9

IsEmpty(*Q*, *status*)

This sub algorithm compares the value of pointer variable *front* with the sentinel value (NULL), and if the value of the *front* variable is NULL it sets the boolean variable *status* to boolean value *true* else to boolean value *false*.

```
1. If ( front = NULL ) then
       Set status = true
   Else
       Set status = false
2. Exit.
```

6.4.2.1.3 Testing Queue for Overflow

Since a queue represented using a linked list can grow to a limit of a computer's memory, therefore overflow condition never occurs. Hence, this operation is not implemented for linked queues.

6.4.2.1.4 Enqueue Operation

To enqueue a new element onto the queue, the element is inserted in the end of the linked list.

Algorithm 6.10

Enqueue(*Q*, *item*)

This sub algorithm allocates a free node, places *item* in the *info* part of the node, set pointer part next to NULL, and finally insert the node at the end of the linked list representing queue Q.

```
1. Set ptr = Address of newly allocated node
2. Set ptr->info = item
3. Set ptr->next = NULL
4. If ( rear = NULL ) then
       Set front = rear = ptr
   Else
       Set rear->next = ptr
       Set rear = ptr
   Endif
5. Return
```

6.4.2.1.5 Dequeue Operation

To dequeue/remove an element from the queue, the element is removed from the beginning of the linked list.

Algorithm 6.11

Dequeue(*Q*, *item*)

This sub algorithm calls sub algorithm *IsEmpty* to see whether the *Q* is empty, and if the answer is yes, it flags "underflow" condition and returns. However, if the *Q* is not empty, it dequeue (removes/deletes) element from front of queue *Q,* and assigns to local variable *item*. The local pointer variable *ptr* is used hold the address of the first node, which will be used later to remove that node from memory.

```
1. Call IsEmpty(Q, status)
2. If ( status = true ) then
       Write: "Underflow"
       Return
   Endif
3. Set item = front->info
```

```
4. Set ptr = front
5. If ( front = rear ) then
      Set front = rear = NULL
   Else
      Set front = front->next
   Endif
6. Delete node at address ptr
7. Return
```

6.4.2.1.6 Accessing Front Element

The element in the front of queue is accessed but it is not removed.

Algorithm 6.12

Peep(*Q*, *item*)

This sub algorithm calls sub algorithm *IsEmpty* to see whether the *Q* is empty, and if the answer is yes, it flags "underflow" condition and returns. However, if the *Q* is not empty, it assigns the front element of linear queue *Q* to local variable *item*.

```
1. Call IsEmpty(Q, status)
2. If ( status = true ) then
      Write: "Underflow"
      Return
   Endif
3. Set item = front->info
4. Return
```

6.4.2.1.7 Disposing a Queue

Because queue is implemented using linked lists, therefore it is programmer's job to write the code to release the memory occupied by the queue.

Algorithm 6.13

Dispose(*Q*, *item*)

This sub algorithm removes/delete the nodes of the linked lists reqpreseting the queue Q from memory one by one. It uses local pointer variable *ptr* to hold the address of the node for deletion later after advancing the pointer variable *front*.

```
1. Repeat steps 2 to 4 While ( front ≠ NULL )
```

```
2.     Set ptr = front
3.     Set front = front->next
4.     Delete node at address ptr
   Endwhile
5. Return
```

6.4.3 Applications of Queues

Some of the applications of queues are listed below:

- There are several algorithms that use queues to solve problems efficiently.
- When the jobs are submitted to a networked printer, they are arranged in order of arrival. Thus, essentially, jobs sent to a printer are placed on a queue.
- There is a kind of computer network where disk is attached to one computer, known as *file server*. Users on other computers are given access to files on a first-come first-served basis, so the data structure is a queue.
- Virtually every real-life line (supposed to be) a queue. For example, lines at ticket counters at cinema halls, railway stations, bus stands, etc., are queues, because the service, *i.e.*, ticket, is provided on first-come first-served basis.

6.5 DEQUE

A *deque*, pronounced as *deck*, a kind of linear queue in which elements can be added/removed at/from either end but not in the middle. The term deque is a contraction of the name *double-ended queue*.

There are two variations of a deque, which are intermediate between a deque and a queue. These are:

- **Input-restricted deque** – which allows insertions only at one end but allows deletions at both ends.
- **Output-restricted deque** – which allows insertions at both ends but allows deletions only at one end.

Deques are introduced here just for academic interest of the students their use in practical situations is almost insignificant.

6.6 PRIORITY QUEUE

A *priorities queue* is a kind of queue in which each element is assigned a priority and the order in which elements are deleted and processed comes from the following rules:

- An element with highest priority is processed first before any element of lower priority.
- Two or more elements with the same priority are processed according to the order in which they were added to the queue.

There can be different criteria's for determining the priority. Some of them are summarized below:

- A shortest job is given higher priority over the longer one.
- An important job is given higher priority over a routine type job. For example, a transaction for on-line booking of an order is given preference over payroll processing.
- In a commercial computer center, the amount you pay for the job can determine priority for your job. Pay more to get higher priority for your job.

6.6.1 Representing a Priority Queue in Memory

There are various ways of representing (maintaining) a priority queue in memory.

- Using a linear linked list
- Using multiple queues, one for each priority
- Using a heap

6.6.1.1 Linear Linked List Representation

In this representation, each node of the linked list will have three fields:

- An information field *info* that hold the element of the queue,
- A priority filed *prn* that holds the priority number of the element, and
- A next pointer filed *link* that holds pointer to next element of the queue.

Further, a node *X* precedes a node *Y* in the linear linked list if either node *X* has higher priority that *Y* or both nodes have same priority but *X* was added to the list before *Y*.

In a given system, we can assign higher priority to lower number or higher number. Therefore, if higher priority is for lower number, we have to maintain linear linked lists sorted on ascending order of the priority. However, if higher priority is for higher number, we have to maintain linear linked lists sorted on descending order of the priority. This way, the element to be processed next is available as the first element of the linked list.

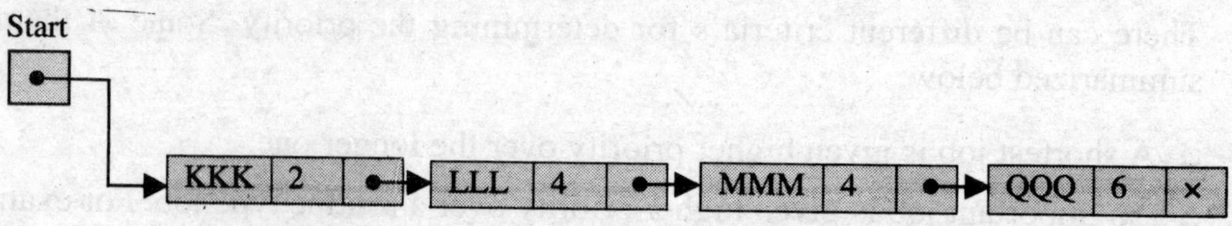

Figure 6.7: A priority queue with 4 elements

Figure 6.7 shows a priority queue with 7 elements, where the element with lower number assigned a higher priority. Element KKK has the highest priority, elements LLL and MMM have equal priority but LLL have arrived first, element QQQ has the lowest priority among the element present in the queue so far.

The main advantage of this representation is that the element to be processed in the priority queue is in the beginning of the list. Therefore, it is very easy to delete and process an element from the priority queue.

The disadvantage of this representation is that since the linked list is to be maintained on the decreasing order of priority of elements (*i.e.*, increasing order of the numbers assigned for priority levels), insertion of a new element will be time consuming since we need to find its correct position in the linked lists, and then element will be inserted.

Dequeue Operation

The dequeue operation is very easy to implement on priority queue, as it involves removing element from the beginning of the linked list.

Algorithm 6.13

Dequeue(*PQ*, *item*)

This sub algorithm removes element from the beginning of the list, *i.e.*, from the front of the priority queue PQ and assigns to variable *item*. It uses local pointer variable *ptr* to hold the address of the first node for deletion later after advancing the pointer of the linked list to second node.

```
1. Set item = start->info
2. Set ptr = start
3. Set start = start->next
4. Delete node at address ptr
   Endwhile
5. Return
```

The whole process implemented by the above algorithm is depicted in Figure 6.8.

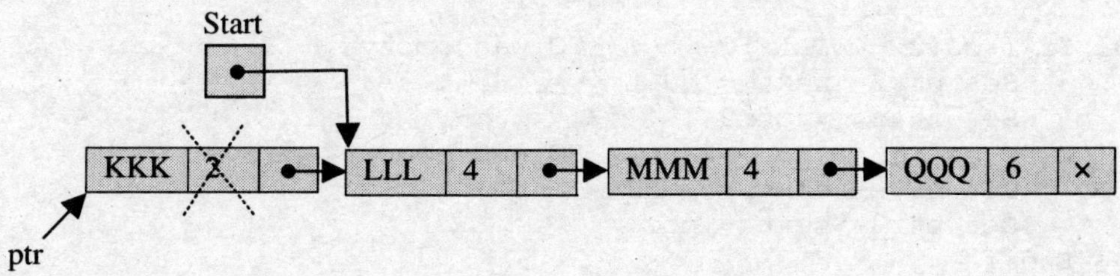

Figure 6.8: Illustration of Dequeue operation on a priority queue

Enqueue Operation

The enqueue operation is bit complicated as it involves finding the correct place to insert the element. To find the correct place, the priority of the element to be inserted is compared with the priority of each element from the beginning of the linked till the element with priority greater that the new element is found. The new element is inserted before that node.

However, if there is no element in linked list having priority greater than the new element, then it is inserted at the end of the linked list.

Since new node is going to be inserted before a given node, we need to keep track of the address of the preceding node.

This complete task of inserting a new element is accomplished as shown below:

Algorithm 6.14

Enqueue(*PQ*, *item*)

This sub algorithm inserts *item* in the priority queue *PQ* in its correct place. It uses local pointer variable *ptr1* to facilitate the traversal, *save* to hold keep track of the address of the preceding node, and ptr2 to hold the address of the newly allocated node.

```
1. Set ptr2 = Address of newly allocated node
2. Set ptr2->info = item
3. Set ptr1 = start
4. Set save = NULL
5. Repeat steps 6 and 7 While ( item < ptr1->info )
6.     Set save = ptr
7.     Set ptr1 = ptr1->next
   Endwhle

8. If ( save = NULL )          // PQ was empty
       Set ptr2->next = NULL
       Set start = ptr2
   Else                        // PQ had some elements
       Set save->next = ptr2
       Set ptr2->next = ptr1
   Endif
9. Return
```

The whole process implemented by the above algorithm is depicted in Figure 6.9.

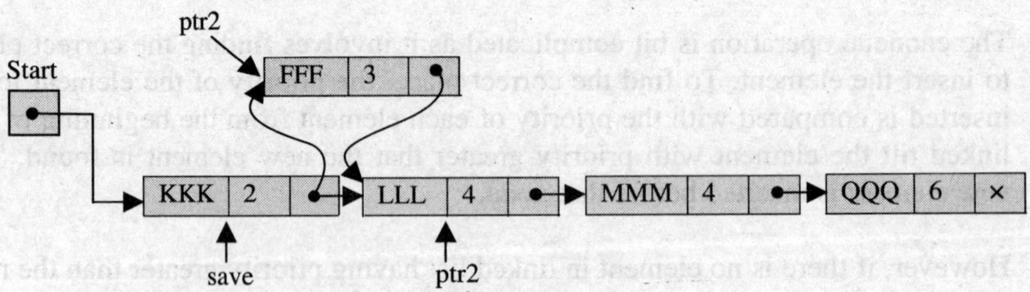

Figure 6.9: Illustration of Enqueue operation on a priority queue

Implementations of other operations (creation/initialization, to check whether it is full, to check whether it is empty and dispose) are trivial and are left as an exercise for the student.

6.6.1.2 Multiple Queue Representation

In this representation, one queue is maintained for each priority number. In order to process an element of the priority queue, element from the first non-empty highest priority number queue is accessed. In order to add a new element to the priority queue, the element is inserted in an appropriate queue for given priority number.

	front	rear
0	0	1
1	-1	-1
2	1	3
3	0	2

PQ

	0	1	2	3	4	5
0	AAA	BBB				
1						
2		PPP	QQQ	RRR		
3	TTT	UUU	VVV			

Figure 6.10: Schematics of a priority queue with 4 priority levels

The priority queue system shown has 4 queues, one for one priority level (0 being highest and 3 being lowest), each one seen as circular and having its own *front* and *rear*. Each queue is allocated same amount of space, say *size*, *i.e.*, number of columns in 2-D array *PQ*.

First queue for highest level priority has 2 elements; queue for the second level priority is empty at this moment, queue for the third level priority has 3 elements; and queue for the fourth level priority also has 3 elements.

The positions of first and last elements in the queues are indicated by the values of their respective *front* and *rear* variables. Observe that *front*[*k*] and *rear*[*k*], for $0 \le k \le 3$ contain the indices of the front and rear elements of row *k* of 2-D array PQ, the row that maintains the queue of elements with priority number *k*.

Dequeue Operation

The dequeue operation first find the first non-empty queue *k*, (for non-empty queue *k*, *front*[*k*] $\neq$ -1), and then removes the front element.

Algorithm 6.15

Dequeue(*PQ*, *item*)

This sub algorithm first finds the first non-empty queue and then removes the front element from it and assigns to variable *item*. This sub algorithm presumes that priority queue is not empty where as individual queue for a given priority level may be empty.

```
1. Set k = 0
2. Repeat steps While ( front[k] ≠ -1 )
3.     Set k = k + 1
   Endwhile
4. Set item = PQ[k][front[k]]
5. If ( front[k] = rear[k] ) then
       Set front[k] = rear[k] = -1
   Else if ( front[k] = size-1 ) then
       Set front[k] = 0
   Else
       Set front[k] = front[k] + 1
   Endif
5. Return
```

Enqueue Operation

The enqueue operation is simple, it just adds the new element with priority *k*, to the queue maintained for that priority level.

Algorithm 6.16

Enqueue(*PQ*, *item*, *k*)

This sub algorithm adds *item* to queue maintained for priority level *k*. This sub algorithm presumes that sufficient space is allocated for each row such that overflow condition will not occur for any individual queue.

```
1. If ( front[k] = -1 ) then  // queue for k initially empty
      Set front[k] = rear[k] = 0
   Else if ( rear[k] = size-1 ) then
      Set rear[k] = 0
   Else
      Set rear[k] = rear[k] + 1
   Endif
2. Set PQ[rear[k]] = item
3. Return
```

Implementations of other operations (creation/initialization, to check whether it is full, to check whether it is empty) are trivial and are left as an exercise for the student.

6.6.1.3 Heap Representation of a Priority Queue

A *heap* is a complete binary tree and with the additional property – the root element is either smallest or largest from its children. If root element of the heap is smallest from its children, it is known as *min heap*. If root element of the heap is largest from its children, it is known as *max heap*.

A priority queue having highest priority for lower number can be represented using *min heap*, and a priority queue having highest priority for higher number can be represented using *max heap*.

The element of the priority queue to be processed next is always in the root node of the heap.

Heaps are discussed in detail in *Chapter 7*, where we will again discuss the representation of priority queue using heap and implementation of dequeue and enqueue operations.

If we compare the effort in adding or removing elements from the priority queue, you will find that heap representation is the best.

SUMMARY

In this chapter, we have learnt about the

- basics of a queue data structure.
- different operations that can be performed on a queues.
- representation of a queue using a linear array.
- concept linear and circular queues when queue is represented using array.
- representation of a queue using linear linked list.
- applications of queues.
- deque data structure in breif.
- priority queues.
- possible ways of representation of a priority queue.
- implementation of operation on a priority queue.

REVIEW EXERCISES

1. What is a queue? Is queue a linear or non-linear data structure?
2. Queue is a special type of list? Comment.
3. How does an array based queue compares with linked list based queue?
4. Why operation to check queue for overflow is not implemented on linked queues?
5. How *peep()* operation differs from *dequeue()* operation?
6. While representing a queue using linked lists, we have implemented additional operation *dispose()* to remove the queue from memory. Why such operation is not implemented for queue represented using an array.
7. How does a linear queue compare with circular queue?
8. What is a deque? What are its variations?
9. What do you understand by priority queue? In what possible ways a priority queue can be represented in memory ?
10. Consider the following queue of characters, where Q is a circular queue which can accommodate maximum of 6 elements:

    front = 2 rear = 4

    Q: ____, A, B, C, ____, ____

    where "____" indicates empty space. Describe the queue Q when the following operations are performed in that sequence.

    (*a*) Enqueue(Q, F)

    (*b*) Dequeue(Q), Dequeue(Q)

    (*c*) Enqueue(Q, K), Enqueue(Q, L), Enqueue(Q, M)

    (*d*) Dequeue(Q), Dequeue(Q)
11. Suppose memory for *n* elements of a circular queue Q is reserved.

    (*a*) Find the number of elements in Q

    (*b*) When Q will be full?
12. Consider the priority queue PQ of following figure:

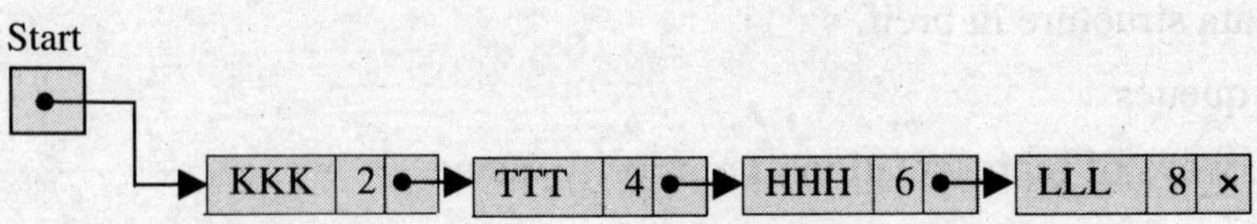

Figure 6.11: A priority queue with 4 elements

Describe the structure of the priority queue PQ, when the following operations are performed in sequence:

(*a*) Elements (SSS, 1), (QQQ, 6), (RRR, 5) and (YYY, 9) are added.
(*b*) Three elements are removed.

13. Consider the priority queue PQ of following figure:

	front	rear
0	0	1
1	-1	-1
2	1	3
3	0	2

PQ

	0	1	2	3	4	5
0	AAA	BBB				
1						
2		PPP	QQQ	RRR		
3	TTT	UUU	VVV			

Figure 6.12: Schematics of a priority queue with 4 priority levels

Describe the structure of the priority queue PQ, when the following operations are performed in sequence:

(*a*) Elements (SSS, 1), (MMM, 2) are added.
(*b*) One element is removed.
(*c*) Elements (CCC, 0), (DDD,1) are added.
(*d*) Two elements are removed.

PROGRAMMING EXERCISES

1. Write a menu driven program to implement a linear queue.
2. Write a menu driven program to implement a circular queue.
3. Write a menu driven program to implement a linked queue.
4. Write a menu driven program to implement a priority queue when the priority queue is represented using linear linked list.
5. Write a menu driven program to implement a priority queue when the priority queue is represented using multiple queues (2-D array).

❑ ❑ ❑

Chapter 7

Trees

Learning Objectives

After reading this chapter, students will be able to

- explain the basic terminology of trees
- explain the types of trees
- explain the way trees can be represented in memory
- demonstrate the common operations on binary and binary search trees
- develop algorithms for operations on binary and binary search trees

7.1 INTRODUCTION

So far in the text we have discussed data structures such as arrays, linked lists, stacks and queues for representing linear and tabular data. These structures in general are not suitable for representing hierarchical data. In hierarchical data we have ancestor-descendant, superior-subordinate, whole-part, or similar relationship among data elements.

The following examples will further illustrate these situations and makes the things more clearer.

Example 7.1: *Family Structure*

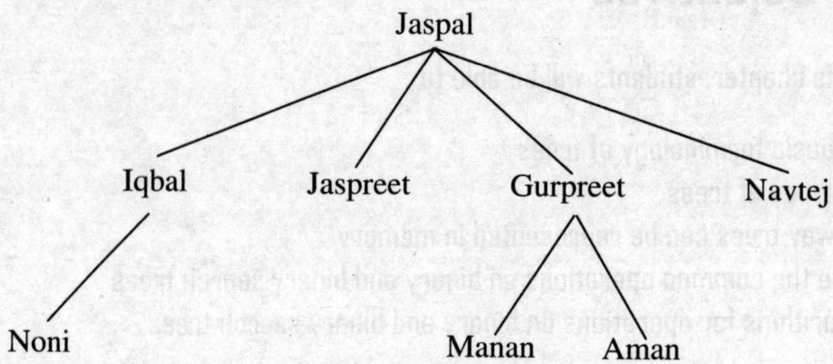

Figure 7.1: Hierarchical structure showing Jaspal's descendants

In above example, the data set is {Jaspal, Iqbal, Jaspreet, Navtej, Gurpreet, Noni, Aman, Manan}.

Therefore, number of element in the data set n = 8. The root of the data set is Jaspal. The remaining elements are divided into four disjoint sets {Iqbal, Noni}, {Jaspreet}, {Gurpreet, Aman, Manan}, and {Navtej}. The root of first disjoint set {Iqbal, Noni} is Iqbal. The remaining element {Noni} is a single element sub tree with Noni as its root. The root of second disjoint set {Gurpreet, Aman, Manan} is Gurpreet. The remaining elements {Aman, Manan} are partitioned into the disjoint sets {Aman} and {Manan}, which are both single element sub trees. The data sets {Jaspreet} and {Navtej} have only one element, and therefore their roots are Jaspreet and Navtej respectively.

Example 7.2: *Business Corporate Structure*

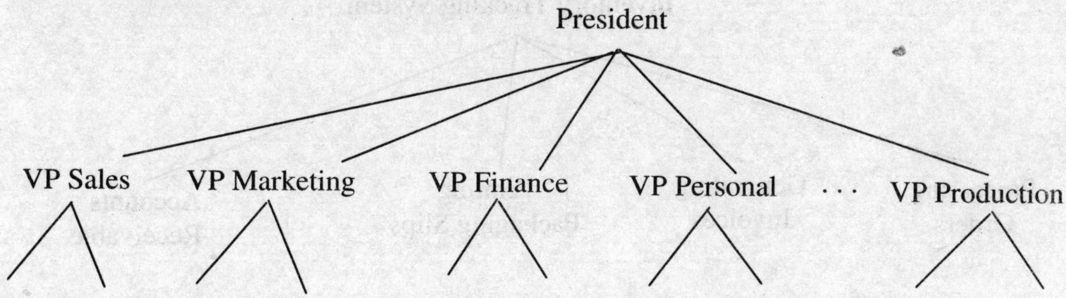

Figure 7.2: Hierarchical administrative structure of a typical business organization

Figure 7.2 shows administrative setup of a typical business organization. The person highest in the hierarchy (president in this case) appears at the top. Those who are next in the hierarchy (vice presidents (VPs) in this case) are shown next in the hierarchy below the president. The vice presidents are the president's immediate subordinates, and the present is their superior. Each vice president, in turn, has his/her subordinates who may themselves have subordinates.

Example 7.3: *Federal Government Structure*

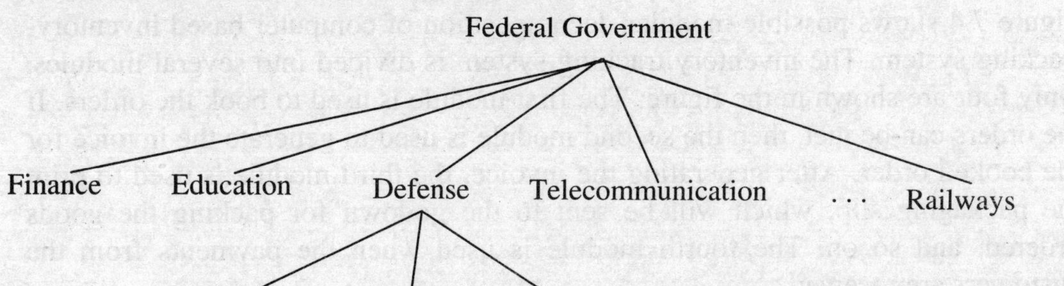

Figure 7.3: Hierarchical structure of a typical federal government

Figure 7.3 shows hierarchical subdivisions of a federal government. At the top, we have entire federal government. At the next level; we have its major subdivisions, *i.e.*, different departments. Each subdivision may have further subdivisions, which will be shown, at the next level. For example, Department of Defense has been subdivided into Army, Navy, and Air Force.

Example 7.4: *Modular Structure of a Computer Program*

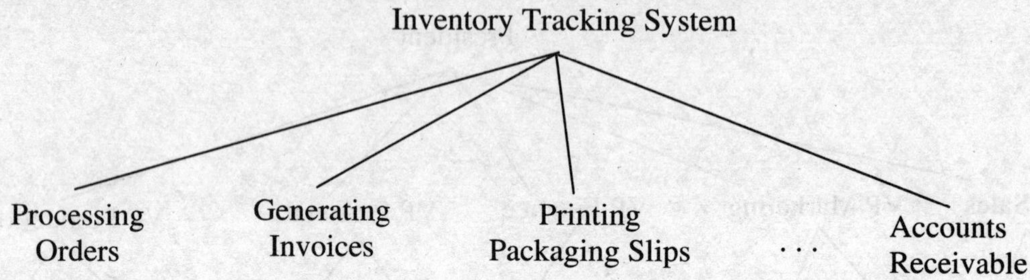

Figure 7.4: Module hierarchy for inventory tracking system

For another example of hierarchical data, consider the popular software development technique referred to as *modularization*. The objective of modularization is to divide the large and complex software system into functionally independent modules (parts) so that each can be developed independently. If necessary, each module may be further divided. It reduces the overall software develop time, as it is much easier to solve several problems than one large one. In addition, different programmers can develop different modules at the same time.

Figure 7.4 shows possible modular decomposition of computer based inventory-tracking system. The inventory tracking system is divided into several modules. Only four are shown in the figure. The first module is used to book the orders. If the orders can be met, then the second module is used to generate the invoice for the booked order. After generating the invoice, the third module is used to print the packaging slip, which will be sent to the godown for packing the goods ordered, and so on. The fourth module is used when the payments from the customers are received.

A tree is an ideal data structure for representing such kind of hierarchical data.

There are many types of trees in data structures such as *general trees*, *binary trees*, *expression trees*, *tournament trees*, *binary search trees*, *threaded trees*, *AVL trees* and B-*trees*, etc.

In this chapter, we will discuss about binary and binary search trees in details while others, *threaded*, *AVL*, etc., are introduced briefly.

7.2 TREE DEFINED

A (*general*) *tree T* is a finite nonempty set of elements. One of these elements is called the *root*, and the remaining elements, if any, are partitioned into trees, which are called the *sub trees* of *T*.

Before moving further, let us have a look at the basic terminology related to trees.

Level of an Element – Very commonly used tree term is level. By definition, the root of the tree is at level 1; its children, if any, are at level 2; their children, if any, are at level 3; and so on. In Figure 7.1, Jaspal is at level 1; Iqbal, Jaspreet, Gurpreet, and Navtej are at level 2; Noni, Aman, and Manan are at level 3.

Degree of an Element – The degree of an element is the number of children it has. The degree of a leaf is zero. In Figure 7.1, Jaspal has degree 4.

Degree of a Tree – The degree of a tree is the maximum of its element degrees. The degree of tree in Figure 7.1 is 4.

Height/Depth of a Tree – If level of the root is denoted by 1, then the maximum level number of the tree is known as its *height* or *depth*.

Internal Node – A node of the tree that have at least one child.

External Node – A node of the tree that have no child. These nodes are also called *leaves*. These nodes are also called *terminal nodes*.

Siblings – All the node having common parent.

Similar Trees – Two trees are said to be similar if they have the same structure (shape). However, they differ in content at corresponding nodes.

Equivalent Trees – Two trees are said to be equivalent if they have the same structure as well as same content at corresponding nodes. These types of trees are also called *copies*.

7.3 BINARY TREES

A *binary tree T* is defined as a finite set of elements, called *nodes*, such that

(*a*) Either *T* is empty (called the *null tree* or *empty tree*), or

(*b*) *T* contains a distinguished node *R*, called the root of *T*, and the remaining nodes of *T* form an ordered pair of disjoint binary trees T_1 and T_2, and are called *left* and *right sub trees* of *R*.

When the binary tree is not empty, one of its elements is called the *root* and the remaining elements, if any, are partitioned into two binary trees, which are called the left and right sub trees of *T*.

A binary tree is drawn with its root at the top. The elements in the left (right) sub tree of the root are drawn below and to the left (right) of the root. Between each element and its children is a line or edge.

The root of left subtree and the right subtree are referred to as left child (also called *left successor*) and right child (also called *left successor*), respectively. We will be using this terminology in our text.

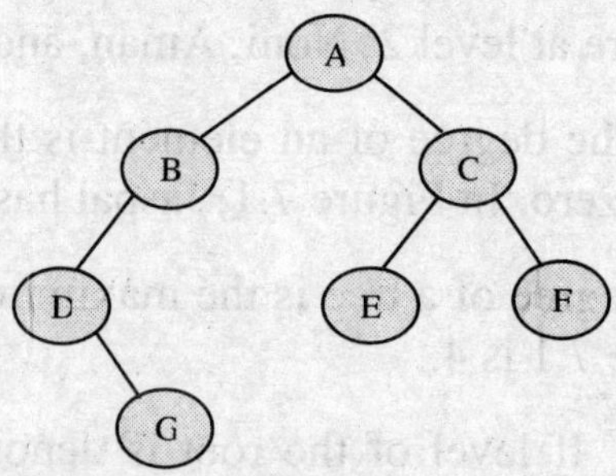

Figure 7.5: Binary tree

Figure 7.5 represents a binary tree *T* as follows:

(*i*) *T* consists of 7 nodes
(*ii*) Root of *T* is the node *A* at the top
(*iii*) A left slanted line from any node indicates a left child of a node, and a right slanted line indicates a right child of a node. Observe that

(*a*) *B* is the root child and *C* is the right child of node *A*.
(*b*) The left child *B* is root of subtree of the node *A* and consists of the nodes *B*, *D*, and *G* while the right child *C* is root of subtree of node *A* and consists of the nodes *C*, *E*, and *F*.

Any node in the binary tree *T* has either 0, 1 or 2 children. The nodes *A* and *C* have two children, the node *B* and *D* have only one child, and the nodes D, E and F have only no child.

You must have observed that the definition of binary tree *T* is recursive since it is defined in terms of binary trees T_1 and T_2. This means that every node *N* of *T* contains a left and a right subtree. When *N* is a terminal node, then both, left as well as right, subtrees are empty.

Example 7.5:

Consider the following binary tree.

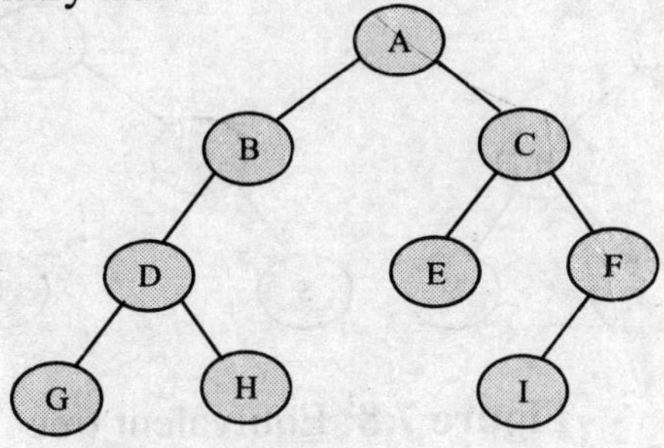

Figure 7.6: Binary tree

- It has 9 nodes.
- Level number of node *A* is 1; *B* and *C* is 2; *D*, *E* and *F* is 3; and *G*, *H* and *I* is 4.
- Its height is 4.
- Nodes *A*, *B*, *C*, *D* and *F* are internal nodes, and nodes *G*, *H*, *E* and *I* are external nodes (terminal nodes or leaves).
- Nodes *B* and *C* are siblings; nodes *E* and *F* are siblings; nodes *G* and *H* are siblings.
- Node *B* is the root of the left subtree of node *A* and node *C* is the root of the right subtree of node *A*. Further, *D* is the root of left subtree of *B* and its right subtree is empty. Node *G* is the root of the left subtree of node *D* and *H* is the root of the right subtree of node *H*. The left and right subtrees of nodes G and H are empty.

  Node *E* is the root of the left subtree of node *C* and node *F* is the root of the right subtree of node *C*. The left and right subtrees of node E. Node *I* is the root of the left subtree of node *D* and its right subtree is empty. Both left and right subtrees of node *I* are empty.

Example 7.6:

Consider the following pair of binary trees.

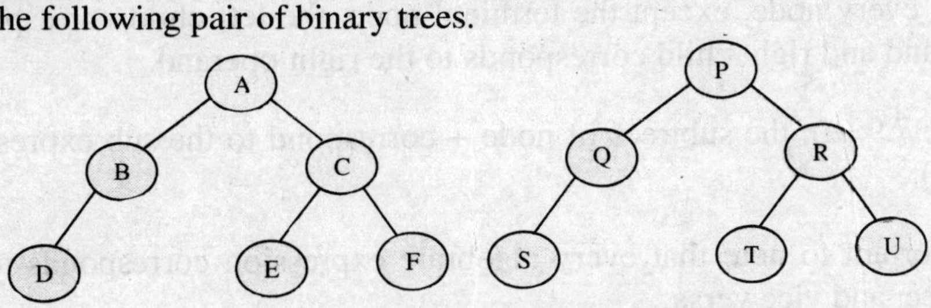

Figure 7.7: Similar trees

These binary trees are similar since they have the same shape.

Example 7.7:

Consider the following pair of binary trees.

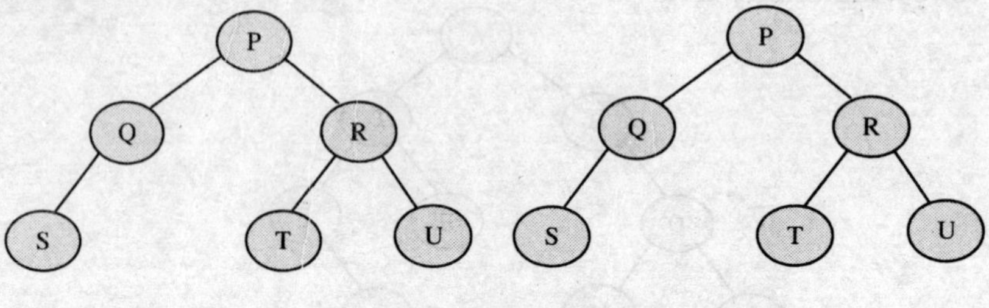

Figure 7.8: Equivalent tree

These binary trees are equivalent (copies) since they have the same shape and same data at corresponding nodes.

Example 7.8:

Binary trees are also used to express arithmetic expressions.

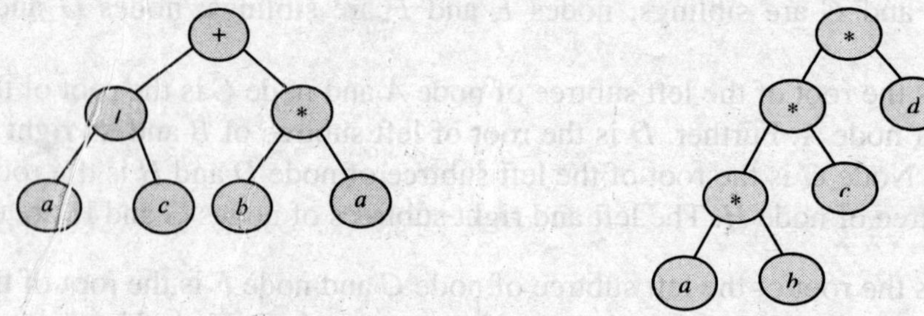

(*a*) $E = (a / c) + (b * d)$ (*b*) $E = (((a * b) * c) * d)$

Figure 7.9: Expression trees

Each operator appears as internal node while each operand appears as external node. At every node, except the terminal node, the left child corresponds to the left operand and right child corresponds to the right operand.

In Figure 7.9 (*a*), the subtrees of node + correspond to the sub expressions (*a*/*c*) and (*b***d*).

It is important to note that every algebraic expression corresponds to a unique binary tree, and vice versa.

7.3.1 Complete Binary Tree

Consider any binary tree T. Each node of binary tree T can have at most two children. Accordingly, each level r of binary tree T can have at most 2^{r-1} nodes, when the root is given level number 1.

Binary tree T is said to be *complete* if all its levels, except the last, have maximum number of possible nodes, and if all the nodes at the last level appear as far as left as possible, *i.e.*, if at the second last level, a node have only one child it will be the left one. Thus, there is a unique complete tree T_n with exactly n node. A complete tree T_6 with 6 nodes is shown in Figure 7.10.

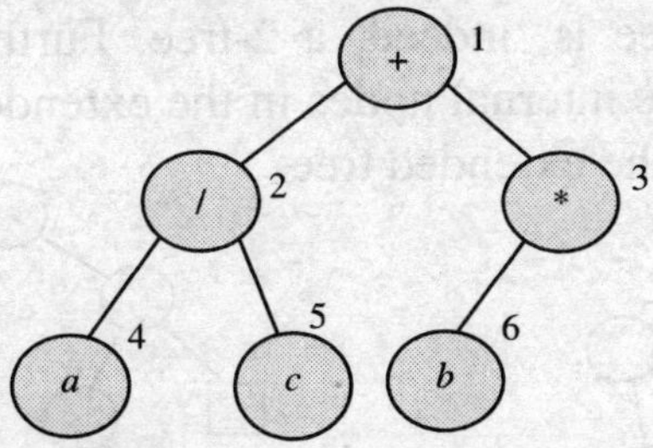

Figure 7.10: Complete binary tree T_6

The nodes of the complete binary tree T_6 are purposely numbered (labeled) from top-to-bottom and left-to-right, level-by-level. With this numbering, one can easily find the children and parent of any node numbered K in the complete binary tree T_n. The left child of node number K is node numbered $2K$ and right child of node number K is node numbered $2K+1$. Similarly, the parent of any node numbered L in the complete binary tree T_n is node number $\lfloor L/2 \rfloor$.

For example, the left and right child of node numbered 2 (K=2) are nodes numbered 4 ($2\times K=2\times 2$) and node numbered 5 ($2\times K+1=2\times 2+1$). The parent of node numbered 5 (L=2) is node numbered 2 ($\lfloor L/2 \rfloor = \lfloor 5/2 \rfloor = 2$).

The height (depth) complete binary tree T_n is given by

$$H_n \text{ or } D_n = \lfloor \log_2 n + 1 \rfloor$$

which is a relatively small number. For example, if a complete binary tree T_n has n = 1024 nodes, then its height

$$H_n = \lfloor \log_2 1024 + 1 \rfloor = \lfloor \log_2 2^{10} + 1 \rfloor = \lfloor 10 + 1 \rfloor = 11$$

7.3.2 Extended Binary Trees: 2-Trees

A binary tree *T* is said to be a *2-tree* or an *extended binary tree* if each node, say *N*, has either 0 or 2 children. In such a case, the nodes with 2 children are called *internal nodes*, the nodes with 0 children are called *external nodes*. Usually the nodes are distinguished in diagram by using circles for internal nodes and squares for external nodes.

The term *extended binary tree* comes from the following operations. Consider any binary tree T, such as the tree in Figure 7.11(*a*). Then *T* may be converted into a 2-tree by replacing each empty subtree by a new node in Figure 7.11(*b*). Observe that the new tree is, indeed, a 2-tree. Furthermore, the nodes in the original tree *T* are now the internal nodes in the extended tree, and the new nodes are the external nodes in the extended tree.

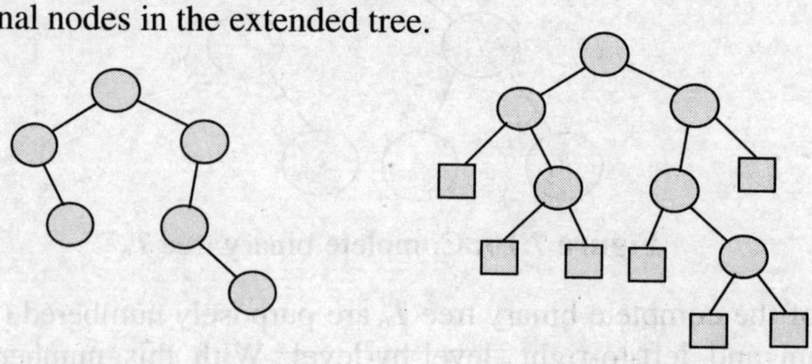

(*a*) Binary tree *T* (*b*) Extended 2-tree

Figure 7.11: Converting a binary tree T into a 2-tree

An important example of a 2-tree is the tree *T* corresponding to any algebraic expression *E* which uses only binary operations. As illustrated in Figure 7.9, the variable in *E* will appear as the external nodes, and the operations in *E* will appear as internal nodes.

7.4 BINARY SEARCH TREES

A *binary search tree T* is a binary tree that may be empty. A non-empty binary search tree satisfies the following properties:

1. Every element has a key (or value) and no two elements have the same key, *i.e.*, all keys are unique.
2. The keys, if any, in left sub tree of the root are smaller than the key in the node.
3. The keys, if any, in right sub tree of the root are larger than the key in the node.
4. The left and right sub trees of root are also binary search trees.

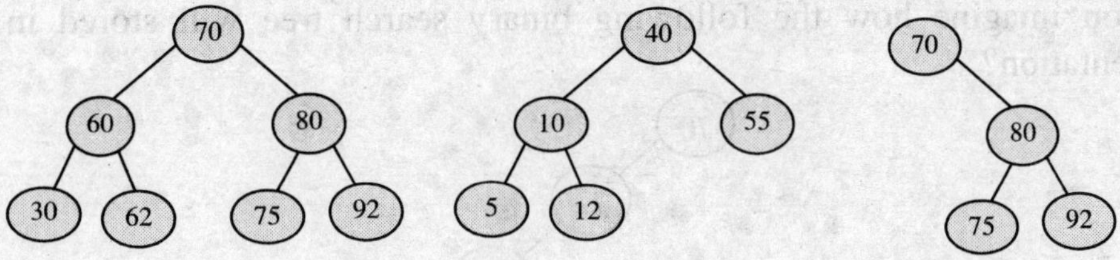

(*a*) (*b*) (*c*)

Figure 7.12: Binary Search trees

7.5 REPRESENTATION OF A BINARY AND BINARY SEARCH TREE

A binary tree and a binary search tree are represented in an identical manner. These can be represented using a linear array (array representation) or linked lists (linked representation). We will discuss these representations one by one and their merits and demerits.

7.5.1 Array Representation

In this representation, the binary (search) tree is represented by storing each element at the array position corresponding to the number assigned to each node, as if the node of a binary (search) tree are numbered starting from 1 and going upto n if n is the number of nodes in the binary (search) tree. In this representation, a binary (search) tree of height h requires an array of size $(2^h - 1)$, in the worst case.

For simplicity, we consider that array is indexed with an index set beginning from 1 not from 0, as consistent with the numbering of the nodes.

1	2	3	4	5	6	7
70	60	80	30	62	75	92

(*a*) Array representation of binary search trees of Figure 7.12(*a*)

1	2	3	4	5	6	7
40	10	55	5	12		

(*b*) Array representation of binary search trees of Figure 7.12(*b*)

1	2	3	4	5	6	7
70		80			75	92

(*c*) Array representation of binary search trees of Figure 7.12(*c*)

Figure 7.13: Array representation of binary search trees of Figure 7.12

Can you imagine how the following binary search tree will stored in array representation?

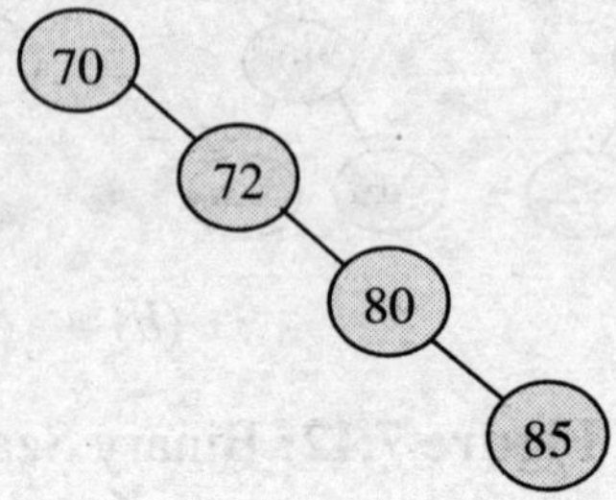

Figure 7.14: A right-skewed binary search tree

The array representation of binary search tree of Figure 7.14 will be as shown in Figure 7.15.

1	2	3	4	5	6	7	8	9	10	11	12	13	14	15
70		72				80								85

Figure 7.15: Array representation of binary search tree of Figure 7.14

This scheme of representation is quite wasteful of space when the binary (search) tree is skewed or number of elements is small as compared to its height.

Hence, array representation is useful only when the binary (search) tree is full or complete.

7.5.2 Linked Representation

The most popular and practical way of representing a binary (search) tree is using links (pointers).

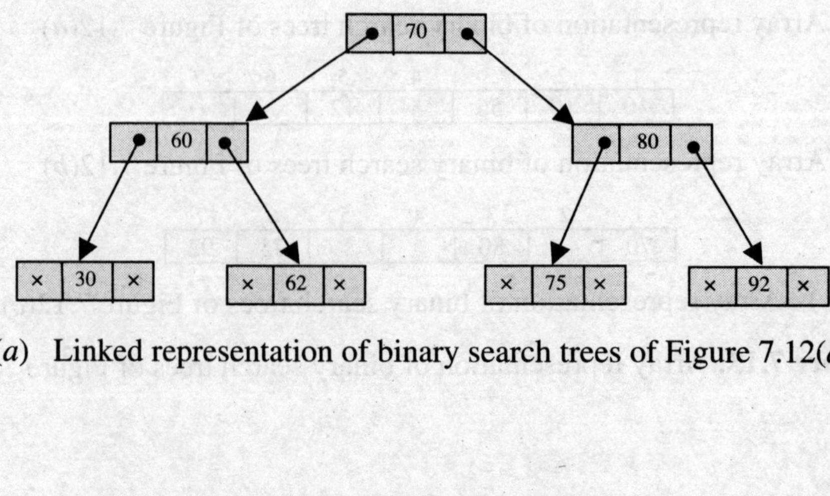

(*a*) Linked representation of binary search trees of Figure 7.12(*a*)

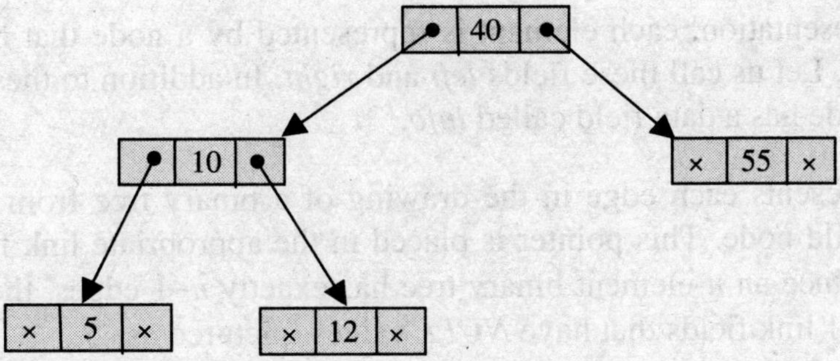

(*b*) Linked representation of binary search trees of Figure 7.12(*b*)

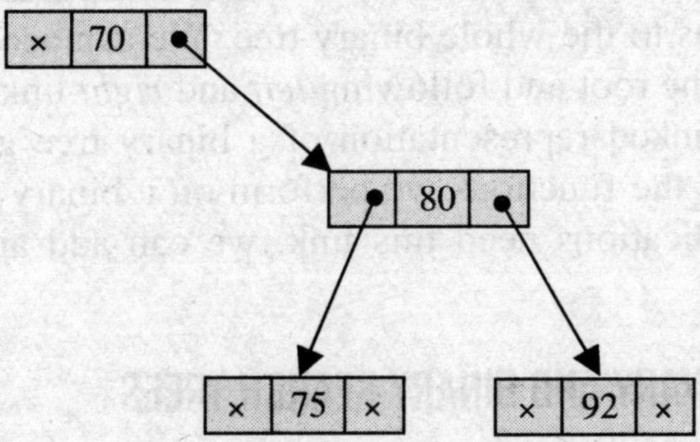

(*c*) Linked representation of binary search trees of Figure 7.12(*c*)

Figure 7.16: Linked representation of binary search trees of Figure 7.12

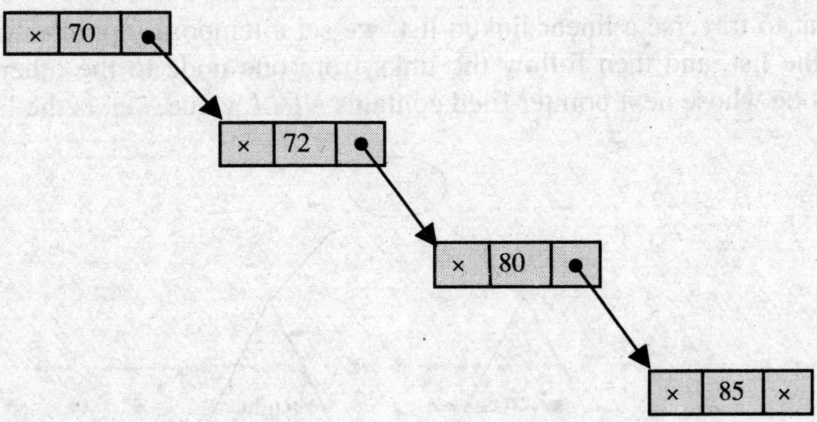

Figure 7.17: Linked representation of binary search trees of Figure 7.14

In linked representation, each element is represented by a node that has exactly two link fields. Let us call these fields *left* and *right*. In addition to these two link fields, each node has a data field called *info*.

An arrow represents each edge in the drawing of a binary tree from the parent node to the child node. This pointer is placed in the appropriate link field of the parent node. Since an *n*-element binary tree has exactly $n-1$ edges, there will be $2n-(n-1) = n+1$ link fields that have *NULL* values (pictured as ×).

In addition to the above node structure, a pointer variable, say *root*, is used to keep track of the root of the binary tree. We will be using this variable to refer to the root node as well as to the whole binary tree. We can access all the nodes in binary tree starting at the root and following *left* and *right* links. The absence of a parent link from the linked representation of a binary tree generally causes no difficulties, as most of the functions we perform on a binary tree do not require this link. If some applications need this link, we can add another link field to each node.

7.6 OPERATIONS ON BINARY AND BINARY SEARCH TREES

In our implementation of operations on binary (search) trees, we will consider linked representation.

7.6.1 Traversing a Binary and Binary Search Tree

Recall that to traverse a linear linked list, we set a temporary pointer variable to *head* of the list, and then follow the links from one node to the other until we reach a node whose next pointer filed contains *NULL* value, *i.e.*, is the last node.

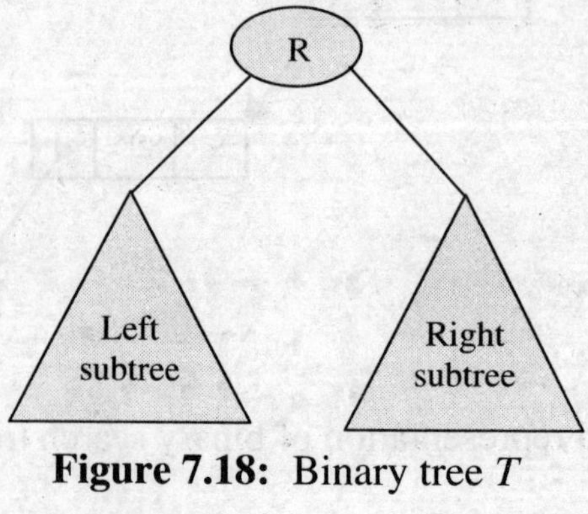

Figure 7.18: Binary tree *T*

Similarly, we can set a pointer variable to the root of the tree. But where do we go from there – to the left child or the right child? Do we process the root first or the leaves first? Therefore, based on the way the nodes in the tree are traversed, the traversal is classified in one of the following categories for a binary tree *T* with root R as shown in Figure 7.18.

- **Pre-order traversal** – the traversal order is
  - o Process the root R
  - o Traverse the left sub tree of R in pre-order
  - o Traverse the right sub tree of R in pre-order
- **In-order traversal** – the traversal order is
  - o Traverse the left sub tree of R in pre-order
  - o Process the root R
  - o Traverse the right sub tree of R in pre-order
- **Post-order traversal** – the traversal order is
  - o Traverse the left sub tree of R in pre-order
  - o Traverse the right sub tree of R in pre-order
  - o Process the root R

Example 7.9:

Consider the following binary tree *T*. Observe that *A* is the root, and left sub tree L_T consists of nodes *B*, *D*, and *E* and the right sub tree R_T consists of nodes *C*, *F*, and *G*.

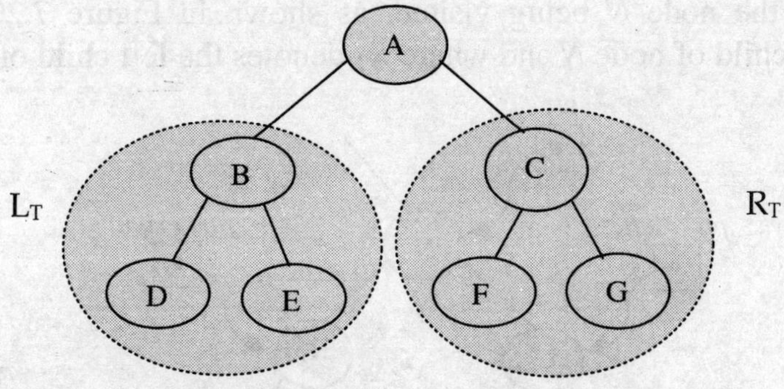

Figure 7.19: An example tree

(*a*) The pre-order traversal of *T* processes *A*, then traverses left sub tree L_T and finally traverses right sub tree R_T. The pre-order of L_T processes its root *B* and then *D* and *E*. The pre-order of R_T processes its root *C* and then *F* and *G*. Thus, the pre-order traversal of tree *T* is *A B D E C F G*.

(*b*) The in-order traversal of *T* first traverses left sub tree L_T, then processes *A* and finally traverses right sub tree R_T. The in-order of L_T processes *D* and then *B* and *E*. The in-order of R_T processes first *F* then *C* and *G*. Thus, the in-order traversal of tree *T* is *D B E A F C G*.

(*c*) The post-order traversal of *T* first traverses left sub tree L_T, then traverses right sub tree R_T and finally processes *A*. The post-order of L_T processes *D* and then *E* and *B*. The post-order of R_T processes first *F* then *G* and *C*. Thus, the post-order traversal of tree *T* is *D E B F G C A*.

Since, binary (search) tree is a recursive data structure by nature, recursive algorithms for performing operation on them are more natural. The recursive algorithms are more concise and well suited for final implementation on computer, but more difficult to simulate (trace). In contrast, the iterative algorithms, which use stack, for performing operations on binary (search) tree may look lengthy and cumbersome but are easy to simulate.

We will consider both type of algorithms, but will use the iterative one to show the implementation of a particular operation.

7.6.1.1 Pre-Order Traversal

The pre-order traversal algorithm uses a pointer variable *ptr* which will contain the location of the node *N* being visited, as shown in Figure 7.20, where L_T denotes the left child of node *N* and where R_T denotes the left child of node *N*.

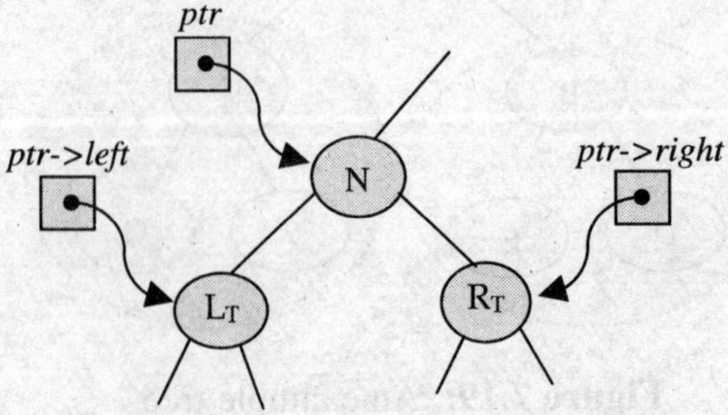

Figure 7.20: Snap shot of part of a binary tree to demonstrate traversal

Outline of Pre-order Traversal Algorithm

To start with push *NULL*, a sentinel value, onto stack, and set *ptr* = *root*. Then repeat the following steps while *ptr* ≠ *NULL*.

(*a*) Proceed down the left most path, using *left->ptr*, rooted at *ptr*, processing, say printing, each node *N* on the path and pushing address of each right child (*ptr->right*), if any, onto the stack. Thus, *ptr* is updated using the assignment statement, *ptr* = *ptr->left*, and traversing down the left stops when *ptr->left* = *NULL*.

(*b*) [Backtracking] Pop stack and assign the popped address to *ptr*. If *ptr* ≠ *NULL* go back to step (*a*); else exit.

Example 7.10:

Consider the following binary tree. We will simulate the iterative version of the above algorithm and show the contents of the stack at each step.

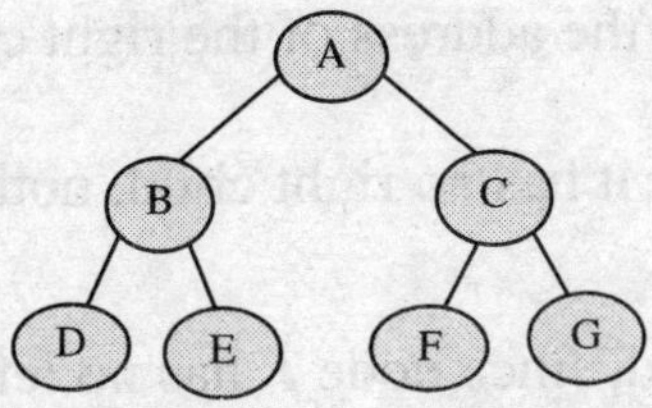

Figure 7.21: Given binary tree *T*

We will use the notation *addr*(*N*) to denote the address of node *N*. And the processing step considering here is printing the vales of the nodes.

1. To start with push *NULL* onto stack, then set *ptr* = *addr*(A)

NULL
STACK

2. Proceed down the left-most path rooted at node *A* as follows:

(*i*) Print *A*, and push the address of the right child *C* onto stack.

addr(*C*)
NULL
STACK

(*ii*) Print *B*, and push the address of the right child *E* onto stack.

(*iii*) Print *D*, and since it has no right child, nothing is pushed into stack.

addr(*E*)
addr(*C*)
NULL
STACK

No other node is processed, since node *D* has no left child.

3. [Backtracking] Pop the stack and assign popped element to *ptr*, therefore *ptr* = *addr*(*E*).

Since *ptr* ≠ *NULL*, go back to step (*a*) of algorithm.

addr(*C*)
NULL
STACK

4. Proceed down the left-most path rooted at node *E* as follows:

(*iv*) Print *E*, and since it has no right child, nothing is pushed into stack.

No other node is processed, since node D has no left child.

addr(*C*)
NULL
STACK

5. [Backtracking] Pop the stack and assign popped element to *ptr*, therefore *ptr* = *addr*(*C*).

Since *ptr* ≠ *NULL*, go back to step (*a*) of algorithm.

NULL
STACK

6. Proceed down the left-most path rooted at node *C* as follows:

(*v*) Print *C*, and push the address of the right child *G* onto stack.

(*vi*) Print *F*, and since it has no right child, nothing is pushed into stack.

No other node is processed, since node *F* has no left child.

addr(*G*)
NULL
STACK

7. [Backtracking] Pop the stack and assign popped element to *ptr*, therefore *ptr* = *addr*(*G*).

Since *ptr* ≠ *NULL*, go back to step (*a*) of algorithm.

NULL
STACK

8. Proceed down the left-most path rooted at node *G* as follows:

(*vii*) Print *G*, and since it has no right child, nothing is pushed into stack.

No other node is processed, since node *G* has no left child.

9. [Backtracking] Pop the stack and assign popped element to *ptr*, therefore *ptr* = *NULL*.

Since *ptr* = *NULL*, the algorithm is completed.

STACK

As seen from steps 2, 4, 6 and 8, the nodes are processed in order *A, B, D, E, C, F, G*.

Formal presentation of iterative as well as recursive algorithms for pre-order traversal is given below:

Algorithm 7.1

PreOrderIterative(***root*** **)**

Here *root* is a pointer variable that holds the address of the root node of the given tree. It uses a stack *S* whose elements are pointers to node of binary (search) tree. It uses a temporary pointer variable *ptr* to hold the address of current node.

```
1. Call Push(S,NULL)
2. Set ptr = root
3. Repeat steps 4 to 6 While ( ptr ≠ NULL )
4.      Write: ptr->info
5.      If ( ptr->right ≠ NULL ) then
            Call Push(S,ptr->right)
        Endif
6.      If ( ptr->left ≠ NULL ) then
            Set ptr = ptr->left
        Else
            Call Pop(S,ptr)
        Endif
   Endwhile
7. Return
```

Algorithm 7.2

PreOrderRecursive(***root*** **)**

Here *root* is a pointer variable that holds the address of the root node of the given tree. It uses recursion to perform the pre-order traversal of a binary (search) tree.

```
1. If ( root ≠ NULL ) then
        Write: root->info
        Call PreOrderRecursive(root->left)
        Call PreOrderRecursive(root->right)
   Endif
2. Return
```

7.6.1.2 In-Order Traversal

The in-order traversal algorithm uses a pointer variable *ptr* which will contain the location of the node *N* being visited. In this algorithm, node is processed only when it is popped from stack.

Outline of In-order Traversal Algorithm

To start with push *NULL*, a sentinel value, onto stack, and set *ptr* = *root*. Then repeat the following steps until NULL is popped from stack.

(*a*) Proceed down the left most path, using *left->ptr*, rooted at *ptr*, pushing each node on the path onto stack, and stop when a node having no left child is pushed onto the stack.

(*b*) [Backtracking] Pop stack and process the node. If a node with a right child is processed, set *ptr* = *ptr->right* and go back to step (*a*). However, if NULL is popped then exit.

Example 7.11:

Consider the following binary tree. We will simulate the iterative version of the above algorithm and show the contents of the stack at each step.

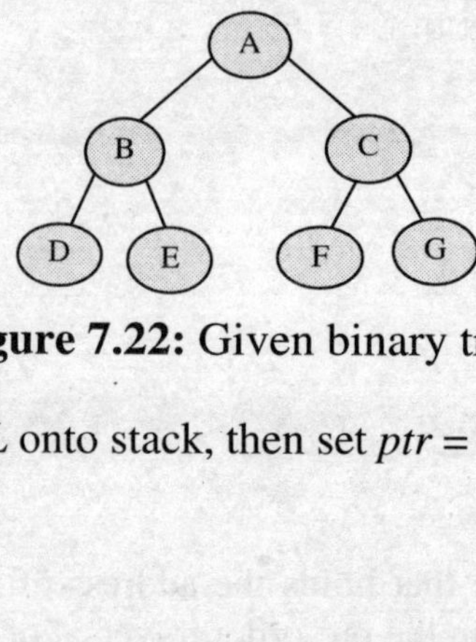

Figure 7.22: Given binary tree *T*

1. To start with push *NULL* onto stack, then set *ptr* = *addr*(A)

2. Proceed down the left-most path rooted at node *A* and pushing the addresses of the nodes *A*, *B*, *D* onto stack:

No other node is pushed since node *D* has no left child.

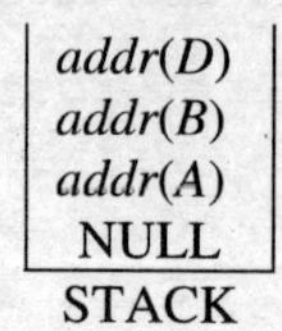

3. [Backtracking] The addresses of node *D* and *B* are popped and nodes *D* and *B* are processed.

- We stop processing at node *B*, since node *B* has a right child. Set *ptr* = *addr*(*E*), go back to step (*a*) of algorithm.

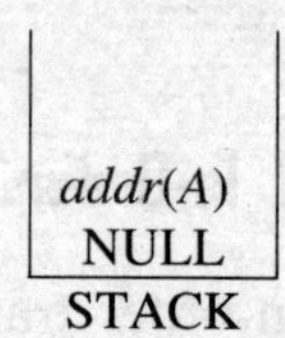

4. Proceed down the left-most path rooted at node *E* and push the address of node *E* onto stack. No other address is pushed since it has no right child as well as no left child.

   addr(*E*)
   addr(*A*)
   NULL
   STACK

5. [Backtracking] The addresses of node *E* and *A* are popped and nodes *E* and *A* are processed.

   We stop processing at node *A*, since node *A* has a right child. Set *ptr* = *addr*(*C*), go back to step (*a*) of algorithm.

   NULL
   STACK

6. Proceed down the left-most path rooted at node *C* and push the address of nodes *C* and *F* onto stack.

   No other address is pushed since node *F* has no left child.

   addr(*F*)
   addr(*C*)
   NULL
   STACK

7. [Backtracking] The addresses of node *F* and *C* are popped and nodes *F* and *C* are processed.

   We stop processing at node *C*, since node *C* has a right child. Set *ptr* = *addr*(*G*), go back to step (*a*) of algorithm.

   NULL
   STACK

8. Proceed down the left-most path rooted at node *G* and push the address of node *G* onto stack. No other address is pushed since it has no right child as well as no left child.

   addr(*G*)
   NULL
   STACK

9. [Backtracking] The address of node *G* is popped and node *G* is processed.

   NULL
   STACK

   Since node *G* has no right child, we pop the stack again, and since this time *NULL* value is popped, the algorithm is completed.

   STACK

As seen from steps 3, 5, 7 and 9, the nodes are processed in order *D, B, E, A, F, C, G*.

Formal presentation of iterative as well as recursive algorithms for in-order traversal is given overleaf.

Algorithm 7.3

InOrderIterative(root)

Here *root* is a pointer variable that holds the address of the root node of the given tree. It uses a stack *S* whose elements are pointers to node of binary (search) tree. It uses a temporary pointer variable *ptr* to hold the address of current node. It also uses a flag variable *done* to control the iteration.

```
1.  Call Push(S,NULL)
2.  Set ptr = root
3.  Set done = false
4.  Repeat steps 5 to 13 While ( not done )
5.     Repeat steps 6 and 7 while ( ptr ≠ NULL )
6.        Call Push(S,ptr)
7.        Set ptr = ptr->left
       Endwhile
8.     Call Pop(S,ptr)
9.     Set flag = true
10.    Repeat steps 11 and 12 While ((ptr≠NULL)and(flag=true))
11.        Write: ptr->info
12.        If ( ptr->right ≠ NULL ) then
              Set ptr = ptr->right
              Set flag = false
           Else
              Call Pop(S,ptr)
           Endif
       Endwhile
13.    If ( ptr  = NULL ) then
          Set done = true
       Endif
    Endwhile
14.Return
```

Algorithm 7.4

InOrderRecursive(***root*** **)**

Here *root* is a pointer variable that holds the address of the root node of the given tree. It uses recursion to perform the in-order traversal of a binary (search) tree.

```
1. If ( tree ≠ NULL ) then
      Call InOrderRecursive(tree->left)
      Write: tree->info
      Call InOrderRecursive(tree->right)
   Endif
2. Exit
```

7.6.1.3 Post-Order Traversal

The post-order traversal algorithm is the most complicated than the other traversal algorithms, because we may have to save a node *N* in two different situations. We distinguish between the two cases by pushing either address of node *N* or negative of address of node *N*, onto stack. Here also, a pointer variable *ptr* is used to contain the address of the node that currently being visited.

Outline of Post-order Traversal Algorithm

To start with push *NULL*, a sentinel value, onto stack, and set *ptr* = *root*. Then repeat the following steps until NULL is popped from stack.

(*a*) Proceed down the left most path, using *left->ptr*, rooted at *ptr*. At each node *N* on the path, push address of node *N* onto stack, and if node *N* has a right child, push negative of address of right child onto stack.

(*b*) [Backtracking] Pop stack and process the nodes with positive address. If negative address is popped then assign the negative of that address (*i.e.*, negative of negative will make it positive) and assign to *ptr*, and go back to step (*a*). However, if NULL is popped then exit.

Example 7.12:

Consider the following binary tree again. We will simulate the iterative version of the above algorithm and show the contents of the stack at each step.

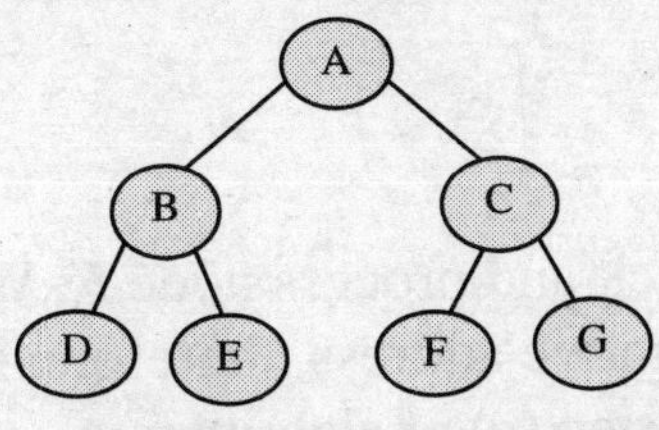

Figure 7.23: Given binary tree *T*

1. To start with push *NULL* onto stack, then set *ptr* = *addr*(A)

NULL
STACK

2. Proceed down the left-most path rooted at node *A* and pushing the address of the node *A*, negative of address of node *C*, address of node *B*, negative of address of node *E*, and finally address of node *D* onto stack.

   No other node is pushed since node *D* has no left child as well as right child.

addr(*D*)
-*addr*(*E*)
addr(*B*)
-*addr*(*C*)
addr(*A*)
NULL
STACK

3. [Backtracking] Pop stack and process node *D*. When we further pop, we get negative address, therefore, we set *ptr* = -*addr*(*E*), go back to step (*a*) of algorithm.

STACK
addr(*B*)
-*addr*(*C*)
addr(*A*)
NULL

4. Proceed down the left-most path rooted at node *E* and push its address on to stack.

   No other node is pushed since node *E* has no left child as well as right child.

STACK
addr(*E*)
addr(*B*)
-*addr*(*C*)
addr(*A*)
NULL

5. [Backtracking] Pop stack and process nodes *E* and *B*. When we further pop, we get negative address, therefore, we set *ptr* = -*addr*(*C*), go back to step (*a*) of algorithm.

STACK
addr(*A*)
NULL

6. Proceed down the left-most path rooted at node *C* and pushing the address of the node *C*, negative of address of node *G*, address of node *F* onto stack.

   No other address is pushed since node *F* has no left child as well right child.

STACK
addr(*F*)
-*addr*(*G*)
addr(*C*)
addr(*A*)
NULL

7. [Backtracking] Pop stack and process node *F*. When we further pop, we get negative address, therefore, we set *ptr* = -*addr*(*G*), go back to step (*a*) of algorithm.

STACK
addr(*C*)
addr(*A*)
NULL

8. Proceed down the left-most path rooted at node *G* and push its address on to stack.

   No other address is pushed since it has no right child as well as no left child.

STACK
addr(*G*)
addr(*C*)
addr(*A*)
NULL

9. [Backtracking] Pop stack and process node *G,* node C, and node *A,* since all addresses of these nodes in stack are positive.

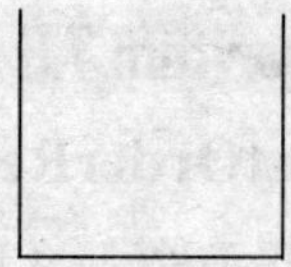

STACK

When we further pop, we get NULL value, and algorithm completes.

As seen from steps 3, 5, 7 and 9, the nodes are processed in order *D, E, B, F, G, C, A.*

Formal presentation of iterative as well as recursive algorithms for in-order traversal is given below:

Algorithm 7.5

PostOrderIterative(root)

Here *root* is a pointer variable that holds the address of the root node of the given tree. It uses a stack *s* whose elements are pointers to node of binary (search) tree. It uses a temporary pointer variable *ptr* to hold the address of current node. It also uses a flag variable *done* to control the iteration.

```
1. Call Push(S,NULL)
2. Set ptr = root
3. Set done = false
4. Repeat steps 5 to 15 While ( not done )
5.    Repeat steps 6 to 8 while ( ptr ≠ NULL )
6.       Call Push(S,ptr)
7.       If ( ptr->right ≠ NULL ) then
             Call Push(S,-(ptr->right))
         Endif
8.       Set ptr = ptr->left
      Endwhile
9.    Call Pop(S,ptr)
10.   Set flag = true
11.   Repeat steps 12 and 13 While ( ptr > 0 )
12.      Write: ptr->info
13.      Call Pop(S,ptr)
      Endwhile
14.   If ( ptr < 0 ) then
         Set ptr = -ptr
      Endif
15.   If ( ptr = NULL ) then
         Set done = true
      Endif
   Endwhile
16.Return
```

Algorithm 7.6

PostOrderRecursive(*root*)

Here *root* is a pointer variable that holds the address of the root node of the given tree. It uses recursion to perform the post-order traversal of a binary (search) tree.

```
1. If ( tree ≠ NULL ) then
       Call PostOrderRecursive(tree->left)
       Call PostOrderRecursive(tree->right)
       Write: tree->info
   Endif
2. Exit
```

Binary search tree has one very interesting property – *property is that if we are given in-order traversal and either of pre-order or post-order traversal; we can construct the binary tree from these traversals.*

Example 7.13:

Consider that a binary tree T has 8 nodes. The pre-order and in-order traversals of binary tree T yield the following sequence of nodes:

Pre-order : A B D E G H C F

In-order : D B G E H A C F

Draw the binary tree *T*.

Solution: The binary tree *T* is drawn as follows:

The first node in the pre-order traversal is always a root node of the binary tree. Thus the root node of the binary tree *T* is node *A*.

After determining the root node of the binary tree, our aim is to find the nodes that comprise the left sub tree and right sub tree of node A. We know from the in-order traversal that first left sub tree is traversed, then root node, and finally the right sub tree. Thus all the nodes to the left of node *A* in in-order traversal comprise its left sub tree. Similarly, all the nodes to the right of node *A* in in-order traversal comprise its right sub tree.

The above procedure partitions the pre-order and in-order traversal sequences as shown below:

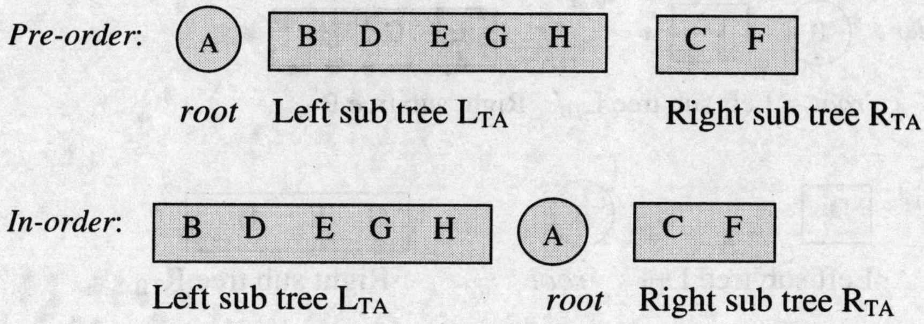

Figure 7.24 shows the partial binary tree constructed so far.

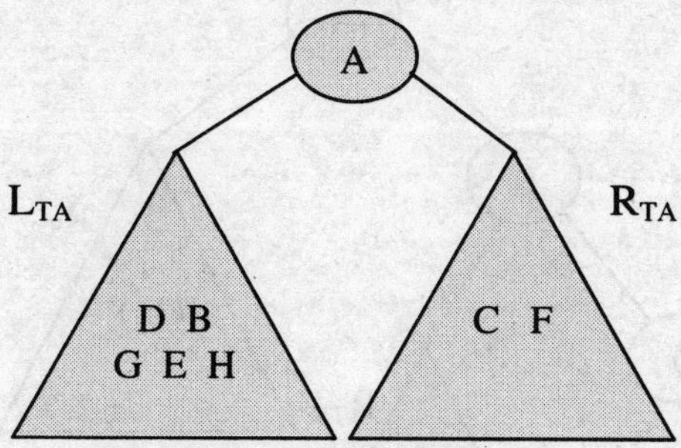

Figure 7.24

In the same way, we can construct the left sub tree L_{TA} and right sub tree R_{TB}. Let us first consider the left sub tree L_{TA}. The pre-order and in-order traversal sequences of the left sub tree L_{TA} are

Pre-order: B D E G H
In-order: D B G E H

From these traversal sequences we find that the root of the sub tree is node B, and its left sub tree consists of a single node D and the right sub tree consists of nodes G, E, and H.

The above procedure partitions the pre-order and in-order sequences as shown below:

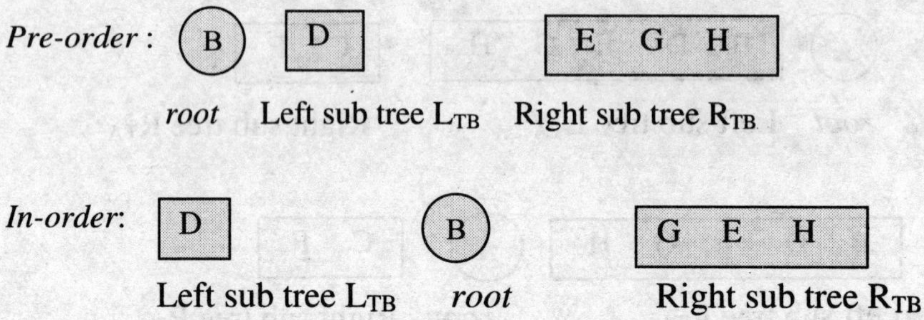

Figure 7.253 shows the partial binary tree constructed so far.

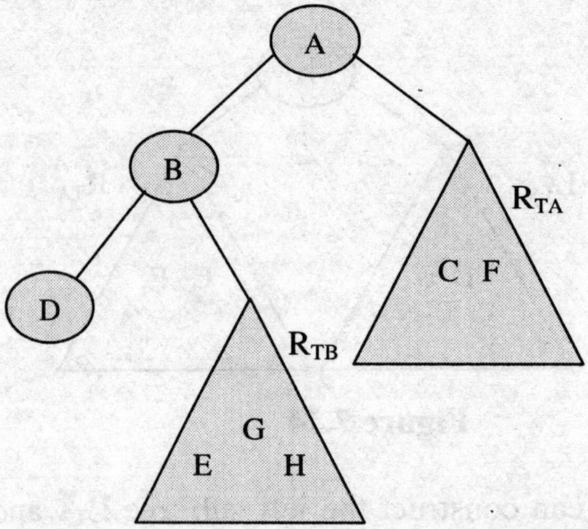

Figure 7.25

Now consider the right sub tree R_{TB}. The pre-order and in-order traversal sequences of R_{TB} are

Pre-order: E G H
In-order: G E H

From these traversal sequences we find that the root of the sub tree R_{TB} is node E, and its left sub tree consists of a single node G and the right sub tree also consists of a single node G.

The above procedure partitions the pre-order and in-order traversal sequences of R_{TB} as shown below:

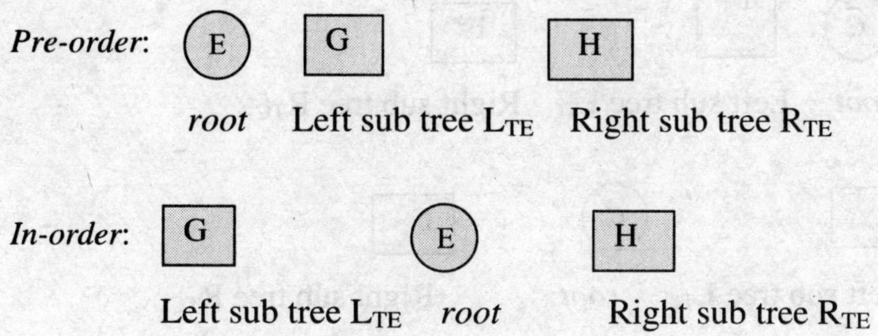

Figure 7.26 shows the partial binary tree constructed so far.

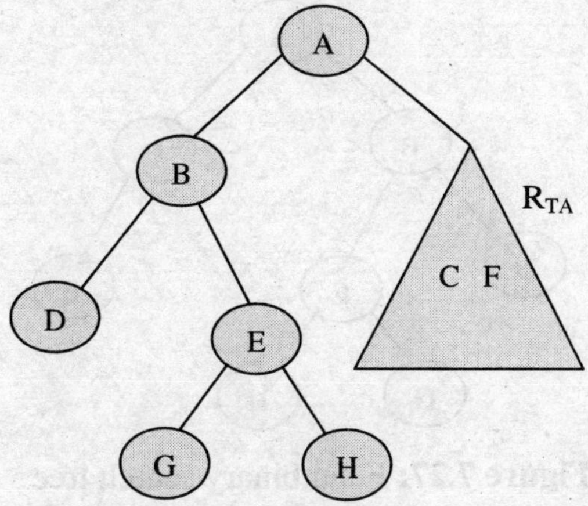

Figure 7.26

Thus we have completed the construction of the left sub tree L_{TA} of node A, which was the root node of the binary tree.

Now we are left with the right sub tree R_{TA}. The pre-order and in-order traversal sequences of R_{TA} are

Pre-order: C F
In-order: C F

From these traversal sequences we find that the root of the sub tree R_{TA} is node C, and its left sub tree is empty and the right sub tree consists of a single node F.

The above procedure partitions the pre-order and in-order traversal sequences of R_{TA} as shown:

Pre-order:

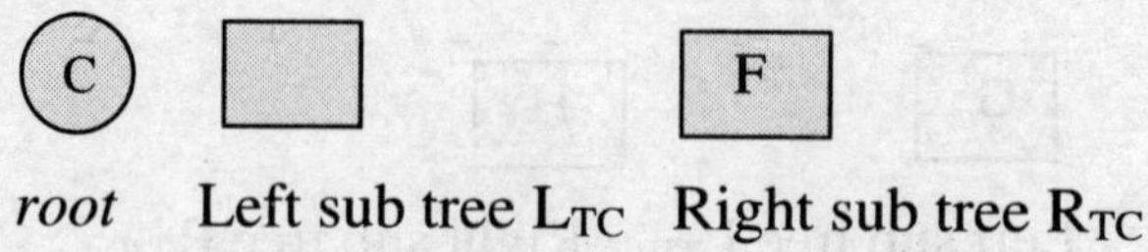

In-order:

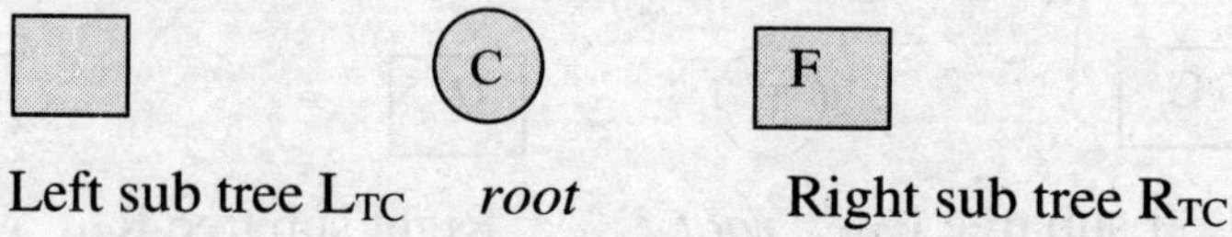

Figure 7.27 shows the binary tree after this step, and this is the final binary tree.

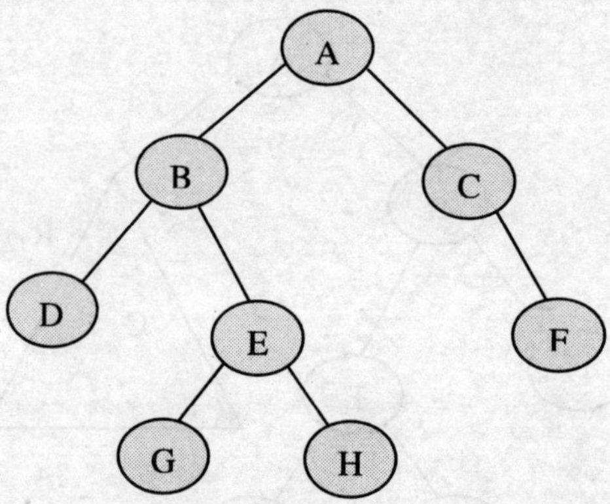

Figure 7.27: Final binary search tree

> The above procedure can be easily modified if the in-order and the post-order traversals of a binary tree are given. The only difference is that the root of the tree will be appearing as the last node in the post-order traversal.

7.6.2 Inserting in a Binary Search Tree

If the binary search tree is initially empty, then the element is inserted as root node; otherwise the new element is inserted as a terminal node. If the element is less than the element in the root node, then the new element is inserted in the left sub tree else right sub tree. Insert operations can also be implemented iteratively as well as recursively.

Outline of Insert Algorithm

To insert a new element *item* in a binary search tree, we proceed as follows:

(*a*) If binary search tree is empty, then new element *item* is inserted as the root node of the new binary search tree.

(*b*) If binary search tree is non-empty, then new element *item* is compared with each node starting with root node. On the way, if element *item* is less than node, we follow the path to the left child otherwise we follow path to the right child. This process is repeated till we reach to any terminal node. At that point, if the element item is less than that terminal node, it is inserted as left child of that terminal node else as right child of that terminal node.

[New element is always inserted as terminal node, never as an internal node.]

The above algorithm is iterative in nature. Element can also be inserted using recursive algorithm that simply states –

- If *tree* is empty then insert *item* as root node;
- If *item* is less than the root node, insert *item* in the left subtree of root node;
- If *item* is greater than the root node, insert *item* in the right subtree of root node;

Example 7.14:

Consider the following binary tree again. Let us simulate the iterative version of the above algorithm while inserting new element 35.

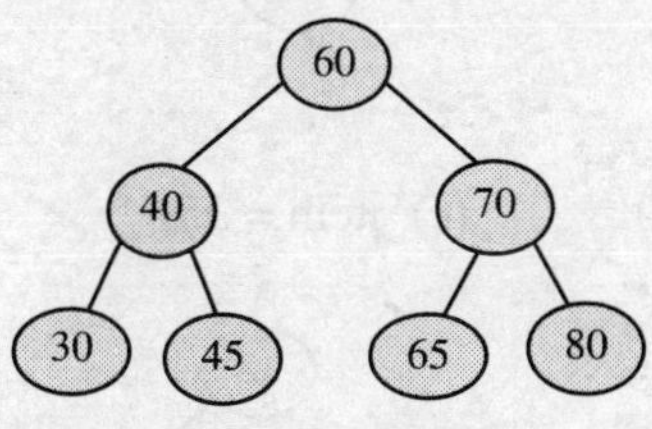

Figure 7.28: Given binary search tree *T*

Solution:

To insert *item* = 35, following steps will be performed

1. Compare *item* = 35 with the root node 60 of given binary search tree *T*. Since 35 < 60, proceed to the left child of 60, which is 40.
2. Compare *item* = 35 with the 40. Since 35 < 40, proceed to the left child of 40, which is 30.
3. Compare *item* = 35 with the 30. Since 35 > 30, proceed to the right child of 30, and since 30 does not have right child.

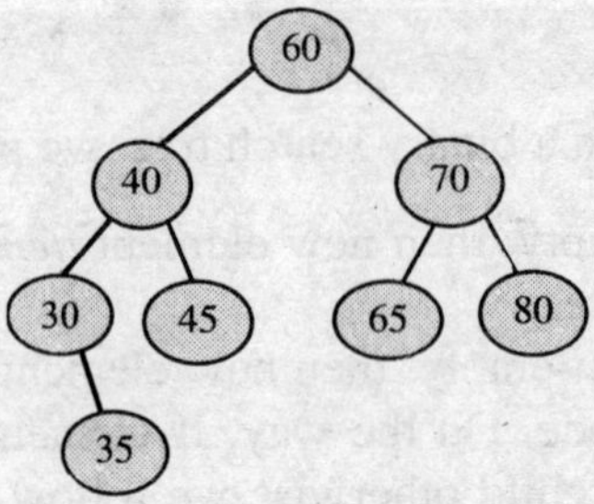

Figure 7.29: New tree with item = 35 inserted. Dark and shaded edges indicate the path followed during the progress of the algorithm.

Example 7.15:

Let us consider the build up of a binary search tree when following six numbers are inserted in an empty binary search tree.

30, 40, 35, 25, 50, 45

Figure 7.28 show the six stages of binary search tree.

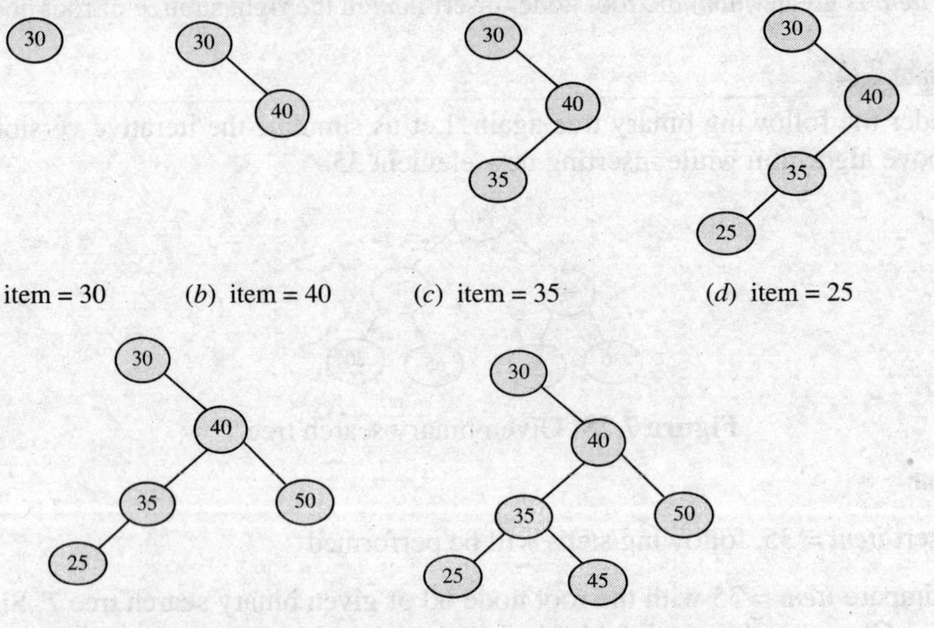

(*a*) item = 30 (*b*) item = 40 (*c*) item = 35 (*d*) item = 25

(*e*) item = 50 (*f*) item = 45

Figure 7.30: Buildup of binary search tree

If the same set of numbers but in different sequence are inserted in an empty binary search tree, the resultant binary search tree will be a different one.

Formal presentation of iterative as well as recursive algorithms for insertion is given below.

Algorithm 7.7

InsertIterative (root, item)

Here *root* is a pointer variable that holds the address of the root node of the given tree. This algorithm inserts a new element *item* in binary search tree. It uses a temporary pointer variable *ptr* to hold the address of newly allocated node. It also uses a flag variable *done* to control the iteration. It also uses pointer variables *nodePtr* and *ParentPtr* for address of the node being checked and its parent, respectively for inserting node at its appropriate place.

```
1. Set ptr = Address of newly allocated node
2. Set ptr->info = item
3. Set ptr->left = NULL
4. Set ptr->right = NULL
5. If ( root = NULL ) then
      Set root = ptr
      Return
   Endif
6. Set parentPtr = NULL
7. Set nodePtr = root
8. Repeat steps 9 to 10 While ( nodePtr ≠ NULL )
9.    Set parentPtr = nodePtr
10.      If ( item < nodePtr->info ) then
             Set nodePtr = nodePtr->left
         Else
             Set nodePtr = nodePtr->right
         Endif
    Endwhile
11.If ( item < parentPtr->info )
      Set parentPtr->left = ptr
  Else
      Set parentPtr->right = ptr
   Endif
12.Return
```

Algorithm 7.8

InsertRecursive (root, item)

Here *root* is a pointer variable that holds the address of the root node of the given tree. This recursive algorithm inserts a new element *item* in binary search tree.

```
1. If ( root = NULL ) then
      Set ptr = Address of newly allocated node
      Set ptr->info = item
      Set ptr->left = NULL
      Set ptr->right = NULL
      Set root = ptr
      Return
   Else If ( item < nodePtr->info ) then
      Call InsertRecursive(root->left,item)
   Else
      Call InsertRecursive(root->right,item)
   Endif
2. Return
```

7.6.3 Searching in a Binary Search Tree

The element in a binary search tree can be searched very quickly. The search operation on binary search tree is similar to applying binary search technique to a sorted linear array. The element to be searched is compared with the root node. If it matches with the root node, then search terminates here; otherwise the search is continued in the left sub tree of the node if the element is less than the root node or in the right sub tree if the element is greater than the root node.

Example 7.16:

Given following binary search tree, search elements (*a*) 30 (*b*) 20.

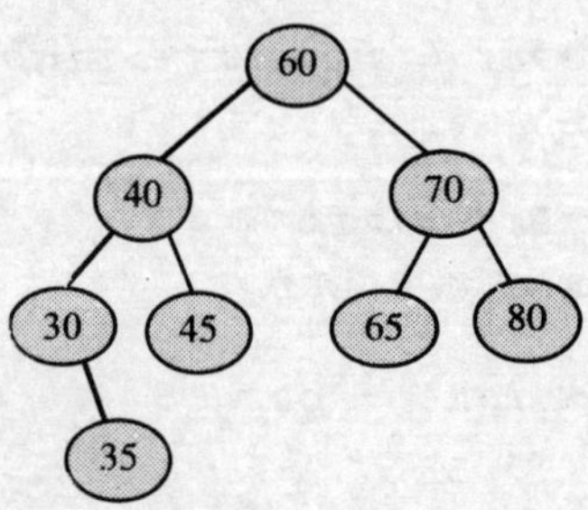

Figure 7.31: Given binary search tree

Solution:

(*a*) To search *item* = 30, following steps will be performed:

1. Compare *item* = 30 with the root node 60 of given binary search tree *T*. Since 30 ≠ 60 and 30 < 60, proceed to the left child of 60, which is 40.
2. Compare *item* = 30 with the 40. Since 30 ≠ 40 and 30 < 40, proceed to the left child of 40, which is 30.
3. Compare *item* = 30 with the 30. Since 30 = 30, search terminates with success.

(*b*) To search *item* = 20, following steps will be performed:

1. Compare *item* = 20 with the root node 60 of given binary search tree *T*. Since 20 ≠ 60 and 20 < 60, proceed to the left child of 60, which is 40.
2. Compare *item* = 20 with the 40. Since 20 ≠ 40 and 20 < 40, proceed to the left child of 40, which is 30.
3. Compare *item* = 20 with the 30. Here 20 ≠ 30 and 20 < 30, and since node 30 does not have a left child, search terminates with failure.

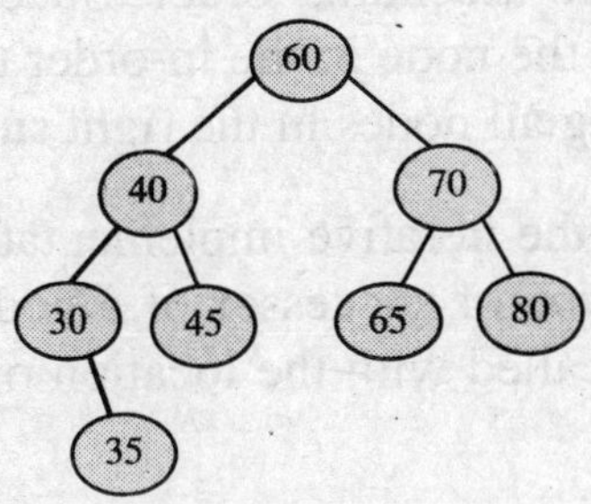

Figure 7.32: Dark and shaded edges indicate the path followed during progress of the search algorithm for *item* = 30.

Formal presentation of iterative search algorithm, which not only find the locations of the node, it also finds the locations of its parent, is given below.

Algorithm 7.9

SearchIterative (*root, item, ploc, loc*)

Here *root* is a pointer variable that holds the address of the root node of the given tree. This algorithm finds the location *loc* of the node *N* containing given element *item* in binary search tree. It also keeps track of the location *ploc* of the parent of the node N.

```
1. If ( root = NULL ) then
      Set loc = NULL
      Return
   Endif
```

```
2. Set ploc = NULL
3. Set loc = root
4. Repeat steps 5 to 7 While ( loc ≠ NULL )
5.     If ( item = loc->info ) then
           Return
       Endif
6.     Set ploc = loc
7.     If ( item < loc->info )
           Set loc = loc->left
   Else
           Set loc = loc->right
       Endif
   Endwhile
8. Return
```

Recursive version of the search algorithm is left as an exercise.

7.6.4 Finding Successor of a Node

When binary search is traversed using in-order traversal, it lists the nodes of the binary search three in the ascending order. Successor of a node is a node that comes immediately after the node in the in-order traversal of a binary search tree and it is the largest among all nodes in the right subtree of that node.

Following listing shows the iterative implementation of the algorithm which not only finds the location *sloc* of successor of a node *N*, it also finds the locations *psloc* of its parent. It is called with the location of the node whose successor we want to find.

Algorithm 7.10

FindSuccessor (*sroot*, *psloc*, *sloc*)

Here *sroot* is a pointer variable that holds the address of the root node of the subtree. This algorithm finds the location *sloc* of the node *N* containing the largest element in the subtree. It also keeps track of the location *psloc* of the parent of the node *N*.

```
1. Set psloc = sroot
2. Set sloc = sroot->right
3. Repeat step 4 and 5 While ( sloc->right ≠ NULL )
4.     Set psloc = sloc
5.     Set sloc = sloc->right
   Endwhile
6. Return
```

Example 7.17:

Given the following binary search tree, find the successor of node 60.

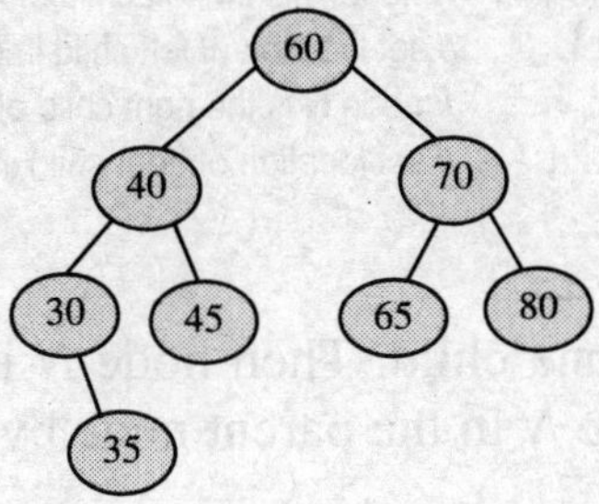

Figure 7.33: Given binary search tree

Solution:

The successor of a node, if it does exist, is always the node with largest value in the right subtree of that node.

Hence, the successor of node 60 is node 65.

7.6.5 Deleting in a Binary Search Tree

Suppose *T* is a binary search tree, and *item* of information is given. In this section, we will describe an algorithm which deletes *item* from *T*.

The deletion algorithm uses iterative search algorithm to find the location *loc* of the node *N* which contains the item and also the location *ploc* of the parent node.

The way node *N* is deleted from the tree primarily depends on the number of children of node *N*.

The following three cases may arise:

Case 1: Node *N* has no children, *i.e.*, it is a terminal node. This will be indicated by the fact that both the pointers, *loc-<left* as well as *loc->right*, will contain NULL value.

Then node *N* is deleted from *T* by replacing the location of node *N* in the parent node by the NULL pointer. *i.e.*, if the node is left child of its parent, then the left pointer of its parent is set to NULL otherwise it will be right child of its parent and accordingly the pointer of its parent is set to NULL.

The following steps will accomplish the task

```
If ( loc->item < ploc->info )      // node N is the left child of its parent
    Set ploc->left = NULL          // set location of left child in parent node to NULL
Else                               // node N is the right child of its parent
    Set ploc->right = NULL         // set location of right child in parent node to NULL
Endif
```

Case 2: Node *N* has only one child. Then node *N* is deleted from *T* by replacing the location of node *N* in the parent node by the only child of node *N*.

The following steps will accomplish the task

```
// store the location of only child in 'ptr'
If ( loc->left ≠ NULL )            // node N has left child as only child
    Set ptr = loc->left
Else                               // node N has right child as only child
    Set ptr = loc->right
Endif
If ( loc->item < ploc->info )      // node N is the left child of its parent
    Set ploc->left = ptr           // set location of left child in the parent node to location of only child
Else                               // node N is the right child of its parent
    Set ploc->right = ptr          // set location of right child in the parent node to location of only child
Endif
```

Case 3: Node *N* has two children. Let *S*(*N*) be the in-order successor of node *N*. Then node *N* is deleted from *T* by replacing the node *N* by *S*(*N*) and then deleting *S*(*N*) from *T* using case 1 or case 2 depending on whether S(N) has no children or only one child.

The following steps will accomplish the task

```
// Let us assume that 'sloc' is the location of the successor S(N) of node N, and
// 'psloc' is the location of parent of S(N)
// replace the node N by its successor S(N)
Set loc->item = sloc->item
// steps to delete S(N)
If ( sloc->left = NULL ) and ( sloc->right = NULL )    // S(N) has no children
    If ( sloc->left ≠ NULL )       // S(N) was left child of its parent
        Set psloc->left = NULL     // set location of left child of its parent node to NULL
    Else                           // S(N) was left child of its parent
        Set psloc->right = NULL    // set location of right child of its parent node to NULL
    Endif
```

```
Else                                    // S(N) has one child
    If ( sloc->left ≠ NULL )            // node S(N) has left child as only child
        Set ptr = sloc->left
    Else                                // node S(N) has right child as only child
        Set ptr = sloc->right
    Endif
    If ( sloc->item < psloc->info )     // node S(N) is the left child of its parent
        Set psloc->left = ptr           // set location of left child in parent node to only child of S(N)
    Else                                // node S(N) is the right child of its parent
        Set psloc->right = ptr          // set location of left child in parent node to only child of S(N)
    Endif
Endif
```

The in-order successor $S(N)$ of a node N is the largest element in the right sub tree of node N. Either it has no children or right child is the only child, *i.e.*, it does not have a left child.

Example 7.18:

Consider the following binary search tree, delete node 42, 65 and 60 from the given tree.

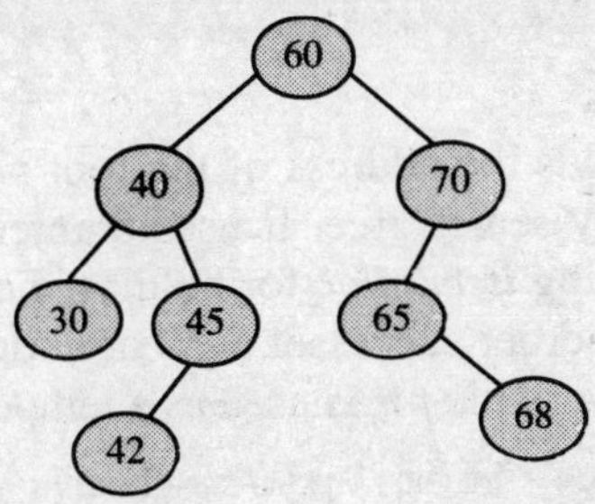

Figure 7.34: Given binary search tree

Solution:

(*a*) To delete node 42:

Node 42 has no children. Since 42 is the left child of its parent, node 45, the location for the left child is set to NULL, and then node 42 is removed from memory.

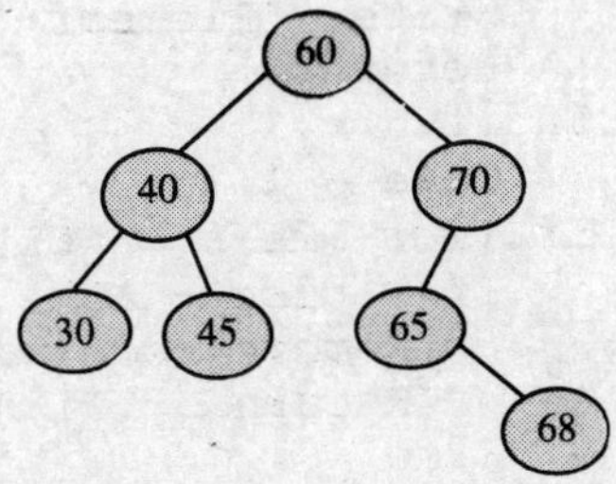

Figure 7.35: Node 42 deleted

(*b*) To delete node 65:

Node 65 has only one child, node 68. Location of node 65 (location of left child of its parent, node 70) is replaced by location of its only child. Finally, node 65 is removed from memory.

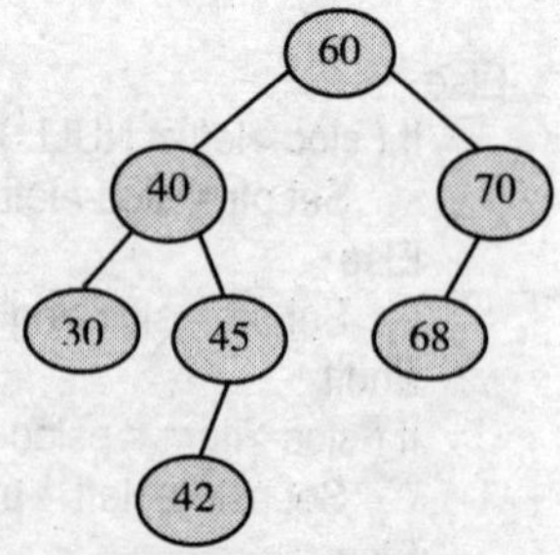

Figure 7.36: Node 65 deleted

(*c*) To delete node 60:

Node 60 has two children, nodes 40 and 70. Successor of node 60 is node 65. Node value 60 is replaced by its successor 65. Then successor is deleted by replacing its location with its child. Finally, the actual node of the successor is removed from memory.

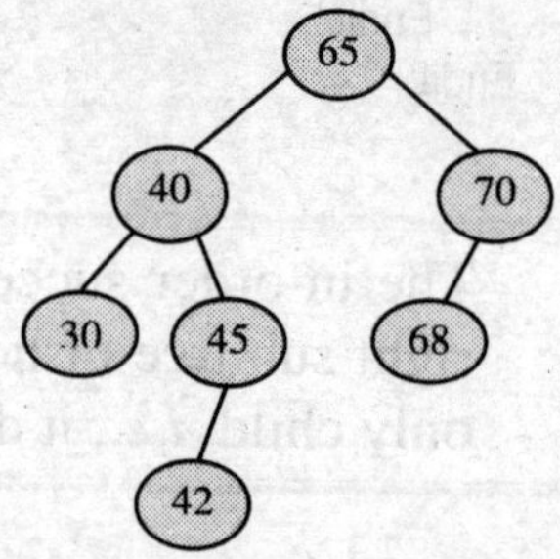

Figure 7.37: Node 60 deleted

Algorithm 7.11

DeleteIterative (root, item)

Here *root* is a pointer variable that holds the address of the root node of the given tree. This algorithm delete *item* from binary search tree. It uses pointer variables — *loc* for holding the location of node *N* containing *item*, *ploc* for holding the location of parent of node *N*, *sloc* for holding location of in-order successor *S*(*N*) of node *N*, *psloc* for holding the location of parent of *S*(*N*). Pointer variable *ptr* is used as a temporary variable.

```
1. Call SearchIterative(root, item, ploc, loc)
2. If ( loc = NULL ) then
      Write: "Element ", item," not found"
      Return
   Endif
   // Case - 1
3. If (loc->left = NULL) AND (loc->right = NULL) then
      If ( ploc = NULL ) then     // node N is the only node in tree
         Remove node with address loc
         Return
      Else
         If ( loc->item < ploc->info )
            Set ploc->left = NULL
         Else
            Set ploc->right = NULL
         Endif
         Remove node with address loc
         Return
      Endif
```

```
   Endif
   // Case - 2
4. If (loc->left ≠ NULL) OR (loc->right ≠ NULL) then
      If ( loc->left ≠ NULL )
         Set ptr = loc->left
      Else
         Set ptr = loc->right
      Endif
      If ( loc->item < ploc->info )
         Set ploc->left = ptr
      Else
         Set ploc->right = ptr
      Endif
      Remove node with address loc
      Return
      Endif
   Endif
   // Case - 3
5. Call FindSuccessor(loc, psloc, sloc)
6. Set loc->item = sloc->item
7. If ( sloc->left = NULL ) and ( sloc->right = NULL )
      If ( sloc->left ≠ NULL )
         Set psloc->left = NULL
      Else
         Set psloc->right = NULL
      Endif
   Else
      If ( sloc->left ≠ NULL )
         Set ptr = sloc->left
      Else
         Set ptr = sloc->right
      Endif
      If ( sloc->item < psloc->info )
         Set psloc->left = ptr
      Else
         Set psloc->right = ptr
      Endif
      Remove node with address sloc
   Endif
8. Return
```

7.7 AVL TREES

We can guarantee O($\log_2 n$) performance for each search tree operation by ensuring that the search tree height is always O($\log_2 n$). Trees with a worst-case height of O($\log_2 n$) are called *balanced trees*. One of the popular balanced trees is *AVL tree*, which was introduced by *Adelson-Velskii* and *Landis*.

If T is a nonempty binary tree with T_L and T_R as its left and right sub tree, then T is an AVL tree if and only if

1. $|h_L - h_R| \leq 1$, where h_L and h_R are the heights of T_L and T_R, respectively, and
2. T_L and T_R are AVL trees.

An *AVL search tree* is a binary search tree that is also an *AVL tree*. The height of an empty (null) AVL tree is taken as −1.

Representation of an AVL Tree

The node in an *AVL* tree will have an additional field *bf* (for balance factor) in addition to the structure of a node in a binary search tree.

The value for field *bf* is chosen as

$$bf = \begin{cases} -1 & \text{if } h_L < h_R \\ 0 & \text{if } h_L = h_R \\ +1 & \text{if } h_L > h_R \end{cases}$$

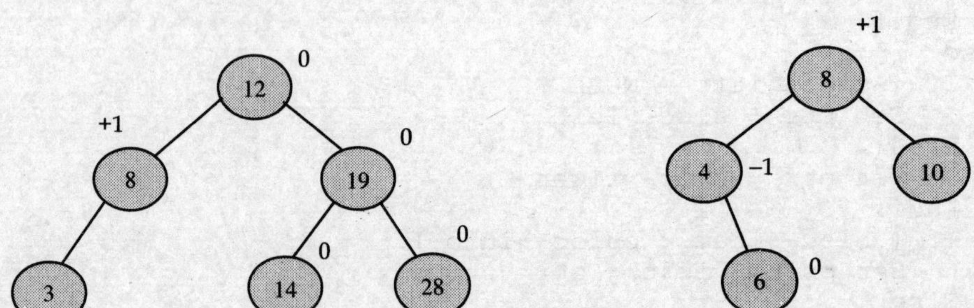

Figure 7.38: AVL trees

7.8 THREADED BINARY TREES

On carefully examining the linked representation of a binary tree T, you will find that approximately half of the pointer fields (*left* and *right* pointer fields that hold the address of the left child and right child, respectively) contain NULL entries (pictured as ×) in these fields. The space occupied by these NULL entries can be utilized to store some kind of valuable information.

One possible way to utilize this space is that we can store special pointer that point to nodes higher in the tree, *i.e.*, ancestors. These special pointers are called *threads*, and the binary tree having such pointers is called *a threaded binary tree*.

Threads in a binary tree must be distinguished from normal pointers. In the graphical representation of a threaded binary tree, the threads are shown by dotted lines. In computer memory, an extra field, called *tag* or *flag* is used to distinguish a thread from a normal pointer.

There are many ways to thread a binary tree. These are

- The right NULL pointer of each node can be replaced by a thread to the successor of that node under in-order traversal called a *right thread*, and the tree will be called a *right-threaded tree*.
- The left NULL pointer of each node can be replaced by a thread to the predecessor of that node under in-order traversal called a *left thread*, and the tree will be called a *left-threaded tree*.
- Both left and right NULL pointers can be used to point to predecessor and successor of that node, respectively, under in-order traversal. Such a tree is called a *fully threaded tree*.

A threaded binary tree where only one thread is used is also known as *one-way* threaded tree and where both the threads are used is also known as *two-way* threaded tree.

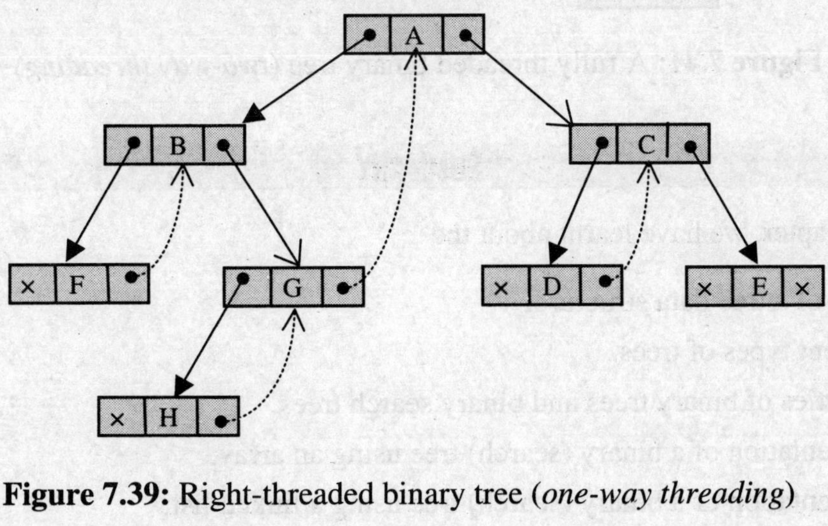

Figure 7.39: Right-threaded binary tree (*one-way threading*)

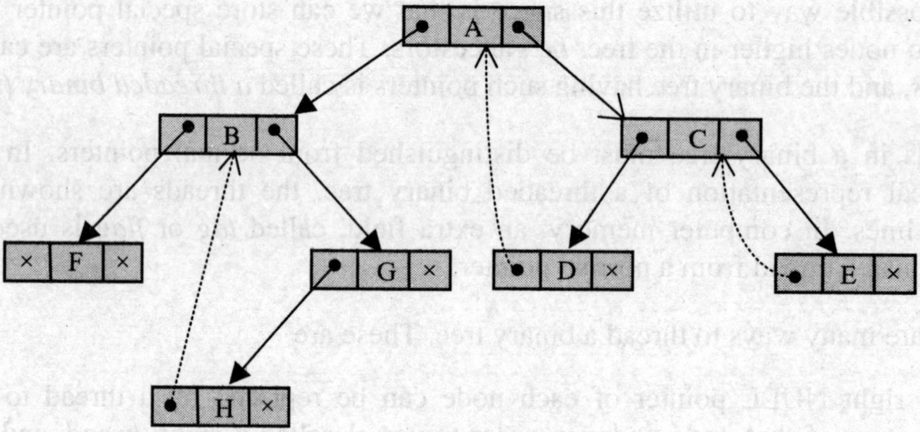

Figure 7.40: Left-threaded binary tree (*one-way threaded*)

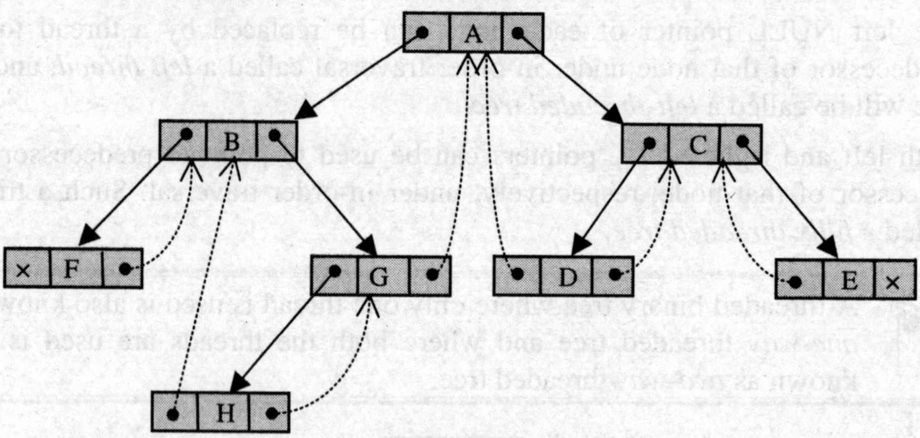

Figure 7.41: A fully threaded binary tree (*two-way threading*)

SUMMARY

In this chapter, we have learnt about the

- basics of a tree data structure.
- different types of trees.
- properties of binary trees and binary search trees.
- representation of a binary (search) tree using an array.
- representation of a binary (search) tree using a linked list.
- implementation of various operations on binary (search) trees.

- threaded binary trees.
- AVL of trees.

REVIEW EXERCISES

1. Answer the following questions in the context of given binary tree.
   (*a*) Which nodes are leave nodes?
   (*b*) Which is the root node?
   (*c*) What is the height of the tree?
   (*d*) Which nodes are non-leave nodes?
   (*e*) Which nodes are descendents of node C?
   (*f*) Which nodes are ancestors of node L?
   (*g*) What is the pre-order traversal of tree?
   (*h*) What is the in-order traversal of tree?
   (*i*) What is the post-order traversal of tree?
   (*j*) What is the level-order traversal of tree?

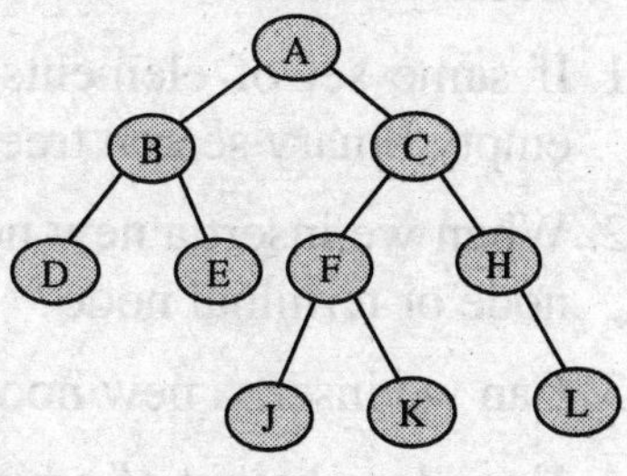

Figure 7.

2. For a binary search tree T, its pre-order and in-order traversals are as follows:

   Pre-order : A B L M K N P Q
   In-order : L B M A N K Q P

   Draw the binary search tree T.

3. For a binary search tree T, its in-order and post-order traversals are as follows:

   In-order : D C K E A H B Q J I
   Post-order : D K E C H Q J I B A

   Draw the binary search tree T.

4. For a binary search tree T, its pre-order and in-order traversals are as follows:

   Pre-order : A B E H Q R C D K L M
   In-order : B Q R H E A D L K M C

   (*a*) What is the height of the tree?
   (*b*) What are the internal nodes?
   (*c*) What is its post-order traversal?

5. What do you by a complete binary tree? Draw one such binary tree?
6. What is the maximum number of nodes at *k*th level of a binary tree?

7. Why binary trees, usually, are not represented using arrays?
8. Binary search tree combines the best worlds of arrays and linked lists into one structure. Comment.
9. Compare and contrast between a binary and a binary search tree.
10. Name the operations that are specific to binary search trees not to binary trees.
11. If same set of elements but in different order are inserted in two different empty binary search trees, will you get identical binary search trees?
12. When we insert a new node in a binary search tree, will it become an internal node or terminal node?
13. Can we insert a new node as an internal node?
14. How does height of a binary search tree affect its performance?
15. If there are 27 nodes in a complete binary tree, what will be its height? Also tell how many nodes will be in the last level.
16. What are the different operations that modify a tree?
17. Which of the operations on binary search tree is more complex and why?
18. How an AVL tree differs from a binary search tree? How AVL trees are represented in computer memory?
19. What is a thread? How is it useful?
20. What are the advantages of threading a binary (search) tree?

PROGRAMMING EXERCISES

1. Write a menu driven program to simulate various operations described on a binary search tree.

❑ ❑ ❑

Chapter 8

Sorting and Searching

Learning Objectives

After reading this chapter, students will be able to

- understand the sorting process
- understand and write algorithms for various sorting algorithms
- understand the searching process
- understand and write algorithms for various searching algorithms
- understand the merging process
- understand and write algorithm for merging of sorted arrays

8.1 INTRODUCTION

Sorting is the process of arranging the elements in some logical order. This logical order may be ascending or descending in case of numeric values or dictionary order in case of alphanumeric values. We do, almost, use this process daily in our routine activities. For example, we do arrange our class notes in increasing order of date in order to refer them quickly later on. Like this there are many situations, which you can enumerate.

Searching is the process of finding the location of given element in the linear array. The search is said to be successful if the given element is found, *i.e.*, the element does exists in the array; otherwise unsuccessful.

Merging is the process of combining the elements of two similar structures, such as linear arrays, into a single structure.

In this chapter, we will discuss various sorting methods, searching methods, and merging.

8.2 SORTING

As mentioned earlier, sorting is the process of arranging the elements in some logical order. This logical order may be ascending or descending in case of numeric values or dictionary order in case of alphanumeric values.

We will cover the following sorting methods:

- Bubble sort
- Selection sort
- Insertion sort
- Merge sort
- Quick sort
- Heap sort

For all the methods, we will consider a linear array *a* of size *n* whose elements are to be sorted in ascending order. You can modify them for the descending order just by reversing the comparison operation. To be consistent with C/C++ language conventions, the elements of the array have index in the range 0..*n*–1.

8.2.1 Bubble Sort Revisited

We have already discussed this method in *Chapter 3*. Here, again we will discuss for the completeness of the concerned topic as per requirement of the syllabus.

The Bubble sort method requires $(n-1)$ pass to sort an array. In each pass every element $a[i]$ is compared with $a[i+1]$, for $i = 0$ to $(n-k)$, where k is the pass number and if they are out of order i.e. if $a[i] > a[i+1]$, they are swapped. This will cause the largest element move or bubble up. Thus after the end of first pass the largest element in the array will be placed in nth position, and on each successive pass, the next largest element is placed at position $(n-1)$, $(n-2)$, ..., 2, respectively.

For more clarity, carefully examine the following steps.

Pass 1:

Step 1. If $a[0] > a[1]$ then swap $a[0]$ and $a[1]$.
Step 2. If $a[1] > a[2]$ then swap $a[1]$ and $a[2]$.
⋮
Step $n-1$. If $a[n-2] > a[n-1]$ then swap $a[n-2]$ and $a[n-1]$.

Pass 2:

Step 1. If $a[0] > a[1]$ then swap $a[0]$ and $a[1]$.
Step 2. If $a[1] > a[2]$ then swap $a[1]$ and $a[2]$.
⋮
Step $n-2$. If $a[n-3] > a[n-2]$ then swap $a[n-3]$ and $a[n-2]$.

⋮

Pass *k*:

Step 1. If $a[0] > a[1]$ then swap $a[0]$ and $a[1]$.
Step 2. If $a[1] > a[2]$ then swap $a[1]$ and $a[2]$.
⋮
Step $n-k$. If $a[n-k+1] > a[n-k]$ then swap $a[n-k+1]$ and $a[n-k]$.

⋮

Pass *n*–1:

Step 1. If $a[0] > a[1]$ then swap $a[0]$ and $a[1]$.

After $(n-1)$ passes, the array will be sorted in ascending order.

Example 8.1:

To illustrate the working of bubble sort method, consider the sorting of the following array in ascending order.

12 40 3 2 15

Solution:

Note that, the output of a given pass becomes the input for the next pass. The sorting process is self explanatory. In each pass, one element, shown as shaded, reaches to its final position. Given array can be shown as

a[0]	*a*[1]	*a*[2]	*a*[3]	*a*[4]
12	40	3	2	15

Pass-1:

a[0]	*a*[1]	*a*[2]	*a*[3]	*a*[4]
12	**40**	3	2	15

(*a*) Compare *a*[0] and *a*[1]. Since *a*[0] < *a*[1] (12 < 40), no action is taken.

a[0]	*a*[1]	*a*[2]	*a*[3]	*a*[4]
12	**40**	**3**	2	15

(*b*) Compare *a*[1] and *a*[2]. Since *a*[1] > *a*[2] (40 > 3), swap these elements.

a[0]	*a*[1]	*a*[2]	*a*[3]	*a*[4]
12	3	**40**	**2**	15

(*c*) Compare *a*[2] and *a*[3]. Since *a*[2] > *a*[3] (40 > 2), swap these elements.

a[0]	*a*[1]	*a*[2]	*a*[3]	*a*[4]
12	3	2	**40**	**15**

(*d*) Compare *a*[3] and *a*[4]. Since *a*[3] > *a*[4] (40 > 15), swap these elements.

a[0]	*a*[1]	*a*[2]	*a*[3]	*a*[4]
12	3	2	15	40

Thus, after first pass, the largest element, 40, has moved to its final position. However, the rest of the numbers, which may have changed their positions, are yet to be sorted. The shaded part shows the elements that have been sorted.

For the remaining passes, only comparisons and swaps, if required, are shown.

Pass-2:

a[0]	*a*[1]	*a*[2]	*a*[3]	*a*[4]	Action
12	3	2	15	40	Swap
3	12	2	15	40	Swap
3	2	12	15	40	No swap
3	2	12	15	40	

After second pass, the second largest element, 15, has moved to its final position.

Pass-3:

a[0]	*a*[1]	*a*[2]	*a*[3]	*a*[4]	Action
3	2	12	15	40	Swap
2	3	12	15	40	No swap
2	3	12	15	40	

After third pass, the third largest element, 12, has moved to its final position.

Pass-4:

$a[0]$	$a[1]$	$a[2]$	$a[3]$	$a[4]$	Action
(2)	(3)	12	15	40	No swap
2	3	12	15	40	

After fourth pass, the fourth largest element, 3, has moved to its final position. Thus, the array is completely sorted in 4 passes.

The above sorting process can also be visualized as shown below:

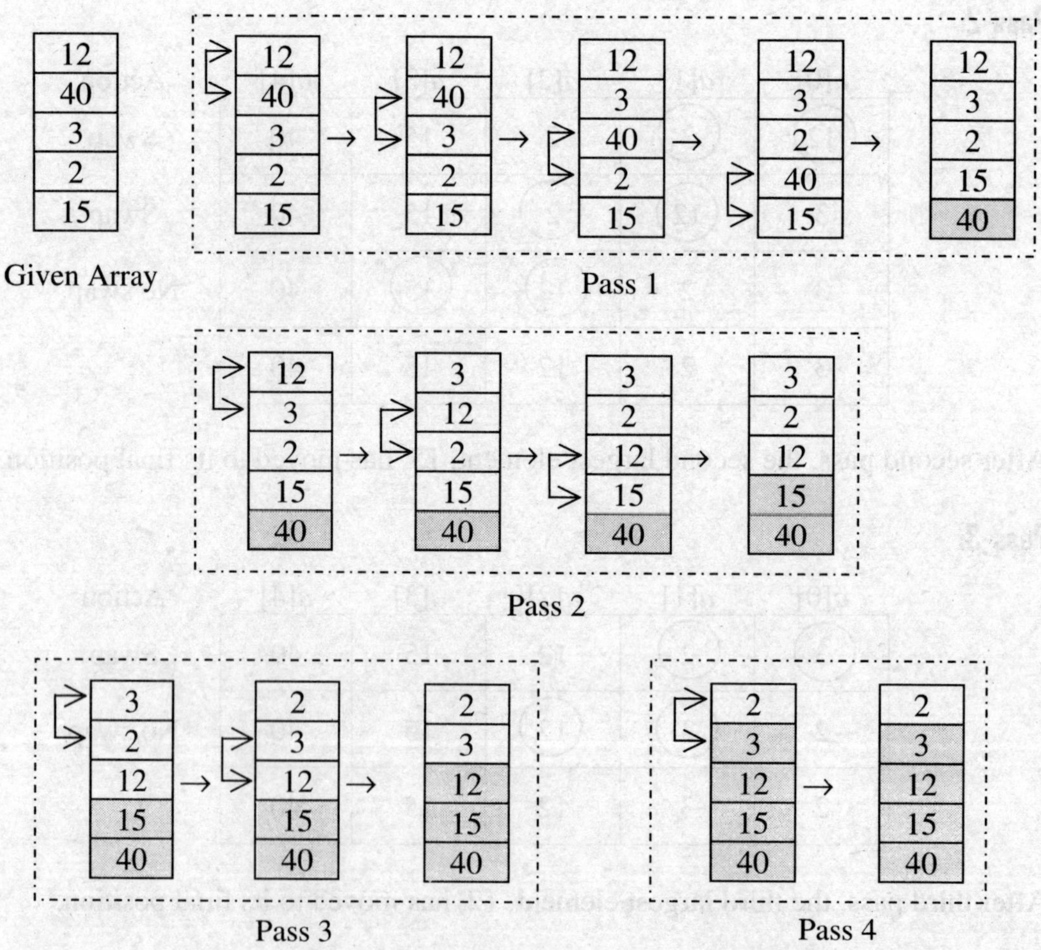

Figure 8.1: Illustration of Bubble sort method

Performance Analysis

After $(n-1)$ passes, the array will be sorted in ascending order. As you must have noticed, the first pass requires $(n-1)$ comparisons, the second pass requires $(n-2)$,...., kth pass requires $(n-k)$, and the last pass requires only one comparison. Therefore, total comparisons are

$$f(n) = (n-1) + (n-2) + (n-3) + \ldots + (n-k) + \ldots + 3 + 2 + 1 = n(n-1)/2 = O(n^2)$$

Algorithm 8.1

BubbleSort(*a*, *n*)

Here *a* is a linear array with *n* elements in memory. This algorithm sorts the elements in the ascending order. It uses a temporary variable *temp* to facilitate the exchange of two values and variable *i* to is used as loop control variable.

```
1. Repeat steps 2 and 3 For k = 1 to (n-1) in steps of +1
2.    Repeat step 3 For j = 0 to (n-k-1) in steps of +1
3.        If ( a[j] > a[j+1] ) then
              Set temp = a[j]        // swap a[j] and a[j+1]
              Set a[j] = a[j+1]
              Set a[j+1] = temp
          Endif
      Endfor
   Endfor
4. Exit
```

8.2.2 Selection Sort

Selection sort method also requires $(n-1)$ pass to sort an array. In the first pass, find the smallest element from elements $a[0]$, $a[1]$, $a[2]$, . . ., $a[n-1]$ and swap with the first element, *i.e*, $a[0]$. In the second pass, find the smallest element from elements $a[1]$, $a[2]$, $a[3]$, . . ., $a[n-1]$ and swap with $a[1]$. And so on.

For more clarity, carefully examine the following steps.

Pass 1:

- Find the location *loc* of the smallest element in the entire array, *i.e.*, $a[0]$, $a[1]$, $a[2]$,...., $a[n-1]$.
- Interchange $a[0]$ & $a[loc]$. Then $a[0]$ is trivially sorted.

Pass 2:

- Find the location *loc* of the smallest element in the sub array *a*[1], *a*[2], *a*[3],. . ., *a*[*n*–1].
- Interchange *a*[1] & *a*[*loc*]. Then elements *a*[0] and *a*[1] are sorted, since *a*[0] ≤ *a*[1].

⋮

Pass *k*:

- Find the location *loc* of the smallest element in the sub array *a*[*k*], *a*[*k*+1], *a*[*k*+2],. . ., *a*[*n*–1].
- Interchange *a*[*k*] & *a*[*loc*]. Then elements *a*[0], *a*[1], *a*[2], . . ., *a*[*k*] are sorted.

⋮

Pass *n*–1:

- Find the location *loc* of the smaller of the elements *a*[*n*–2], *a*[*n*–1].
- Interchange *a*[*n*–2] & *a*[*loc*]. Then elements *a*[0], *a*[1], *a*[2], . . ., *a*[*n*–1] are sorted.

After (*n*–1) passes, the array will be sorted in ascending order.

Example 8.2:

To illustrate the working of the selection sort method, consider the following array *a* with 7 elements as

20, 35, 40, 100, 3, 10, 15

Solution:

In each iteration *i*, we find the location *loc* of the smallest element in the unsorted part of the array. If *loc* ≠ *i* then element at *i* and *loc* are swapped.

	a[0]	*a*[1]	*a*[2]	*a*[3]	*a*[4]	*a*[5]	*a*[6]
Given Array *a*	20	35	40	100	3	10	15

Pass 1:

$a[0]$	$a[1]$	$a[2]$	$a[3]$	$a[4]$	$a[5]$	$a[6]$
20	35	40	100	3	10	15

$i = 0$
$loc = 4$

Interchange elements $a[0]$ & $a[4]$, *i.e.*, 20 & 3 to obtain following array.

Pass 2:

$a[0]$	$a[1]$	$a[2]$	$a[3]$	$a[4]$	$a[5]$	$a[6]$
3	35	40	100	20	10	15

$i = 1$
$loc = 5$

Interchange elements $a[1]$ & $a[5]$, *i.e.*, 35 & 10 to obtain following array.

Pass 3:

$a[0]$	$a[1]$	$a[2]$	$a[3]$	$a[4]$	$a[5]$	$a[6]$
3	10	40	100	20	35	15

$i = 2$
$loc = 6$

Interchange elements $a[2]$ & $a[6]$, *i.e.*, 40 & 15 to obtain following array.

Pass 4:

$a[0]$	$a[1]$	$a[2]$	$a[3]$	$a[4]$	$a[5]$	$a[6]$
3	10	15	100	20	35	40

$i = 3$
$loc = 4$

Interchange elements $a[3]$ & $a[4]$, *i.e.*, 100 & 20 to obtain following array.

Pass 5:

$a[0]$	$a[1]$	$a[2]$	$a[3]$	$a[4]$	$a[5]$	$a[6]$
3	10	15	20	100	35	40

$i = 4$
$loc = 5$

Interchange elements $a[4]$ & $a[5]$, *i.e.*, 100 & 35 to obtain following array.

Pass 6:

$a[0]$	$a[1]$	$a[2]$	$a[3]$	$a[4]$	$a[5]$	$a[6]$
3	10	15	20	35	100	40

$i = 5$
$loc = 6$

Interchange elements $a[5]$ & $a[6]$, *i.e.*,100 & 40 to obtain following sorted array.

$a[0]$	$a[1]$	$a[2]$	$a[3]$	$a[4]$	$a[5]$	$a[6]$
3	10	15	20	35	40	100

Figure 8.2: Successive passes of selection sort method

The shaded part shows the part of the array sorted so for after each iteration. In each iteration, one element is added on the right of the sorted part.

To implement the selection sort algorithm, we need a routine to find the location *loc* of the smallest element among the elements *a*[*k*–1], *a*[*k*+1], *a*[*k*+2],. . ., *a*[*n*–1], during *k*th pass.

Algorithm 8.2

SelectSmallestElement(*a*, *n*, *k*, *loc*)

Here *a* is a linear array of size *n*. This sub-algorithm finds the location *loc* of the smallest element among *a*[*k*–1], *a*[*k*+1], *a*[*k*+2],..., *a*[*n*–1]. Temporary variable *small* is used to hold the current smallest element and variable *j* is used as loop control variable.

```
1. Set small = a[k-1]
2. Set loc = k-1
3. Repeat step 4 For j = k to (n-1) in steps of +1
4.      If ( a[j] < small ) then
            Set small = a[j]
            Set loc = j
        Endif
   Endfor
5. Exit
```

The selection sort algorithm can now be formulated as

Algorithm 8.3

SelectionSort1(*a*, *n*)

Here *a* is a linear array with *n* elements in memory. This algorithm sorts the elements in the ascending order. It uses a temporary variable *temp* to facilitate the exchange of two values, variable *loc* is used to hold the index of the smallest element, and variable *i* to is used as loop control variable.

```
1. Repeat steps 2 and 3 For i = 1 to (n-1) in steps of +1
2.    Call SelectSmallestElement( a, n, i, loc )
3.      If ( i ≠ loc ) then
           Set temp = a[i-1]
           Set a[i-1] = a[loc]
           Set a[loc] = temp
        Endif
   Endfor
4. Exit
```

However, the steps required finding the location of the smallest element can also be coded in the main algorithm as shown overleaf.

Algorithm 8.4

SelectionSort2(***a, n*** **)**

Here *a* is a linear array with *n* elements in memory. This algorithm sorts the elements in the ascending order. Temporary variable *small* is used to hold the current smallest element, temporary variable *temp* to facilitate the exchange of two values and variable *i* and *j* are used as loop control variables.

```
1.  Repeat steps 2 to 6 For i = 1 to (n-1) in steps of +1
2.     Set small = a[i-1]
3.     Set loc = i-1
4.     Repeat step 5 For j = i to (n-1) in steps of +1
5.        If ( a[j] < small ) then
             Set small = a[j]
             Set loc = j
          Endif
       Endfor
6.     If ( i ≠ loc ) then
          Set temp = a[i-1]
          Set a[i-1] = a[loc]
          Set a[loc] = temp
       Endif
    Endfor
7. Exit
```

Performance Analysis

As you must have noticed, the first pass requires $(n-1)$ comparisons to find the location *loc* of smallest element, the second pass requires $(n-2)$, ..., kth pass requires $(n-k)$, and the last pass requires only one comparison. Therefore total comparisons are

$$f(n) = (n-1) + (n-2) + (n-3) + \ldots + (n-k) + \ldots + 3 + 2 + 1$$
$$= n(n-1)/2 = O(n^2)$$

Note that in bubble sort, the sorted part of the array extends from right to left. In selection sort, the sorted part of the array extends from left to right. Thus, in both the methods, only one element is added to sorted part of the array in each pass, because of this property these methods are also called *methods of incremental sorts*.

8.2.3 Insertion Sort

This algorithm is very popular with bridge players when they first sort their cards. In this procedure, we pick up a particular value and then insert it at the appropriate place in the sorted sub list, *i.e.*, during kth iteration the element $a[k]$ is inserted in its proper place in the sorted sub array $a[1], a[2], a[3], \ldots, a[k-1]$. This task is accomplished by comparing $a[k]$ with $a[k-1]$, $a[k-2]$, $a[k-3]$, and so on until the first element $a[j]$ such that $a[j] \leq a[k]$ is found. Then each of the elements $a[k-1], a[k-2], \ldots, a[j+1]$ are moved one position up, and then element $a[k]$ is inserted in $(j+1)$st position in the array.

For more clarity, carefully examine the following steps.

Pass 1: $a[1]$ is inserted either before or after $a[0]$ so that $a[0]$ and $a[1]$ are sorted.

Pass 2: $a[2]$ is inserted either before $a[0]$ or between $a[0]$ and $a[1]$ or after $a[1]$ so that the elements $a[0], a[1], a[2]$ are sorted.

Pass 3: $a[3]$ is inserted either before $a[0]$ or between $a[0]$ and $a[1]$ or between $a[1]$ and $a[2]$ or after $a[2]$ so that the elements $a[0], a[1], a[2], a[3]$ are sorted.

⋮

Pass *k*: $a[k]$ is inserted in proper place in the sorted sub array $a[0], a[1], a[2], \ldots, a[k-1]$ so that after insertion, the elements $a[0], a[1], a[2], \ldots, a[k-1], a[k]$ are sorted.

⋮

Pass *n*–1: $a[n-1]$ is inserted in proper place in the sorted sub array $a[0], a[1], a[2], \ldots, a[n-2]$, so that after insertion, the elements $a[0], a[1], a[2], \ldots, a[n-1]$ are sorted.

Thus, after $(n-1)$ passes, the array will be sorted in ascending order.

Example 8.3:

To illustrate the working of the insertion sort method, consider the following array a with 7 elements as

35, 20, 40, 100, 3, 10, 15

Solution: Given array *a*

a[0]	*a*[1]	*a*[2]	*a*[3]	*a*[4]	*a*[5]	*a*[6]
35	20	40	100	3	10	15

Pass 1:

a[0]	*a*[1]	*a*[2]	*a*[3]	*a*[4]	*a*[5]	*a*[6]
35	20	40	100	3	10	15

Since *a*[1] < *a*[0], insert element *a*[1] before *a*[0] giving the following array.

Pass 2:

a[0]	*a*[1]	*a*[2]	*a*[3]	*a*[4]	*a*[5]	*a*[6]
20	35	40	100	3	10	15

Since *a*[2] > *a*[1], no action is performed.

Pass 3:

a[0]	*a*[1]	*a*[2]	*a*[3]	*a*[4]	*a*[5]	*a*[6]
20	35	40	100	3	10	15

Since *a*[3] > *a*[2], again no action is performed.

Pass 4:

a[0]	*a*[1]	*a*[2]	*a*[3]	*a*[4]	*a*[5]	*a*[6]
20	35	40	100	3	10	15

Since *a*[4] is less than *a*[3], *a*[2], *a*[1] as well as *a*[0], therefore insert *a*[4] before *a*[0], giving the following array.

Pass 5:

a[0]	*a*[1]	*a*[2]	*a*[3]	*a*[4]	*a*[5]	*a*[6]
3	20	35	40	100	10	15

Since *a*[5] is less than *a*[4], *a*[3], *a*[2], and *a*[1], therefore insert *a*[5] before *a*[1], giving the following array.

Pass 6:

a[0]	*a*[1]	*a*[2]	*a*[3]	*a*[4]	*a*[5]	*a*[6]
3	10	20	35	40	100	15

Since *a*[6] is less than *a*[5], *a*[4], *a*[3], and *a*[2], therefore insert *a*[6] before *a*[2], giving the following sorted array.

$a[0]$	$a[1]$	$a[2]$	$a[3]$	$a[4]$	$a[5]$	$a[6]$
3	10	15	20	35	40	100

Figure 8.3: Successive passes of insertion sort method

In insertion sort, we cannot identify which part of the array is sorted after each pass. Only after going through all the passes, we get the array completely sorted. We can say that elements are inserted random pattern whose may move in their positions.

Algorithm 8.5

InsertionSort(***a*, *n*** **)**

Here *a* is a linear array with *n* elements in memory. This algorithm sorts the elements in the ascending order. It uses a temporary variable *temp* to facilitate the exchange of two values and variable *j* and *k* are used as loop control and index variables.

```
1. Repeat steps 1 to 8 For k = 1 to (n-1) in step of +1
2.      Set temp = a[k]
3.      Set j = k-1
4.      Repeat steps 5 and 6 While ((temp < a[j]) and (j ≥ 0))
5.         Set a[j+1] = a[j]
6.         Set j = j-1
        Endwhile
7.      Set a[j+1] = temp
8.      Set k = k + 1
   Endfor
9. Exit
```

The above algorithm moves the elements up by one position till the correct slot for the element is found and then inserts the element at that slot.

Performance Analysis

The worst case performance occurs when the elements of the input array are in descending order. In that case, the first pass requires one comparison, the second pass requires two comparisons, third pass requires three comparisons, . . ., *k*th pass requires (k–1), and the finally the last pass requires (n–1) comparisons.

Therefore, total number of comparisons is

$$f(n) = 1 + 2 + 3 + \ldots + (n\text{-}k) + \ldots + (n-3) + (n-2) + (n-1) = n(n-1)/2$$
$$= O(n^2)$$

8.2.4 Merge Sort

Merge sort is a sorting algorithm that uses the idea of *divide and conquers*. This algorithm divides the array into two halves, sorts them separately, and then merges them. This procedure is recursive, with the base criteria — the number of elements in the array are not more than 1.

Suppose variable *beg* and *end* represents the index of the first and last element of the array respectively, the merge sort can be defined recursively as

```
If ( beg < end ) then
   Divide the list into two halves
   Mergesort the left half
   Mergesort the right half
   Merge the two-sorted halves into one sorted list
Endif
```

Example 8.5:

To illustrate the working of the merge sort method, consider the following array *a* with 7 elements as

33, 26, 35, 29, 18, 10, 24

Solution:

The first step of mergesort is to divide the array into two sub arrays. Thus we divide the array into

33, 26, 35, 29 and 18, 10, 24

and first consider the left sub array. It is again divided into two sub arrays as

33, 26 and 35, 29

For each of these sub arrays, we again apply the same method, dividing each of these into sub arrays of one element each. Sub arrays of size one, of course, require no sorting. Finally, we start merging the sub arrays to obtain a sorted array.

The sub arrays 33 and 26 merge to give the sorted array 26, 33 and the sub arrays 35 and 29 merge to give sorted array 29, 35.

At the next step, we merge these two-sorted sub arrays of size two to obtain a sorted array of size four as

26, 29, 33, 35

Now the left half of the given array is sorted, we do the same steps on the right half. First, we divide it into two sub arrays as

18, 10 and 24

The first of these is divided into two sub arrays of size one, which are merged to give 10, 18. The second sub array, 24, has size one, so needs no sorting. Now these are merged to give the sorted array

10, 18, 24

Finally, the sorted sub arrays of size four and three are merged to give

10, 18, 24, 26, 29, 33, 35

The above sorting process can also be visualized as shown in Figure 8.4.

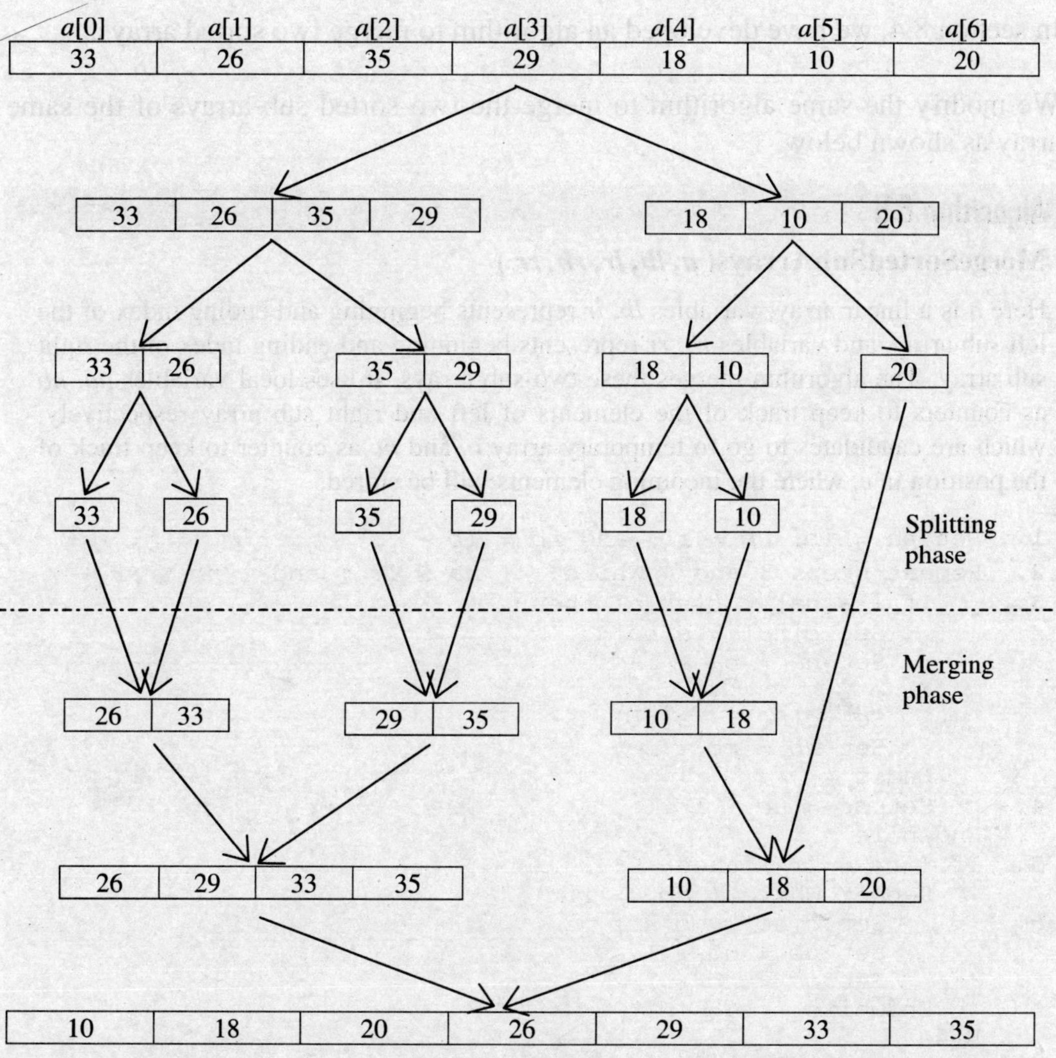

Figure 8.4: Illustration of successive steps of Merge sort

In section 8.4, we have developed an algorithm to merge two sorted arrays.

We modify the same algorithm to merge the two-sorted sub arrays of the same array as shown below.

Algorithm 8.6

MergeSortedSubArrays(***a, lb, lr, rb, rr*** **)**

Here *a* is a linear array, variables *lb*, *lr* represents beginning and ending index of the left sub array, and variables *rb*, *rr* represents beginning and ending index of the right sub array. The algorithm merges these two sub arrays. It uses local variables *na*, *nb* as counters to keep track of the elements of left and right sub array respectively, which are candidates to go to temporary array *c*, and *nc* as counter to keep track of the position in *c*, where the incoming elements will be stored.

```
1.  Set na = lb, nb = rb, and nc = lb
2.  Repeat steps 3 and 4 While ( ( na ≤ lr ) and ( nb ≤ rr ) )
3.      If ( a[na] < b[nb] ) then
            Set c[nc] = a[na]
            Set na = na + 1
        Else
            Set c[nc] = a[nb]
            Set nb = nb + 1
        Endif
4.      Set nc = nc + 1
    Endwhile
5.  If ( na > lr ) then
        Repeat While ( nb <= rr )
            Set c[nc] = b[nb]
            Set nb = nb + 1
            Set nc = nc + 1
        Endwhile
    Else
        Repeat While ( na <= lr )
            Set c[nc] = b[na]
            Set na = na + 1
            Set nc = nc + 1
        Endwhile
    Endif
6.  Repeat step 7 For k = lb to rr in steps of +1
7.      Set a[k] = c[k]
    Endfor
8.  Exit
```

After the procedure for merging to halves is defined, the various steps required for Mergesort are summarized in algorithm 8.7.

Algorithm 8.7

MergeSort(***a*****,** ***beg*****,** ***end*** **)**

Here *a* is a linear array with lower bound *beg* and upper bound *end*. The algorithm sorts the array using merge sort method. It uses variable *mid* to represent the index of the element at which array will be divided into two halves.

```
1.  If ( beg < end ) then
        Set mid = ( beg + end ) / 2
        Call MergeSort( a, beg, mid )
        Call MergeSort( a, mid + 1, end )
        Call MergeSortedSubArrays(a, beg, mid, mid+1, end)
    Endif
2.  Exit
```

The recursive procedure *mergeSort()* will be called from the calling function by the call statement as *mergeSort*(*a*, 0, *n*–1), where *a* in an array of size *n*.

Performance Analysis

The major work is done in the merge procedure, which is an O(*n*) operation. The merge procedure is called from merge-sort procedure after the array is divided into two halves, and each half has been sorted. In each of the recursive calls, one for left half and one for right half, the array is divided into halves, thus dividing the array into four segments. At each level, the number of segments doubles. Therefore, the total divisions are $\log_2 n$.

Hence, total number of comparisons

$$f(n) = n \times \log_2 n$$

$$= O(n \log_2 n)$$

The only disadvantage of merge sort is that it uses an extra temporary array, of the same size as that of input array, to merge the two halves. The elements of the temporary array are copied back to the original array before the next merging.

8.2.5 Quick Sort

We have already discussed this method in *Chapter 3*. Here, again we will discuss for the completeness of the concerned topic as per requirement of the syllabus.

Quicksort is a sorting algorithm that also, like merge sort, uses the idea of *divide and conquer*. This algorithm finds the element, called *pivot*, that partitions the array into two halves in such a way that the elements in the left sub array are less than and the elements in the right sub array are greater than the partitioning element. Then these two subarrays are sorted separately. This procedure is recursive in nature with the base criteria – the number of elements in the array are not more than 1.

Suppose variable *beg* and *end* represents the index of the first and last element of the array respectively, the quick sort can be defined recursively as

```
If ( beg < end ) then
   Find the location of the pivot such that it partitions the
   array into two halves
   Quicksort the left half
   Quicksort the right half
Endif
```

The main task in quick sort is to find the element that partitions the array into two halves and to place it at its proper location in the array. Usually, the procedure places the first element in the array at its final location. This task is performed as stated below.

To begin with, set the index of the first element of the array to *loc* and *left* variables, and index of the last element of the array to *right* variable. Then proceed as follows:

1. Beginning with the element pointed to by *right*, the array is scanned from right to left, comparing each element on the way with the element pointed to by *loc*, till either
   (a) Element smaller than the element pointed to by *loc* is found. In this case, the elements are interchanged and procedure continues with step 2.
   (b) If the value of the *right* variable becomes equal to the value of *loc*, the procedure terminates here. This condition indicates that the element is placed in its final position *loc*.

2. Beginning with the element pointed to by *left*, the array is scanned from left to right, comparing each element on the way with the element pointed to by *loc*, till either
   (a) Element greater than the element pointed to by *loc* is found. In this case, the elements are interchanged and procedure continues with step 1.
   (b) If the value of the *left* variable becomes equal to the value of *loc*, the procedure terminates here. This condition indicates that the element is placed in its final position *loc*.

As this procedure terminates, the first element, pivot, of original the array will be placed at *loc*, its final location in the sorted array. The elements to left of it will be less than this element and elements to its right will be greater than this element.

Example 8.5:

To illustrate the above procedure, consider the array

25 10 30 15 20 28

Solution:

Here the pivot element is 25.

To begin with set *loc* = 0, *left* = 0, *right* = 5 as

a[0]	*a*[1]	*a*[2]	*a*[3]	*a*[4]	*a*[5]
25	10	30	15	20	28
↑					↑
loc *left*					*right*

Start scanning elements from right. Since *a*[*loc*] < *a*[*right*], we decrease the value of variable *right* to get

a[0]	*a*[1]	*a*[2]	*a*[3]	*a*[4]	*a*[5]
25	10	30	15	20	28
↑				↑	
loc *left*				*right*	

Now, *a*[*loc*] > *a*[*right*], interchange these elements to get

a[0]	*a*[1]	*a*[2]	*a*[3]	*a*[4]	*a*[5]
20	10	30	15	25	28
↑				↑	
left				*loc* *right*	

Now start scanning elements from left. Since *a*[*loc*] > *a*[*left*], we increase the value of variable *left* to get

a[0]	*a*[1]	*a*[2]	*a*[3]	*a*[4]	*a*[5]
20	10	30	15	25	28
	↑			↑	
	left			*loc* *right*	

Since again *a*[*loc*] > *a*[*left*], we increase the value of variable *left* to get

a[0]	*a*[1]	*a*[2]	*a*[3]	*a*[4]	*a*[5]
20	10	30	15	25	28
		↑		↑	
		left		*loc* *right*	

Now *a*[*loc*] < *a*[*left*], interchange these elements to get

a[0]	*a*[1]	*a*[2]	*a*[3]	*a*[4]	*a*[5]
20	10	25	15	30	28
		↑		↑	
		loc *left*		*right*	

Now again start scanning elements from right. Since *a*[*loc*] < *a*[*right*], we decrease the value of variable *right* to get

a[0]	*a*[1]	*a*[2]	*a*[3]	*a*[4]	*a*[5]
20	10	25	15	30	28
		↑	↑		
		loc *left*	*right*		

Now, $a[loc] > a[right]$, interchange these elements to get

$a[0]$	$a[1]$	$a[2]$	$a[3]$	$a[4]$	$a[5]$
20	10	15	25	30	28
		↑	↑		
		left	*loc* *right*		

Now again start scanning elements from left. Since $a[loc] > a[left]$, we increase the value of variable *left* to get

$a[0]$	$a[1]$	$a[2]$	$a[3]$	$a[4]$	$a[5]$
20	10	15	25	30	28
			↑		
			loc *left* *right*		

Since *left* becomes equal to *loc*, thus indicating the termination of the procedure.

The element 25 is placed in its final position and it divides the array into two sub arrays as

20 10 15 (Left sub array) and 30 28 (Right sub array)

As you can see, the elements in the left sub array are smaller than 25, and elements in the right sub array are greater than 25.

This means that element 25 is correctly placed in its final position and it partitions the remaining elements in two sub arrays where elements in the left sub array are less than it and elements in the right sub array are greater it..

The above partitioning step is repeated with each sub array containing 2 or more elements. Since, we can work on one sub array at a time, we must be able to keep track of the second sub array. This task is accomplished either using stack explicitly (iterative implementation) or implicitly (recursive implementation). Both the implementations are given in this section.

The complete sorting process is visualized in Figure 8.5.

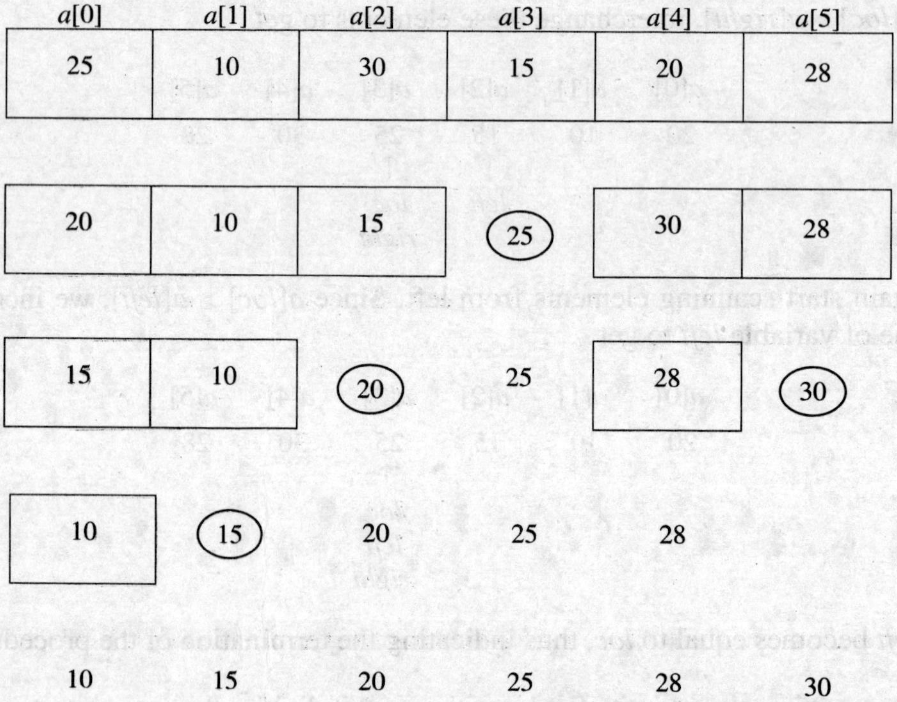

Figure 8.5: Illustration of successive steps of Quick sort, here circled element is the partitioning element (also called *pivot* element)

Algorithm 8.8

PartitionArray(***a, beg, end, loc*** **)**

Here *a* is a linear array in memory, and *beg* and *end* represents the lower bound and upper bound of the sub array in question. It partition the array into two halves by placing the partitioning element at index *loc*, which is its final position.

```
1.  Set left = beg, right = end, loc = beg
2.  Set done = false
3.  Repeat steps 4 to 10 While ( not done )
4.      Repeat step 5 While (a[loc]≤a[right]) and (loc≠right))
5.          Set right = right − 1
        Endwhile
6.      If ( loc = right ) then
            Set done = true
        Else if ( a[loc] > a[right] ) then
            Interchange a[loc] and a[right]
            Set loc = right
        Endif
```

```
7.        If ( not done ) then do step 8
8.           Repeat step 9 While (a[loc]≥a[left]) and (loc≠left))
9.              Set left = left + 1
             Endwhile
10.          If ( loc = left ) then
                Set done = true
             Else if ( a[loc] < a[left] ) then
                Interchange a[loc] and a[left]
                Set loc = left
             Endif
          Endif
    Endwhile
11. Exit
```

The QuickSort algorithm in recursive form takes the following shape

Algorithm 8.9

QuickSortRecursive(*a*, *lb*, *ub*)

Here *a* is a linear array of size *n* (>1) in memory. This algorithm sorts this array in ascending order using quick sort method. The variable *loc* is used to hold the index of splitting element.

```
1.  If ( lb < up ) then
2.     Call PartitionArray( a, lb, ub, loc )
3.     Call QuickSortRecursive( a, lb, loc – 1 )
4.     Call QuickSortRecursive( a, loc + 1, ub )
    Endif
5.  Exit
```

Recursive procedure *quickSortRecursive()* can be called from the calling function by the call statement as *quickSortRecursive(a, 0, n –*1), where *a* in an array of size *n*.

The QuickSort algorithm in iterative form takes the following shape

Algorithm 8.9

QuickSortIterative(*a*, *n*)

Here *a* is a linear array of size *n* (>1) in memory. This algorithm sorts this array in ascending order using quick sort method, handling the left sub array first and then the right sub array. The variable *loc* is used to hold the index of splitting element. To keep track of the sub arrays it uses stack, of integers, explicitly.

```
1.   CreateStack(STK)
2.   Call Push(STK, 0)           // push lower index of starting array
3.   Call Push(STK, n-1)         // push upper index of starting array
4.   Repeat steps 5 to 11 While STK is not empty
5.      Call POP(STK, ub)        // pop upper index into up
6.      Call POP(STK, lb)        // pop upper index into lb
7.      Call PartitionArray( a, lb, ub, loc )
8.      Call Push(STK, loc+1)    // push lower index of right subarray
9.      Call Push(STK, ub)       // push upper index of right subarray
10.     Call Push(STK, lb)       // push lower index of left subarray
11.     Call Push(STK, loc-1)    // push upper index of left subarray
     Endwhile
12.  Exit
```

Iterative procedure *quickSortIterative()* can be called from the calling function by the call statement as *quickSortIterative(a, n)*, where *a* in an array of size *n*.

Performance Analysis

To find the location of the element that splits the array into two sections is an O(n) operation, because every element in the array is compared to the dividing element.

After the division, each section is examined separately. If the array is split approximately in half (which is not usually), then there will be $\log_2 n$ splits.

Therefore, the total comparisons are

$$f(n) = n \times \log_2 n = O(n \log_2 n)$$

Quick sort is sensitive to the order of the input data. And it gives the worst case performance when the elements are already in the ascending order. Then it divides the array into sections of 1 and (n–1) elements in each call. Thus, there will be (n–1) partitions, in all.

Therefore, in this case, the total number of comparisons

$$f(n) = n \times (n - 1) = O(n^2)$$

The efficiency of quick Sort is affected by the initial order of elements.

8.2.6 Heap Sort

Before discussing heapsort method to sort an array in ascending order, we need to be familiar with a heap data structure.

A *heap* is a binary tree that satisfies the following properties:

- Shape property
- Order property

By the *shape property* we mean that heap must be a complete binary tree, whereas by *order property* we mean that for every node in a heap, the value stored in that node is greater than or equal to the value in each of its children. A heap that satisfies these properties is known as *max heap*. However, if the order property is such that for every node in the heap, the value stored in a node is less than or equal to the value in each of its children, the corresponding heap is known as *min heap*.

A heap is represented in memory using a linear array, *i.e.*, by *sequential representation* as shown in Figure 8.6.

We know that the maximum value in a *max heap* is in the root node, because of the order property. We can take advantage of this situation by using a heap to help us to sort the given array *a* with *n* elements in ascending order.

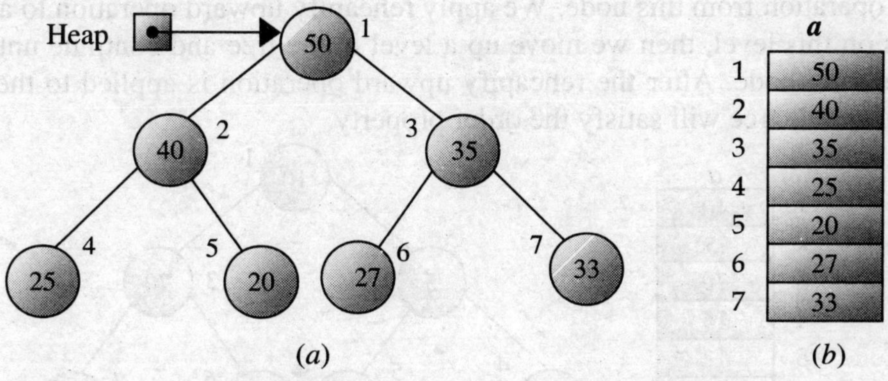

Figure 8.6: (*a*) Max heap (*b*) Sequential representation of Max heap

The general approach of heapsort method is as follows:

1. From the given array, build the initial max heap.
2. Interchange the root (maximum) element with the last element.
3. Use *downheap* operation from root node to rebuild the heap of size one less than the starting.
4. Repeat steps 2 and 3 until we are left with a heap with size equal to 1.

Building a Heap

To have a look at how the heap relates to array of unsorted elements. The Figure 8.5 shows unsorted array and its equivalent binary tree.

We want that the elements of the unsorted array must satisfy the order property of heaps. Let us first have a look at the binary tree to see that is there any part of the binary tree that already satisfies the order property. Observe that all the leaf nodes (subtrees with only single node) are heaps. In Figure 8.6(*b*), the subtrees whose roots contain values 15, 12, 35, and 50 are heaps because they are root nodes.

Now let us look at the first leftmost non-leaf node, the one containing value 5. The subtree rooted at this node is not a heap, and it is the root of the subtree that is heap. And we have already seen how to fix this problem using reheapify upward operation from this node. We apply reheapify upward operation to all the subtrees on this level, then we move up a level in the tree and continue until we reach the root node. After the reheapify upward operation is applied to the root node, the whole tree will satisfy the order property.

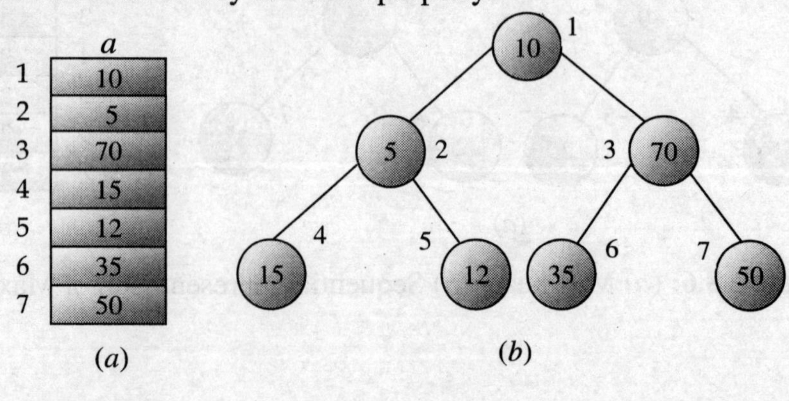

Figure 8.6: (*a*) Unsorted array *a*, (*b*) Equivalent binary tree

The heap building process, also popularly known as *heapify*, is illustrated for the given unsorted array *a* in Figure 8.7.

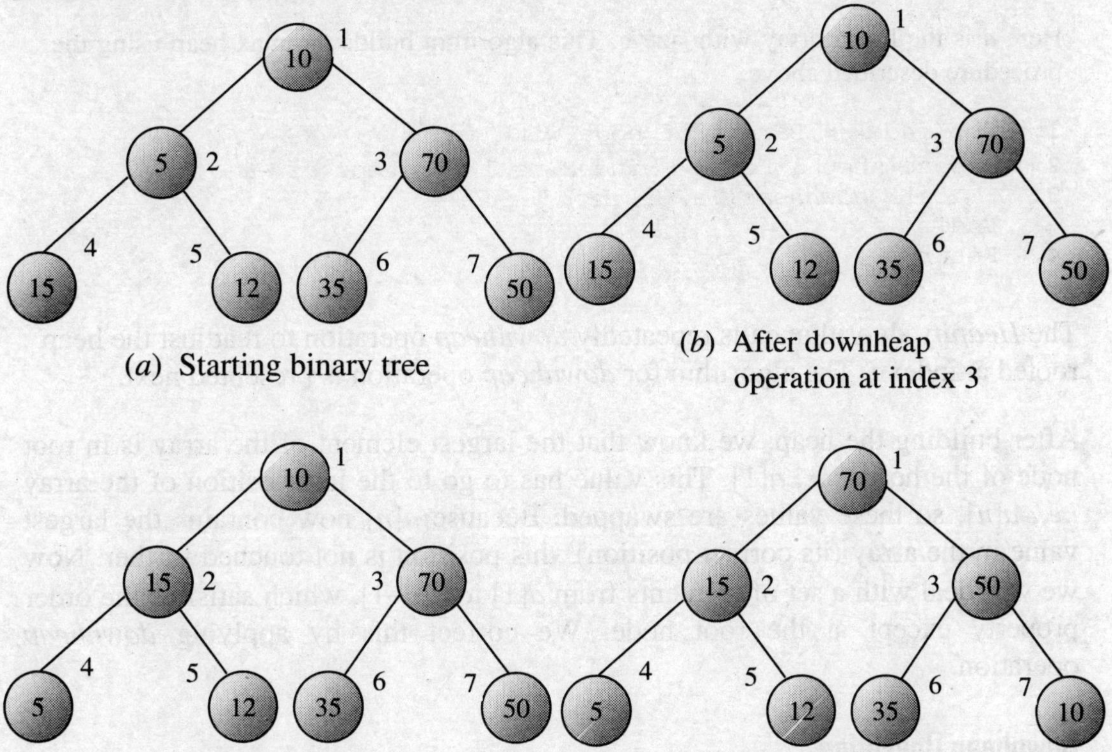

(*a*) Starting binary tree

(*b*) After downheap operation at index 3

(*c*) After downheap operation at index 2

(*d*) After downheap operation at index 1

Figure 8.7: Illustration of heap building process

The binary tree of Figure 8.7(*d*) represents a *max* heap.

	$a[1]$	$a[2]$	$a[3]$	$a[4]$	$a[5]$	$a[6]$	$a[7]$
Original array A	10	5	70	15	12	35	50
After reheapify upward							
From index 3	10	5	70	15	12	35	50
From index 2	10	15	70	5	12	35	50
From index 1	70	15	50	5	12	35	10

Figure 8.8: Illustration of changing contents of array *a*

Algorithm 8.5

Heapify(*a*, *n*)

Here *a* is the linear array with size *n*. This algorithm builds the max heap using the procedure described above.

```
1.  Set index = Parent of node with index n
2.  Repeat step 3 For i = index to 1 in steps of -1
3.     Call downheap( a, i, n )
    Endif
4.  Return
```

The *Heapify* algorithm calls repeatedly *downheap* operation to readjust the heap rooted at index *i*. The algorithm for *downheap* operation is presented next.

After building the heap, we know that the largest element of the array is in root node of the heap, *i.e.*, *a*[1]. This value has to go to the last position of the array *i.e.*, *a*[*n*], so these values are swapped. Because *a*[*n*] now contains the largest value in the array (its correct position), this position is not touched further. Now we will deal with a set of elements from *a*[1] to *a*[*n*–1], which satisfies the order property except at the root node. We correct this by applying *downheap* operation.

Downheap Operation

This operation involves moving the elements down from a particular node until either it ends up in a position where the order property is satisfied or we hit the leaf node. This operation in the text will be referred to as *downheap* operation and works as follows:

Interchange the value of the node with the value of the child that is the largest among its children. For example, if the value of the left child is the largest, the node is interchanged with its left child, and then the down heap operation is repeated from its left child onward. Similar is the case if the right child is largest. Then start downheap operation from that child with which the value of the node was interchanged. This operation is recursive.

Algorithm 8.1

Downheap(a, start, finish)

Here *a* is a linear array, *start* is the index of the element from where downheap operation is to start, and *finish* is index of the last (bottom) element of the heap. The variable *index* is used to keep track of the index of the largest child.

```
1.  If ( a[start] is not a leaf node ) then
        Set index = index of the child with largest value
        If ( a[start] < a[index] ) then
            Swap a[start] and a[index]
            Call Downheap( a, index, finish )
        Endif
    Endif
2.  Return
```

At this point, we know that the next largest element in the array is in the root node of the new heap. To put this element in the correct position in the array, we interchange it with the element $a[n-1]$. Now two largest elements are in their final position, and we are left dealing with elements from $a[1]$ to $a[n-2]$. This process is repeated until all the elements are in their correct position, *i.e.*, until heap contains only single element, which is the smallest element in the array.

Sorting Process

Putting things together, the complete algorithm for Heap sort will look like as shown below.

Algorithm 8.12

HeapSort(***a, n*** **)**

Here *a* is a linear array of size *n* in memory. This algorithm sorts this array in ascending order using Heap sort method. It call *heapify* sub algorithm to build the initial heap and *downheap* sub algorithms rebuild the heap of reduced size after each iteration.

```
1. Call Heapify( a, n )
2. Repeat steps 3 and 4 For i = n to 2 in steps of -1
3.    Interchange elements a[1] and a[i]
4.    Call downheap( a, 1, i-1  )
   Endif
5. Exit
```

Example 8.7:

Let us consider a working example to illustrate the working of heapsort algorithm.

For this purpose consider array: 10, 5, 70, 15, 12, 35, 50

Solution:

	a[1]	*a*[2]	*a*[3]	*a*[4]	*a*[5]	*a*[6]	*a*[7]
After heapify operation	70	15	50	5	12	35	10
Swap	10	15	50	5	12	35	70
Downheap	50	15	35	5	12	10	70
Swap	10	15	35	5	12	50	70
Downheap	35	15	10	5	12	50	70
Swap	12	15	10	5	35	50	70
Downheap	15	12	10	5	35	50	70
Swap	5	12	10	15	35	50	70
Downheap	12	5	10	15	35	50	70
Swap	10	5	12	15	35	50	70
Downhcap	10	5	12	15	35	50	70
Swap	5	10	12	15	35	50	70
Final sorted array	**5**	**10**	**12**	**15**	**35**	**50**	**70**

Figure 8.9: Illustration of effect of heapsort on array *a*

In the discussion of heapsort algorithm, we are considering that the array is indexed from 1 to *n* not from 0 to *n*–1.

The above sorting process can also be visualized as shown overleaf.

Given array is

10, 5, 70, 15, 12, 35, 50

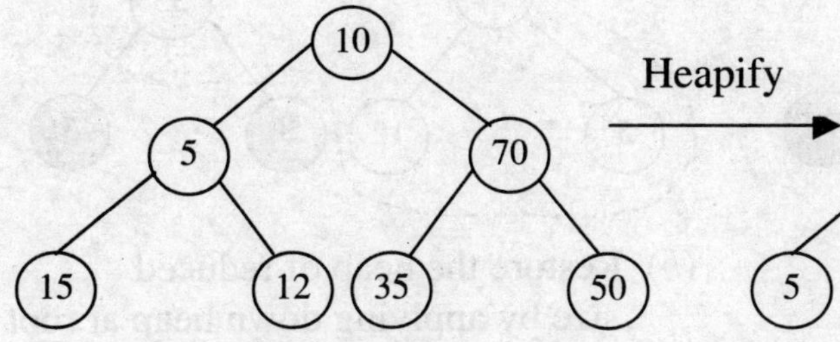

(*a*) Equivalent binary tree

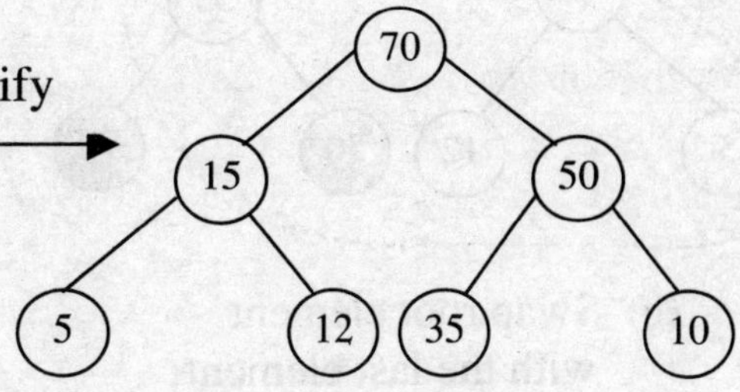

(*b*) Max heap

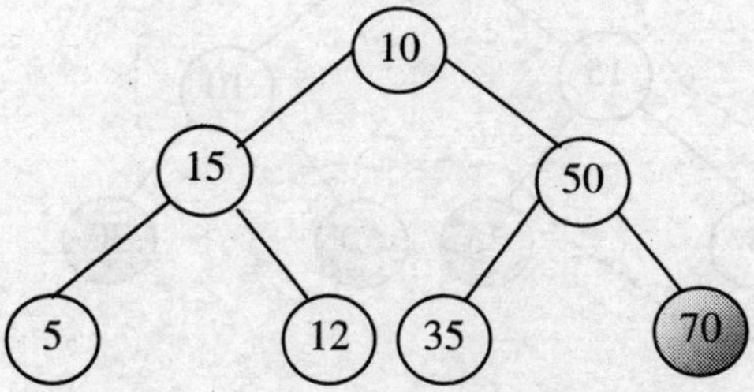

(*c*) Swap root element with the last element

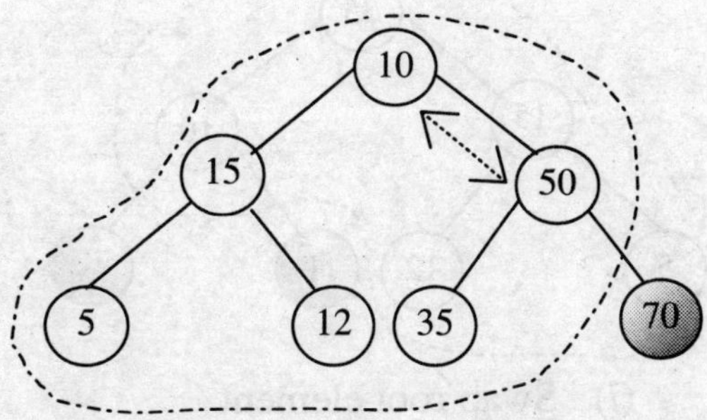

(*d*) Apply downheap operation from root to the reduced heap

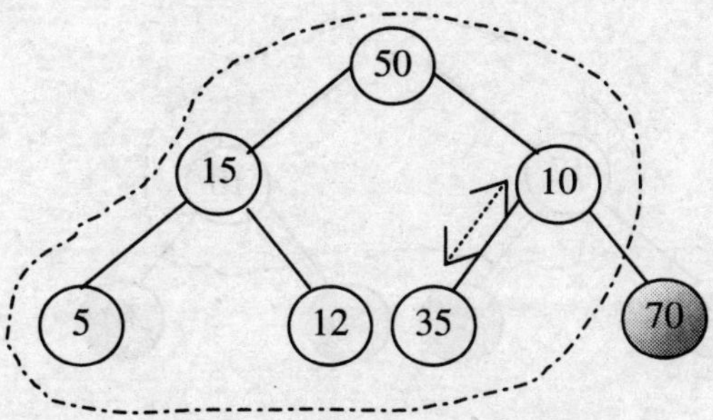

(*e*) Apply downheap operation from node with value 10

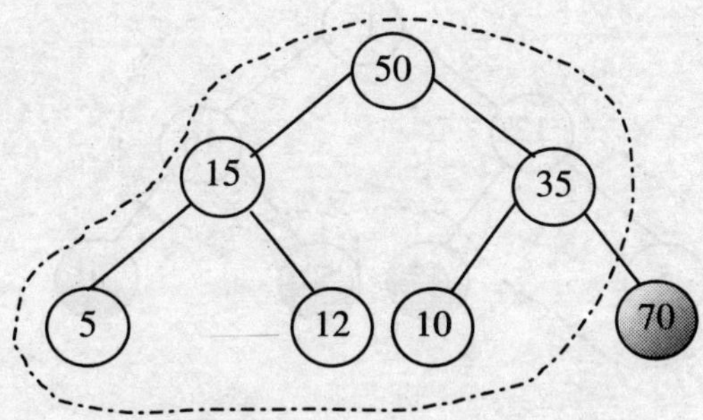

(*f*) Here the order property of heap is restored

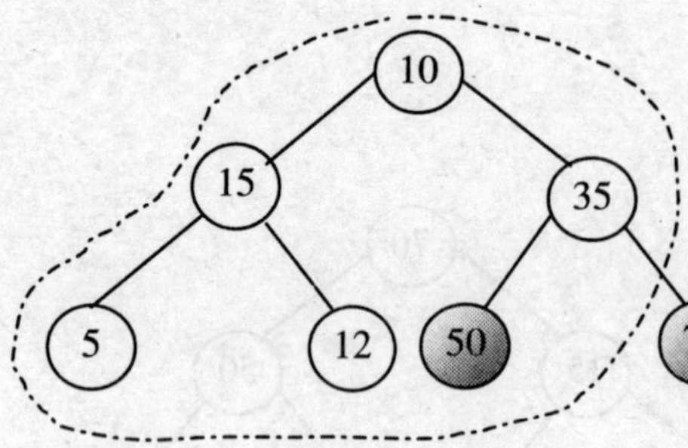

(*g*) Swap root element with the last element

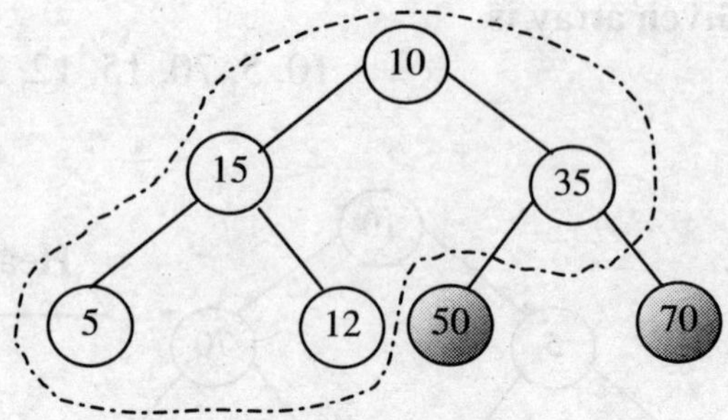

(*h*) Restore the heap of reduced size by applying down heap at root

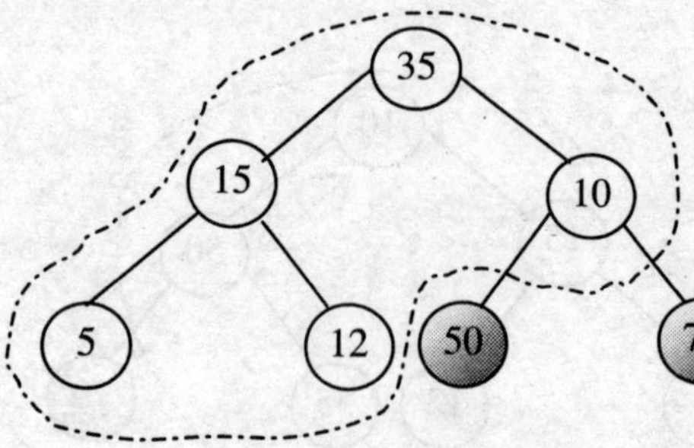

(*i*) Swap root element wth the last element

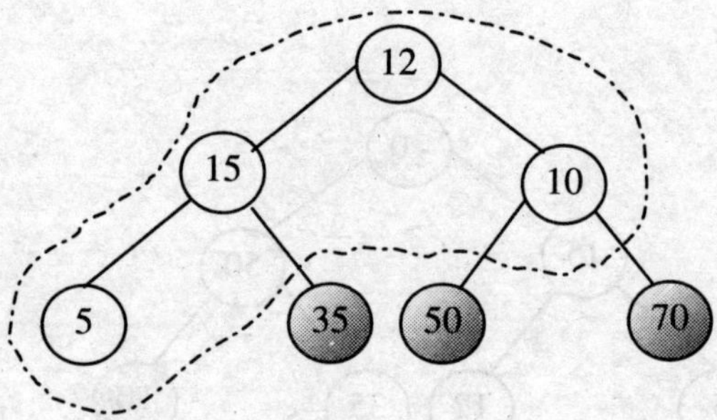

(*j*) Again restore the heap of reduced size by applying down heap at root

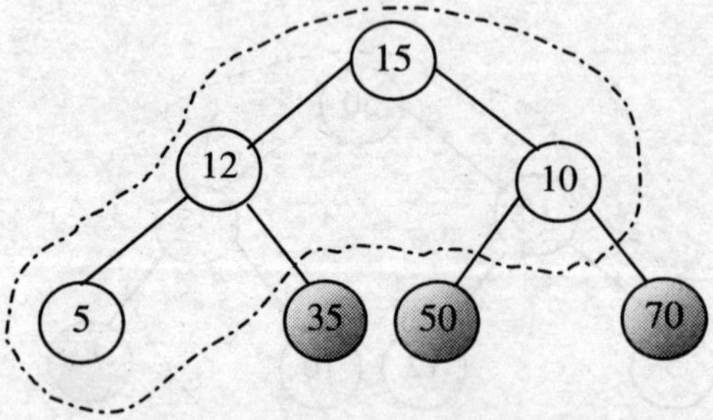

(*k*) Swap root element with the last element

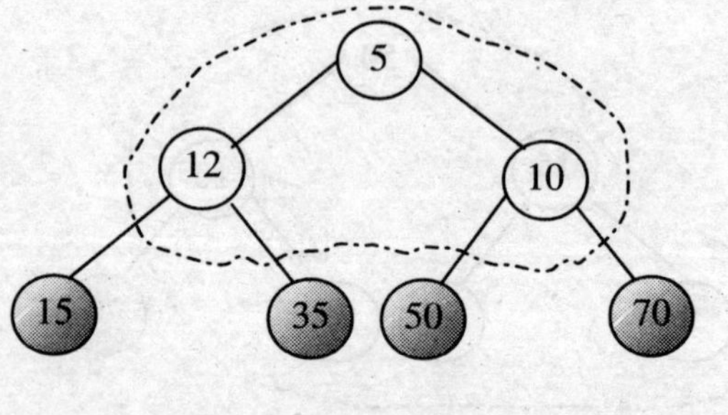

(*l*) Again restore the heap of reduced size by applying down heap at root

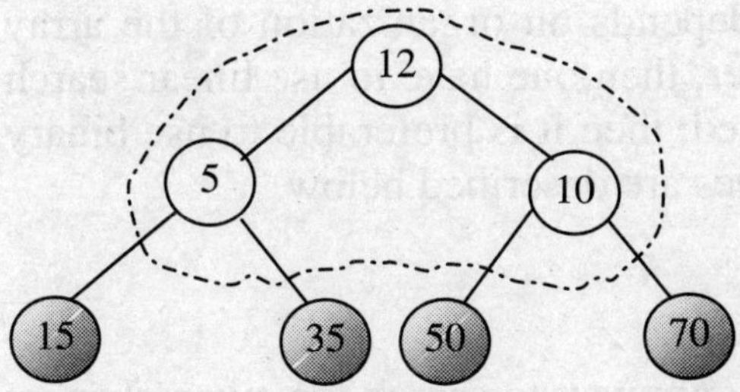

(*m*) Swap root element with the last element

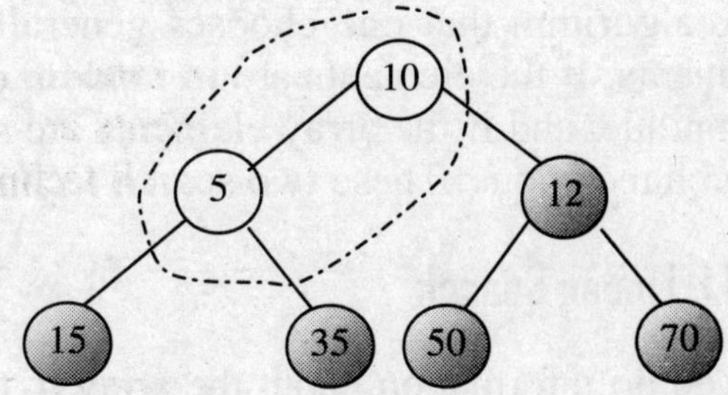

(*n*) Here property of the heap of Reduced size is not disturbed

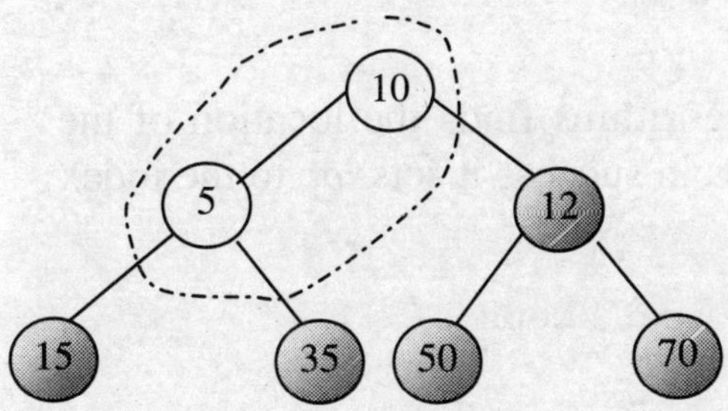

(*o*) Swap root element with the last element

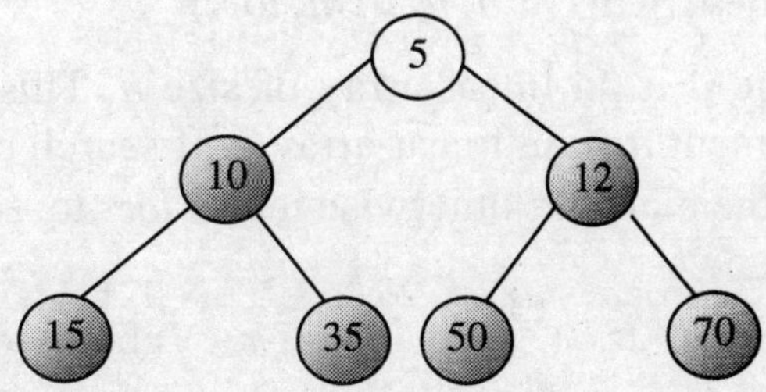

(*p*) The sorting process is complete, and the resultant binary tree represents the array sorted in ascending order.

Figure 8.: Visual illustration of working of heap sort method

8.3 SEARCHING

Searching is the process of finding the location of given element in the linear array. The search is said to be successful if the given element is found, *i.e.*, the element does exists in the array; otherwise unsuccessful. There are two approaches to search operation:

- Linear search
- Binary search

We have already discussed these methods in *Chapter 3*. Here, again we will discuss for the completeness of the concerned topic as per requirement of the syllabus.

The algorithm that one chooses generally depends on organization of the array elements. If the elements are in random order, then one have to use linear search technique, and if the array elements are sorted, then it is preferable to use binary search technique. These two search techniques are described below.

8.3.1 Linear Search

Given no information about the array *a*, the only way to search for given element *item* is to compare *item* with each element of *a* one by one. This method, which traverses *a* sequentially to locate *item* is called *linear search* or *sequential search*.

Algorithm 8.14

LinearSearch(*a*, *n*, *item*, *loc*)

Here *a* is an linear array of size *n*. This algorithms finds the location of the element *item* in linear array *a*. If search ends in success it sets *loc* to the index of the element; otherwise it sets *loc* to –1.

```
1.  Repeat step 2 For i = 0 to (n-1) in steps of +1
2.     If ( a[i] = item ) then
          Set loc = i
          Return
       Endif
    Endfor
3.  Set loc = -1
4.  Return
```

Performance Analysis

In the best possible case, the *item* may occur at first position. In this case, the search operation terminates in success with just one comparison. However, the worst case occurs when either the item is present at last position or missing from the array. In the former case, the search terminates in success with *n* comparisons. In the later case, the search terminates in failure with *n* comparisons.

Thus, we find that in worst case the linear search is $O(n)$ operations.

8.3.2 Binary Search

Suppose the elements of the array *A* are sorted in ascending order (if the elements are numbers) or dictionary order (if the elements are strings). The best searching algorithm, called *binary search,* is used to find the location of the given element. We do use this approach in our daily life. For example, suppose we want to find the meaning of the term *modem* in a computer dictionary. Obviously, we don't search page by page. We open the dictionary in the middle (roughly) to determine which half contains the term being sought. Then for the subsequent search one half is discarded, and we search in the other half. This process is continued till other we have located the required term or that term is missing from the dictionary, which will be indicated by the fact that at the end we will be left with only one page.

Example 8.9:

To illustrate working of binary search technique, consider following sorted array *a* with 7 elements: 3, 10, 15, 20, 35, 40, 60, and we want to search element 15.

Solution:

	a[0]	*a*[1]	*a*[2]	*a*[3]	*a*[4]	*a*[5]	*a*[6]
Given Array *a*	3	10	15	20	35	40	60

To start with, we take $beg = 0$, $end = 6$, and compute location of the middle element as

$$mid = (beg + end) / 2 = (0 + 6) / 2 = 3$$

Since $a[mid]$, *i.e.*, $a[3] \neq 15$, and $beg < end$. We start next iteration.

As $a[mid] = 20 > 15$, therefore, we take $end = mid - 1 = 3 - 1 = 2$, where as *beg* remains unchanged. Thus

$$mid = (beg + end) / 2 = (0 + 2) / 2 = 1$$

Since $a[mid]$, *i.e.*, $a[1] \neq 15$, and $beg < end$. We start next iteration.

As $a[mid] = 10 < 15$, therefore, we take $beg = mid + 1 = 1 + 1 = 2$, where as *end* remains unchanged.

Since $beg = end$, again compute location of the middle element as

$$mid = (beg + end) / 2 = (2 + 2) / 2 = 2$$

Since $a[mid]$, *i.e.*, $a[2] = 15$, the search terminates on success.

The element 15 is found at index 2.

Algorithm 8.15

BinarySearch(***a, n, item, loc*** **)**

Here *a* is an linear array of size *n*. This algorithms finds the location of the element *item* in sorted (ascending) linear array *a*. If search ends in success it sets *loc* to the index of the element; otherwise it sets loc to −1. Here variables *beg* and *end* to keep track of the first element and last element of the array to be searched, and variable *mid* is used as index of the middle element of the array under consideration.

```
1.  Set beg = 0
2.  Set end = n-1
3.  Set mid = ( beg + end ) / 2
4.  Repeat steps 5 and 6 While ((beg ≤ end) and (a[mid] ≠ item))
5.      If ( item < a[mid] ) then
           Set end = mid-1
        Else
           Set beg = mid+1
        Endif
6.      Set mid = ( beg + end ) / 2
    Endwhile
7.  If ( beg > end ) then
        Set loc = -1
    Else
        Set loc = mid
    Endif
8.  Exit
```

Performance Analysis

In each iteration, the search is reduced to one half of the array. Therefore, for n elements in the array, there will be $\log_2 n$ iterations or recursive calls. Thus, the complexity of binary search is $O(\log_2 n)$. This complexity will be same irrespective of the position of the element, even if it is not present in the array.

8.4 MERGING

Merging is the process of combining the elements of two similar structures (linear arrays) into a single structure. Suppose that two arrays are unsorted, we can combine them end to end, *i.e.*, we can first put elements of array *a* into third array *c*, and then the elements of the second array *b* are placed after it in array *c*.

This process is illustrated in Figure 8.9.

Array a	12	40	–3	2					
Array b	15	5	7	10	60				
Array c	12	40	–3	2	15	5	7	10	60

Figure 8.9: Merging end-to-end

But in most cases, we may have sorted arrays and our aim is to combine them in such a way that the combined array is also in the sorted order. One straightforward approach is to join them end to end, and then sort the combined array. But this approach in not efficient and economical. The best approach is to compare the elements of the given array, and based on this comparison, decide which element should go first to the third array.

This process is illustrated in Figure 8.10, for arrays sorted in the ascending order.

Array a	–3	2	12	40					
Array b	5	7	10	15	60				
Array c	–3	2	5	7	10	12	15	40	60

Figure 8.10: Merging of sorted arrays

In case of sorted arrays, to start with, compare first element of array a (element –3) with the first element of array b (element 5), and put the smallest of these (–3) into array c. Since first element of array a is put in array c. Next we compare second element of array a (element 2) with the first element of array b (element 5), since 2 is the smallest, put it into c. Next compare third element of a (element 12) with first element of b (element 5), since 5 is the smallest, put it into c. Next compare third element of a (element 12) with second element of b (element 7), since 7 is the smallest, put it into c, and so on. When one array is exhausted, the elements of the other array are copied one by one to c. To accomplish the above task, we use counters to keep track of the current element which is a candidate to go in c, and the position in c where it will be stored.

Algorithm 8.16

MergingSortedArrays(***a, m, b, n, c*** **)**

Here *a* and *b* are sorted (ascending) linear arrays of size *m* and *n*, respectively. This algorithm merges these arrays, by comparing their elements, into array c, which will be of size *m*+*n*. It uses variables *na* and *nb* to keep track of the respective elements of arrays *a* and *b*, and a variable *nc* to keep track of index in array *c* where the incoming element (either from array *a* or *b*) will be stored.

```
1:   Set na = 0, nb = 0, and nc = 0
2.   Repeat steps 3 and 4 While ( ( na ≤ m ) and ( nb ≤ n ) )
3.      If ( a[na] < b[nb] ) then
           Set c[nc] = a[na]
           Set na = na + 1
        Else
           Set c[nc] = a[nb]
           Set nb = nb + 1
        Endif
4.      Set nc = nc + 1
     Endwhile
5.   If ( na = m ) then          // array a is exhausted
        Repeat While ( nb < n )
           Set c[nc] = b[nb]
           Set nb = nb + 1
           Set nc = nc + 1
        Endwhile
     Else                        // array b is exhausted
        Repeat While ( na <= m )
           Set c[nc] = b[na]
           Set na = na + 1
           Set nc = nc + 1
        Endwhile
     Endif
6.   Exit
```

Performance Analysis

The input to this algorithrn consists of the total number r (= $m + n$) of elements of a and b. each comparison assigns an element to array c, which eventually has r elements. According the number $f(r)$ of comparison cannot exceed r:

$$f(r) \leq r = O(r)$$

which means, the merging algorithm can be run in linear time.

SUMMARY

In this chapter, we have learnt about the

- working of different sorting methods.
- algorithms of different sorting methods.
- performance of different sorting methods.
- working of different searching methods.
- algorithms of different searching methods.
- performance of different searching methods.
- working of merging the sorted arrays.
- algorithm for merging of two sorted arrays on ascending order.
- performance of merging technique.

REVIEW EXERCISES

1. What is sorting? What is its importance?
2. How do quick sort and heap sort compare as far as performance is concerned?
3. Can you implement quick sort method without recursion? If yes, show its implementation.
4. How would you implement merge sort method without recursion?
5. Sort the list 213, 145, 456, 700, 515, 295, 674, 925 using bucket sort method.
6. Sort the list 3, 1, 4, 7, 5, 2, 6, 9 using merge sort method.
7. How the heap sort processes the list 142, 34, 77, 23, 18, 100, 72 in order to sort it in the descending order?
8. How the quicksort processes the list 42, 34, 75, 23, 18, 100, 10, 72 in order to sort it in the descending order?
9. Here is an array of ten integers:

   5 3 8 9 1 7 0 2 6 4

   Rewrite this array after the FIRST iteration of the selection sort in order to sort it in ascending order.
10. Here is an array of ten integers:

    5 3 8 9 1 7 0 2 6 4

    Rewrite this array after the TWO iterations of the insertion sort in order to sort it in ascending order.

11. Here is an array, which has just been partitioned by the first step of quick sort in order to sort it in the ascending order:

    3, 0, 2, 4, 5, 8, 7, 6, 9

    Which of these elements could be the pivot?
13. Here is an array of ten integers:

    5 3 8 9 1 7 0 2 6 4

    Suppose we partition this array using quick sort's partition function and using 5 as the pivot. Rewrite the resulting array after the partition finishes.
14. Fill in the following table for the times to sort an array of *n* items. Use only Big-O notation.

Method	Worst Case Performance
Bubble sort	
Insertion sort	
Merge sort	
Quick sort	
Selection sort	
Heap sort	

PROGRAMMING EXERCISES

1. Write a program to sort an array of integers in the descending order using bubble sort.
2. Write a program to sort an array of integers in the descending order using selection sort.
3. Write a program to sort an array of integers in the descending order using insertion sort.
4. Write a program to sort a list of student names in dictionary order using any method of your choice.
5. Write a program to sort an array of integers in the descending order using quick sort.
6. Write a program to sort an array of integers in the descending order using heap sort.

Appendix A

Implementation of Selected Data Structures & Algorithms Using C Language

Learning Objectives

After reading this appendix, students will be able to develop C programs for the data structure and algorithms described in text and asked in the form of programming exercises.

A.2 *Data Structures*

Listing A.1

```
/*
*  Program to sort an array of integers in ascending order using
*  bubble sort method
*/
#include<stdio.h>
#include<conio.h>
/*----  function prototype  ----*/
void bubbleSortMethod( int a[], int n );
void main()
{
    int i, n, a[50];
    clrscr();
    printf( "\nEnter size of array : " );
    scanf( "%d", &n );
    printf( "\nEnter %d elements of array\n\n", n );
    for ( i = 0; i < n; i++ )
        scanf( "%d", &a[i] );
    bubbleSortMethod( a, n );
    printf( "\n\nSorted list of elements\n\n" );
    for ( i = 0; i < n; i++ )
       printf( "%d\t", a[i] );
    printf( "\n");
} /*---- end of main function ----*/
void bubbleSortMethod( int a[], int n )
{
    int j, k, temp;
    for ( k = 1; k < n; k++ ) {
        for ( j = 0; j < n-k; j++ ) {
           if ( a[j] > a[j+1] ) {
               temp  = a[j];
               a[j]  = a[j+1];
               a[j+1] = temp;
           }
        }
    }
}
```

Listing A.2

```
/*
*   Program to demonstrate the use of binary search to search
*   a given element in a sorted array in ascending order
*/
#include <stdio.h>
#include <conio.h>
/*---  function prototype  ---*/
int binarySearchRecursive(int a[], int lb, int ub, int item);
void main()
{
    int a[50], i, n, item, loc;
```

```
    clrscr();
    printf("\nEnter size of array : " );
    scanf("%d", &n );
    printf("\nEnter %d elements in ascending order\n", n);
    for ( i = 0; i < n; i++ )
        scanf( "%d", &a[i] );
    printf( "\nEnter element to search : " );
    scanf( "%d", &item );
    loc = binarySearchRecursive(a, 0, n-1, item);
    if ( loc == -1 )
        printf( "\nElement not found. . .\n" );
    else
        printf( "\nElement found at index %d\n", loc );
}
int binarySearchRecursive(int a[], int lb, int ub, int item)
{
    int mid;
    if ( lb > ub )
        return -1;
    else
    {
        mid = ( lb + ub ) / 2;
        if ( item == a[mid] )
            return mid;
        else if ( item < a[mid] )
            return binarySearchRecursive(a, lb, mid-1, item );
        else
            return binarySearchRecursive(a, mid+1, ub, item );
    }
}
```

Listing A.3

```
/*
*  Program to illustrate implementation of linear linked list
*/
#include <stdio.h>
#include <conio.h>
/*------ defining structure of a node  -------*/
typedef struct nodeType {
    int info;
    struct nodeType *next;
} node;
node *head = NULL;         /*  head of list as global variable  */
/*-------   function prototypes    -------*/
void traverse();
node *search( int item );
void insertAtBeginning( int item );
void insertAfterElement( int item, int after );
void insertAtEnd( int item );
void deleteFromBeginning();
```

```
void deleteFromEnd();
void deleteAfterElement( int after );
void deleteList();
void main()   /*  main function  starts from here  */
{
    int choice, element, after;
    while ( 1 )
    {
        clrscr();
        printf( "         Options available \n" );
        printf( "++++++++++++++++++++++++++++++++ \n\n" );
        printf( "  1.  Insert at beginning\n" );
        printf( "  2.  Insert at end\n" );
        printf( "  3.  Insert after a given element\n" );
        printf( "  4.  Traverse in order\n" );
        printf( "  5.  Delete from beginning\n" );
        printf( "  6.  Delete from end\n" );
        printf( "  7.  Delete after a given element\n" );
        printf( "  8.  Exit\n\n" );
        printf( "Enter your choice ( 1-8 ) : " );
        scanf( "%d", &choice );
        switch ( choice )
        {
            case 1 : printf( "\nEnter element : " );
                     scanf( "%d", &element );
                     insertAtBeginning( element );
                     break;
            case 2 : printf ( "\nEnter element : " );
                     scanf( "%d", &element );
                     insertAtEnd( element );
                     break;
            case 3 : printf( "\nEnter element : " );
                     scanf( "%d", &element );
                     printf("\nEnter element after " );
                     printf("which to insert : " );
                     scanf( "%d", &after );
                     insertAfterElement( element, after );
                     break;
            case 4 : if ( head == ( node * ) NULL )
                         printf( "\nList is empty ... " );
                     else
                         traverse();
                     printf(  "\n\nPress any key to continue..." );
                     getch();
                     break;
            case 5 : deleteFromBeginning();
                     break;
            case 6 : deleteFromEnd();
                     break;
            case 7 : printf( "\nEnter element after " );
                     printf( " which to delete : " );
                     scanf( "%d", &after );
                     deleteAfterElement( after );
```

```
                    break;
            case 8: deleteList();
                    return;
        }
    }
}  /****** end of main function ******/
void traverse()
{
    node *ptr;
    ptr = head;
    while ( ptr != NULL ) {
        printf( "%d\n", ptr->info );
        ptr = ptr->next;
    }
}
node *search( int item )
{
    node *ptr;
    ptr = head;
    while ( ( ptr != NULL ) && ( ptr->info != item ) )
       ptr = ptr->next;
    return head;
}
void insertAtBeginning( int item )
{
   node *ptr;
   ptr = ( node * ) malloc( sizeof( node ) );
   ptr->info  = item;
   ptr->next =  head;
   head = ptr;
}
void insertAtEnd( int item )
{
    node *ptr, *loc;
    ptr =  ( node * ) malloc( sizeof( node ) );
    ptr->info  = item;
    ptr->next =  ( node * ) NULL;
    if ( head == NULL )   /* list initially empty */
        head =  ptr;
    else
    {
        loc = head;
        while ( loc->next != NULL )
            loc = loc->next;
        loc->next = ptr;
    }
}
void insertAfterElement( int item, int after )
{
    node *ptr, *loc;
    loc = search( after );
    if ( loc == NULL )      /*  element 'after' not found  */
        return;
    ptr = ( node * ) malloc ( sizeof ( node ) );
```

```
    ptr->info = item;
    ptr->next = loc->next;
    loc->next = ptr;
}
void deleteFromBeginning()
{
    node *ptr;
    if ( head == NULL )
        return;
    else {
        ptr = head;
        head = head->next;
        free( ptr );
    }
}
void deleteFromEnd()
{
    node *ptr, *loc;
    if ( head == NULL )
        return;
    else if ( head->next == NULL ) {
        ptr = head;
        head = NULL;
        free ( ptr );
    } else {
        loc = head;
        ptr = head->next;
        while ( ptr->next != NULL ) {
            loc = ptr;
            ptr = ptr->next;
        }
        loc->next = NULL;
        free (ptr);
    }
}
void deleteAfterElement( int after )
{
    node *ptr, *loc;
    loc = search( after );
    if ( loc == NULL )
        return;
    ptr = loc->next;
    loc->next = ptr->next;
    free (ptr);
}
void deleteList()
{
    node *ptr;
    while ( head != NULL ) {
        ptr = head;
        head = head->next;
        free ( ptr );
    }
}
```

Listing A.4

```
/*
*  Program to illustrate implementation of doubly linked list
*/
#include <stdio.h>
#include <conio.h>
/*------ defining structure of a node  -------*/
typedef struct nodeType {
    struct nodeType *prev;
    int info;
    struct nodeType *next;
} node;
node *head=NULL, *tail=NULL; /*head & tail as global variables */
/*-------   function prototypes    -------*/
void traverseInOrder();
void traverseInReverseOrder();
node *search( int item );
void insertAtBeginning( int item );
void insertAtEnd( int item );
void insertAfterElement( int item, int after );
void insertBeforeElement( int item, int before );
void deleteFromBeginning();
void deleteFromEnd();
void deleteBeforeElement( int before );
void deleteAfterElement(int after );
void deleteList();
void main()  /*---- main function starts ----*/
{
   int choice, element, after, before;
   createEmptyList ( &head, &tail );
   while ( 1 )
   {
       clrscr();
       printf( "          Options available \n" );
       printf( "++++++++++++++++++++++++++++++++++++ \n\n" );
       printf( "   1. Insert at beginning\n" );
       printf( "   2. Insert at end\n" );
       printf( "   3. Insert after a given element\n" );
       printf( "   4. Insert before a given element\n" );
       printf( "   5. Traverse in order\n" );
       printf( "   6. Traverse in Reverse order\n" );
       printf( "   7. Delete from beginning\n" );
       printf( "   8. Delete from end\n");
       printf( "   9. Delete after a given element\n" );
       printf( "  10. Delete before a given element\n" );
       printf( "  11. Exit\n\n");
       printf( "Enter your choice ( 1-11 ) : " );
       scanf( "%d", &choice );
       switch ( choice ) {
         case 1 : printf("\nEnter element : " );
                  scanf("%d", &element );
                  insertAtBeginning( element );
                  break;
```

```
         case 2 : printf("\nEnter element : " );
                  scanf("%d", &element );
                  insertAtEnd( element );
                  break;
         case 3 : printf("\nEnter element : " );
                  scanf("%d", &element );
                  printf("\nEnter element after which ");
                  printf("to insert : ");
                  scanf("%d", &after );
                  insertAfterElement( element, after );
                  break;
         case 4 : printf("\nEnter element : " );
                  scanf("%d", &element );
                  printf("\nEnter element before which ");
                  printf(" to insert : ");
                  scanf( "%d", &before );
                  insertBeforeElement( element, before );
                  break;
        case 5 : if ( head == NULL )
                    printf( "\nList is empty ... " );
                  else
                    traverseInOrder();
                  printf("\n\nPress any key to continue...");
                  getch();
                  break;
        case 6 : if ( head == NULL )
                    printf( "\nList is empty ... " );
                  else
                    traverseInReverseOrder();
                  printf("\n\nPress any key to continue...");
                  getch();
                  break;
        case 7 : deleteFromBeginning();
                  break;
        case 8 : deleteFromEnd();
                  break;
        case 9 : printf("\nEnter element after ");
                 printf(" which to delete : ");
                  scanf( "%d", &after );
                  deleteAfterElement( after );
                  break;
        case 10: printf("\nEnter element before ");
                  printf("\nwhich to delete : ");
                  scanf( "%d", &before );
                  deleteBeforeElement( before );
                  break;
        case 11: deleteList();
                  exit(1);
      }
   }
}  /****** end of main function ******/
void traverseInOrder()
{
    node *ptr = head;
```

```
    while ( ptr != NULL ) {
       printf( "%d   ", ptr->info );
       ptr = ptr->next;
    }
}
void traverseInReverseOrder()
{
    node *ptr = tail;
    while ( ptr != NULL ) {
        printf( "%d   ", ptr->info );
        ptr = ptr->prev;
    }
}
node *search( int item )
{
    node *ptr = head;
    while ( ptr != NULL ) {
        if ( ptr->info == item )
             return ptr;
        ptr = ptr->next;
    }
    return NULL;
}
void insertAtBeginning( int item )
{
    node *ptr;
    ptr = ( node * ) malloc(sizeof(node));
    ptr->info = item;
    if ( head == NULL ) {
        ptr->next = ptr->prev = NULL;
        head = tail = ptr;
    } else {
        ptr->prev = NULL;
        ptr->next = head;
        head->prev = ptr;
        head = ptr;
    }
}
void insertAtEnd( int item )
{
    node *ptr;
    ptr = ( node * ) malloc(sizeof(node));
    ptr->info = item;
    if ( head == NULL ) {
        ptr->next = ptr->prev = NULL;
        head = tail = ptr;
    } else {
        ptr->next = NULL;
        ptr->prev = tail;
        tail->next = ptr;
        tail = ptr;
    }
}
```

```
void insertAfterElement( int item, int after )
{
    node *ptr, *loc;
    loc = search ( after );
    if ( loc == NULL )
        return;
    ptr = ( node * ) malloc ( sizeof ( node ) );
    ptr->info  = item;
    if ( loc->next == NULL ) {
        ptr->next = NULL;
        loc->next = ptr;
        ptr->prev = tail;
        tail = ptr;
    } else {
        ptr->prev = loc;
        ptr->next = loc->next;
        (loc->next)->prev = ptr;
        loc->next = ptr;
    }
}
void insertBeforeElement( int item, int before )
{
    node *ptr, *loc;
    loc = search ( before );
    if ( loc == NULL )
        return;
    ptr = ( node * ) malloc ( sizeof ( node ) );
    ptr->info = item;
    if ( loc->prev == NULL ) {
        ptr->prev = NULL;
        loc->prev = ptr;
        ptr->next = head;
        head = ptr;
    } else {
        ptr->prev = loc->prev;
        ptr->next = loc;
        (loc->prev)->next = ptr;
        loc->prev = ptr;
    }
}
void deleteFromBeginning()
{
    node *ptr;
    if ( head == NULL )
        return;
    ptr = head;
    if ( head == tail )    /* one element only */
        head = tail = NULL;
    else {
        (ptr->next)->prev = NULL;
        head = ptr->next;
    }
    free(ptr);
}
```

```
void deleteFromEnd()
{
    node *ptr;
    if ( head == NULL )
        return;
    ptr = tail;
    if ( head == tail )    /* one element only */
        head = tail = NULL;
    else {
        (ptr->prev)->next = ( node * ) NULL;
        tail = ptr->prev;
    }
    free(ptr);
}
void deleteAfterElement( int after )
{
    node *ptr, *loc;
    loc = search ( after );
    if ( loc == NULL )
        return;
    else if ( (loc->next)->next == NULL ) {
        ptr = loc->next;
        loc->next = NULL;
        tail = loc;
        free ( ptr );
    } else {
        ptr = loc->next;
        loc->next = ptr->next;
        (ptr->next)->prev = loc;
        free (ptr);
    }
}
void deleteBeforeElement( int before )
{
    node *ptr, *loc;
    ptr = head;
    loc = search( before );
    if ( loc == NULL )
        return;
    else if ( (loc->prev)->prev == NULL ) {
        ptr = loc->prev;
        loc->prev = NULL;
        head = loc;
        free(ptr);
    } else {
        ptr = loc->prev;
        loc->prev = ptr->prev;
        (ptr->prev)->next = loc;
        free(ptr);
    }
}
void deleteList()
{
    node *ptr;
```

```
    while ( head != NULL ) {
        ptr = head;
        head = head->next;
        free(ptr);
    }
    tail = NULL;
}
```

Listing A.5

```
/*
*  Program to demonstrate use of stack in converting expression
* from infix notation to postfix notation
*/
#include<stdio.h>
#include<conio.h>
typedef struct nodeType {
    char info;
    struct nodeType *next;
} stack;
stack *top = NULL;  // empty stack to start with
typedef enum { false, true } boolean;
/*----  function prototypes ----*/
boolean isEmpty();
void push( char value );
char pop();
char peep();
void disposeStack();
void infixToPostfix( char *source, char *target );
int getPriority( char op );
void main()
{
   char *infixExp = "", *postfixExp = "";
   clrscr();
   printf("\nEnter arithmetic expression in infix notation\n\n" );
   gets(infixExp);
   infixToPostfix( infixExp, postfixExp );
   printf("\nEquivalent expression in postfix notation is\n\n");
   puts(postfixExp);
   getch();
} /*---- end of main function ----*/
void infixToPostfix( char *source, char *target )
{
   char *s, *t;
   s = source;
   t = target;
   while ( *s )
   {
      if ( ( *s == ' ' )||( *s == '\t' ) ) {
         s++;
         continue;
      } else if ( *s == '(' ) {
```

```
            push( *s );
            s++;
        } else if ( *s == ')' ) {
            while ( ( !isEmpty() )&&( peep() != '(' ) ) {
                *t = pop();
                t++;
                *t = ' ';   /*  add one space  */
                t++;
            }
            if ( isEmpty() ) {
                printf( "\nError: Incorrect expression \n" );
                disposeStack();
                return;
            }
            pop(); /* remove left parenthesis from stack  */
            s++;
        } else if ( isdigit( *s ) || isalpha( *s ) ) {
            *t = *s;
            t++;
            *t = ' ';   /*  add one space  */
            t++;
            s++;
        } else if (*s=='+'||*s=='-'||*s=='*'||*s=='/'||*s=='%') {
            while ((!isEmpty())&&( peek() != '(' ) &&
                ( getPriority( peep() ) >= getPriority( *s ) ) )
            {
                *t = pop();
                t++;
                *t = ' ';   /*  add one space  */
                t++;
            }
            push( *s );
            s++;
        } else {
            printf("\nError:Incorrect element in expression\n");
            disposeStack();
            return;
        }
    }
    while ( ( !isEmpty() ) && ( peek() != '(' ) ) {
        *t = pop( &top );
        t++;
        *t = ' ';   /*  add one space  */
        t++;
    }

    if ( peep() == '(' ) {
        printf( "\nError: Incorrect expression\n" );
        disposeStack();
        return;
    }
    *t = '\0'; /*  terminate the string by null character   */
}
```

```
int getPriority( char op )
{
    int priority;
    if ( op == '/' || op == '*' || op == '%' )
        priority = 1;
    else if ( op == '+' || op == '(' )
        priority = 0;
    return priority;
}
boolean isEmpty()
{
    if ( top == NULL )
      return true;
    else
      return false;
}
void push( char value )
{
    stack *ptr;
    ptr = ( stack * ) malloc( sizeof( stack ) );
    if ( ptr == NULL ) {
       printf( "\nUnable to allocate memory for new node..."
);
       printf( "\nPress any key to exit..." );
       getch();
    }
    ptr->info = value;
    ptr->next = top;
    top = ptr;
}
char pop()
{
    char temp;
    stack *ptr;
    temp = top->info;
    ptr = top;
    top = top->next;
    free(ptr);
    return temp;
}
char peep()
{
    return top->info;
}
void disposeStack()
{
    stack *ptr;
    while ( top != NULL )
    {
       ptr = top;
       top = top->next;
       free (ptr);
    }
}
```

Listing A.6

```
/*
*  Program to demonstrate the use of stack in evaluating arithmetic
*  expression in postfix notation. Stack is implemented using a
*  linked list
*/
#include<stdio.h>
#include<conio.h>
typedef struct nodeType {
    float info;
    struct nodeType *next;
} stack;
stack *top = NULL;  // empty stack to start with
typedef enum { false, true } boolean;
boolean isEmpty();
void push( float value );
float pop();
void disposeStack();
float evaluatePostfixExpression( char *exp );
void main()
{
    float value;
    char *postfixExp = "";
    clrscr();
    printf("\nEnter arithmetic expression in postfix notation\n");
    gets(postfixExp);
    value = evaluatePostfixExpression(postfixExp);
    printf( "\nValue of expression = %.4f\n", value );
    getch();
} /*---- end of main function ----*/
float evaluatePostfixExpression( char *exp )
{
     char c;
     float op1, op2, value;
     while ( *exp ) {
         if (*exp == ' ' || *exp == '\t' || *exp == ',') {
             exp++;
             continue;
         }
         if ( isdigit( *exp ) )
             push( (float)(*exp - '0'));  /*convert to value*/
         else {
             op2 = pop();
             op1 = pop();
             switch ( *exp ) {
                case '+' : value = op1 + op2;
                           break;
                case '-' : value = op1 - op2;
                           break;
                case '/' : value = op1 / op2;
                           break;
                case '*' : value = op1 * op2;
                           break;
```

```
            case '%' : value = (int)op1 % (int)op2;
                       break;
            default  : printf( "\nIllegal operation ... %x7\n"
);
                       disposeStack();
                       return;
          }
          push( value );
        }
        exp++;
    }
    return ( pop() );
}
boolean isEmpty()
{
  if ( top == NULL )
     return true;
  else
    return false;
}
void push( char value )
{
   stack *ptr;
   ptr = ( stack * ) malloc( sizeof( stack ) );
   if ( ptr == NULL ) {
      printf( "\nUnable to allocate to memory for new node..." );
      printf( "\nPress any key to exit..." );
      getch();
   }
   ptr->info = value;
   ptr->next = top;
   top = ptr;
}
char pop()
{
   char temp;
   stack *ptr;
   temp = top->info;
   ptr = top;
   top = top->next;
   free(ptr);
   return temp;
}
void disposeStack()
{
   stack *ptr;
   while ( top != NULL )
   {
      ptr = top;
      top = top->next;
      free (ptr);
   }
}
```

Listing A.7

```
/*
* Program to demonstration the implementation of various operations
* on a circular queue represented using a linear array
*/
#include<stdio.h>
#include<conio.h>
# define  MAX  15
typedef enum { false, true } boolean;
int front = -1, rear = -1;   /* initialized to empty status */
int elements[MAX];
boolean isEmpty();
boolean isFull();
void enqueue( int );
int dequeue();
int peep();
void main()
{
   int choice, element;
   do
   {
      clrscr();
      printf( "\nOptions available \n" );
      printf( "++++++++++++++++++++ \n\n" );
      printf( "    1. Enqueue\n" );
      printf( "    2. Dequeue\n" );
      printf( "    3. Peep\n" );
      printf( "    4. Exit\n\n" );
      printf( "Enter your choice ( 1-4 ) : ");
      scanf( "%d", &choice );
      switch ( choice ) {
          case 1: if ( isFull() ) {
                     printf("Queue full…");
                     printf("\n\nPress any key to continue");
                     getch();
                  } else {
                     printf( "Enter value : " );
                     scanf( "%d", &element );
                     enqueue( element );
                  }
                  break;
          case 2: if ( isEmpty() ) {
                     printf("Queue full…");
                     printf("\n\nPress any key to continue");
                     getch();
                  } else {
                     printf("Value dequeued is %d \n",dequeue());
                     printf("\nPress any key to continue ... ");
                     getch();
                  }
                  break;
        case 3: if ( isEmpty() ) {
                     printf("Queue full…");
```

```
                  printf("\n\nPress any key to continue");
                  getch();
              } else {
                  printf("Element at front of queue is %d \n",
                          peep());
                  printf("\nPress any key to continue ... ");
                  getch();
              }
        }
    }
    while ( choice != 4 );
} /*---- end of main function ----*/
boolean isEmpty()
{
    if ( front == -1 )
        return true;
    else
        return false;
}
boolean isFull()
{
    if ( (( front == 0 ) && (rear == MAX-1)) || (front == rear+1) )
        return true;
    else
        return false;
}
void enqueue( int value )
{
    if ( front == -1 )
        front = rear = 0;
    else if ( rear == MAX-1 )
        rear = 0;
    else
        rear++;
    elements[rear] = value;
}

int dequeue()
{
     int temp;
     temp = elements[front];
     if ( front == rear )
         front = rear = -1;
     else if ( front == MAX-1 )
         front = 0;
     else
         front++;
     return temp;
}
int peek()
{
     return elements[front];
}
```

Listing A.8

```
/*
* Program to demonstration the implementation of various
* operations on queue represented using linear linked list
*/
#include<stdio.h>
#include<conio.h>
typedef enum { false, true } boolean;
typedef struct nodeType {
   int  info;
   struct nodeType *next;
} node;
node *front = NULL, *rear = NULL;
boolean isEmpty();
void enqueue( int );
int dequeue ();
int peep();
void disposeQueue();
void main()
{
   int choice, element;
   do
   {
      clrscr();
      printf( "\nOptions available \n" );
      printf( "++++++++++++++++++ \n\n" );
      printf( "   1. Enqueue\n" );
      printf( "   2. Dequeue\n" );
      printf( "   3. Peep\n" );
      printf( "   4. Exit\n\n" );
      printf( "Enter your choice ( 1-4 ) : " );
      scanf( "%d", &choice );
      switch ( choice ) {
         case 1: printf( "Enter value : " );
                 scanf( "%d", &element );
                 enqueue( element );
                 break;
         case 2: if ( isEmpty() ) {
                    printf("Queue empty... ");
                    printf("\nPress any key to continue");
                    getch();
                 } else {
                    printf("Value dequeued is %d\n",dequeue());
                    printf("\nPress any key to continue ... ");
                    getch();
                 }
                 break;
         case 3: if ( isEmpty() ) {
                    printf("Queue empty... ");
                    printf("\nPress any key to continue");
                    getch();
                 } else {
                    printf("1st Element in queue is %d\n",
```

```
                        peep());
                   printf("\nPress any key to continue ... ");
                   getch();
                 }
       }
   }
   while ( choice != 4 );
} /*---- end of main function ----*/
boolean isEmpty()
{
   return ( pq->front == NULL ? true : false );
}
void enqueue( int value )
{
   node *ptr;
   ptr = ( node * ) malloc( sizeof( node ) );
   ptr->info = value;
   ptr->next = NULL;
   if ( front == NULL )
      front = rear = ptr;
   else {
      rear->next = ptr;
      rear = ptr;
   }
}
int dequeue()
{
   int temp;
   node *ptr;
   temp = front->info;
   ptr = front;
   if ( front == rear )
      front = rear = NULL;
   else
      front = front->next;
   free( ptr );
   return temp;
}
int peep()
{
    return ( front->info );
}
void disposeQueue()
{
   node *ptr;
   while ( front != NULL ) {
      ptr = front;
      front = front->next;
      free( ptr );
   }
   rear = NULL;
}
```

Listing A.9

```
/*
*  Program to illustrate the implementation of different
*  operations on a Binary Search Tree
*/
#include<stdio.h>
#include<alloc.h>
typedef struct BST_node {
   struct BST_node *left;
   int item;
   struct BST_node *right;
} BST;
void createTree( BST **tree );
void insertElementRecursive( BST **tree, int element );
BST *findLargestElement( BST *tree );
void preorderRecursive( BST *h );
void inorderRecursive( BST *h );
void postorderRecursive( BST *h );
void deleteElement( BST **tree, int element );
void deleteTree( BST **tree );
void main()
{
   int choice, element, height;
   BST *root, *loc;
   createTree(&root);
   while ( 1 )
   {
       clrscr();
       printf( "\n     Options available \n" );
       printf( "++++++++++++++++++++++++++++++ \n\n" );
       printf( "  1. Insert node\n" );
       printf( "  2. Pre-order traversal\n" );
       printf( "  3. In-order traversal\n" );
       printf( "  4. Post-order traversal\n" );
       printf( "  5. Delete node\n" );
       printf( "  6. Exit\n\n");
       printf( "Enter your choice ( 1-6 ) : " );
       scanf( "%d", &choice );
       switch( choice ) {
          case 1 : printf("Element to insert : " );
                   scanf( "%d", &element );
                   insertElement( &root, element );
                   break;
          case 2 : printf("\nPre-order Traversal\n");
                   preorderRecursive(root);
                   printf("\n\nPress any key to continue...");
                   getch();
                   break;
          case 3 : printf("\nIn-order Traversal\n" );
                   inorderRecursive(root);
                   printf("\n\nPress any key to continue...");
                   getch();
                   break;
```

```
            case 4 : printf("\nPost-order Traversal\n" );
                     postorderRecursive(root);
                     printf("\n\nPress any key to continue...");
                     getch();
                     break;
            case 5 : printf("Element to delete : ");
                     scanf( "%d", &element );
                     deleteElement( &root, element );
                     break;
            case 6 : deleteTree(&root);
                     return;
        }
    }
}
void createTree( BST **tree )
{
  *tree = NULL;
}
void insertElementRecursive( BST **tree, int element )
{
   if ( *tree == NULL ) {
      *tree = ( BST * ) malloc ( sizeof ( BST ) );
      (*tree)->item = element;
      (*tree)->left = (*tree)->right = NULL;
   } else {
      if ( element < (*tree)->item )
         insertElementRecursive( &((*tree)->left), element);
      else
         insertElementRecursive( &((*tree)->right), element);
   }
}
BST *findLargestElement( BST *tree )
{
   if ( ( tree == NULL ) || ( tree->right == NULL ) )
      return tree;
   else
      return findLargestElement(tree->right);
}
void preorderRecursive( BST *h )
{
   if ( h != NULL ) {
      printf( "%d  ", h->item );
      preorderRecursive( h->left );
      preorderRecursive( h->right );
   }
}
void inorderRecursive( BST *h )
{
   if ( h != NULL ) {
      inorderRecursive( h->left );
      printf( "%d  ", h->item );
      inorderRecursive( h->right );
   }
}
```

```
void postorderRecursive( BST *h )
{
   if ( h != NULL ) {
      postorderRecursive( h->left );
      postorderRecursive( h->right );
      printf( "%d  ", h->item );
   }
}
void deleteElement( BST **tree, int element )
{
   BST *temp;
   if ( *tree == ( BST* ) NULL ) {
      printf( "\nElement %d not found in BST", element );
      printf( "\n\nPress any key to continue ..." );
      getch();
   }
   else if ( element < (*tree)->item )
      deleteElement( &((*tree)->left), element );
   else if ( element > (*tree)->item )
      deleteElement( &((*tree)->right), element );
   else if ( (*tree)->left && (*tree)->right ) {
      temp = ( BST * ) findLargestElement( (*tree)->left );
      (*tree)->item = temp->item;
      deleteElement( &((*tree)->left), temp->item );
   } else {
      temp = *tree;
      if (((*tree)->left == NULL )&&((*tree)->right == NULL))
         *tree = ( BST *) NULL;
      else if ( (*tree)->left != NULL )
         *tree = (*tree)->left;
      else
         *tree = (*tree)->right;
      free ( temp );
   }
}
void deleteTree( BST **tree )
{
   if ( *tree != NULL ) {
      deleteTree( &((*tree)->left) );
      deleteTree( &((*tree)->right) );
      free ( *tree );
   }
}
```

Listing A.10

```
/* Program to sort an array of integers in ascending order using
*  selection sort method  */
#include<stdio.h>
#include<conio.h>
void selectionSortMethod( int a[], int n );
void main()
```

```
{
    int i, n, a[50];
    clrscr();
    printf( "\nEnter size of array : " );
    scanf( "%d", &n );
    printf( "\nEnter %d elements of array\n\n", n );
    for ( i = 0; i < n; i++ )
        scanf( "%d", &a[i] );
    selectionSortMethod( a, n );
    printf( "\n\nSorted list of elements\n\n" );
    for ( i = 0; i < n; i++ )
       printf( "%d\t", a[i] );
    printf( "\n");
} /*---- end of main function ----*/
void selectionSortMethod( int a[], int n )
{
    int i, loc, j, small;
    for ( i = 1; i < n; i++ ) {
       small = a[i-1];
       loc = i-1;
       for ( j = i; j < n; j++ ) {
          If ( a[j] < small ) {
             small = a[j];
             loc = j;
          }
       }
       If ( loc != (i-1) ) {
          temp = a[i-1];
          a[i-1] = a[loc];
          a[loc] = temp;
      }
   }
}
```

Listing A.11

```
/* Program to sort an array of integers in ascending order using
*  insertion sort method   */
#include<stdio.h>
#include<conio.h>
void insertionSortMethod( int a[], int n );
void main()
{
    int i, n, a[50];
    clrscr();
    printf( "\nEnter size of array : " );
    scanf( "%d", &n );
    printf( "\nEnter %d elements of array\n\n", n );
    for ( i = 0; i < n; i++ )
        scanf( "%d", &a[i] );
    insertionSortMethod( a, n );
    printf( "\n\nSorted list of elements\n\n" );
```

```
    for ( i = 0; i < n; i++ )
        printf( "%d\t", a[i] );
    printf( "\n");
} /*---- end of main function ----*/
void insertionSortMethod( int a[], int n )
{
    int k, temp, j;
    for ( k = 1; k <= n-1; k++ ) {
        temp = a[k];
        j = k-1;
        while ( ( temp < a[j] ) && ( j >= 0 ) ) {
            a[j+1] = a[j];
            j = j-1;
        }
        a[j+1] = temp;
    }
}
```

Listing A.12

```
/* Program to sort an array of integers in ascending order using
*  merge sort method   */
#include<stdio.h>
#include<conio.h>
void mergeSortMethod( int a[], int beg, int end );
void mergingSortedSubArrays(int a[50],int lb,int lr,int rb,int rr);
void main()
{
   int i, n, a[50];
   clrscr();
   printf( "\nEnter size of array : " );
   scanf( "%d", &n );
   printf( "\nEnter %d positive integer elements of array\n\n", n
);
   for ( i = 0; i < n; i++ )
      scanf( "%d", &a[i] );
   mergeSortMethod( a, 0, n-1 );
   printf( "\n\nSorted list of elements\n\n" );
   for ( i = 0; i < n; i++ )
      printf( "%d\t", a[i] );
   printf( "\n");
} /*---- end of main function ----*/
void mergeSortMethod( int a[], int beg, int end )
{
   int mid;
   if ( beg < end )  {
       mid = ( beg + end ) / 2;
       mergeSortMethod( a, beg, mid );
       mergeSortMethod( a, mid+1, end );
       mergingSortedSubArrays( a, beg, mid, mid+1, end );
   }
}
void mergingSortedSubArrays(int a[50],int lb,int lr,int rb,int rr)
{
```

```
    int na, nb, nc, k, c[50];
    na = lb;
    nb = rb;
    nc = lb;
    while ( ( na <= lr ) && ( nb <= rr ) ) {
       if ( a[na] < a[nb] )
          c[nc] = a[na++];
       else
          c[nc] = a[nb++];
       nc++;
    }
    if ( na > lr ) {
       while ( nb <= rr )
          c[nc++] = a[nb++];
    } else {
       while ( na <= lr )
          c[nc++] = a[na++];
    }
    for ( k = lb; k <= rr; k++ )
      a[k] = c[k];
}
```

Listing A.13

```
/* Program to sort an array of integers in ascending order using
*  Quicksort method   */
#include<stdio.h>
#include<conio.h>
typedef enum { false, true } boolean;
int void partitionArray( int a[], int beg, int end );
void quickSortRecursive( int a[], int lb, int ub );
void main()
{
    int i, n, a[50];
    clrscr();
    printf( "\nEnter number of elements in array : " );
    scanf("%d", &n );
    printf( "\nEnter %d elements\n\n", n );
    for ( i = 0; i < n; i++ )
       scanf("%d", &a[i] );
    quickSortRecursive( a, 0, n-1 );
    printf( "\n\nSorted list of elements\n\n" );
    for ( i = 0; i < n; i++ )
       printf("%d\t", a[i] );
    printf("\n");
} /*---- end of main function ----*/
void quickSortRecursive(  int a[], int lb, int ub )
{
    int loc;
    if ( lb < ub ) {
        loc = partitionArray( a, lb, ub );
        quickSortRecursive( a, lb, loc-1 );
```

```
        quickSortRecursive( a, loc+1, ub );
    }
}
int partitionArray( int a[], int beg, int end )
{
    int left, right, temp;
    boolean done;
    left = loc = beg;
    right = end;
    done = false;
    while ( !done )
    {
        while ( ( a[loc] < a[right] ) && ( loc != right ) )
            right--;
        if ( loc == right )
            done = true;
        else {
            temp = a[loc];
            a[loc] = a[right];
            a[right] = temp;
            loc = right;
        }
        if  ( !done ) {
            while ( ( a[loc] > a[left] ) && ( loc != left ) )
                left++;
               if ( loc == left )
                    done = true;
                else {
                    temp = a[loc];
                    a[loc] = a[left];
                    a[left] = temp;
                    loc = left;
                }
        }
    }
}
```

Listing A.14

```
/* Program to sort an array of integers in ascending order using
*  Heap sort method   */
#include<stdio.h>
#include<conio.h>
void heapSortMethod ( int a[], int n );
void downheap( int a[], int start, int finish );
void heapify( int a[], int n );
void main()
{
    int i, n, a[50];
    clrscr();
    printf( "\nEnter size of array : " );
    scanf( "%d", &n );
```

```
    printf( "\nEnter %d integer elements of array\n\n", n );
    for ( i = 1; i <= n; i++ )
       scanf( "%d", &a[i] );
    heapSortMethod( a, n );
    printf( "\n\nSorted list of elements\n\n" );
    for ( i = 1; i <= n; i++ )
       printf( "%d\t", a[i] );
    printf( "\n");
} /*---- end of main function ----*/
void heapSortMethod ( int a[], int n )
{
    int i, temp;
    heapify( a, n );
    for ( i = n; i > 1; i-- ) {
        temp = a[1];
        a[1] = a[i];
        a[i] = temp;
        downheap( a, 1, i-1 );
    }
}
void downheap( int a[], int start, int finish )
{
    int  index, lchild, rchild, maximum, temp;
    lchild = 2*start;
    rchild = lchild + 1;
    if ( lchild <= finish ) {
        maximum = a[lchild];
        index = lchild;
        if ( rchild <= finish ) {
            if ( a[rchild] > maximum ) {
                maximum = a[rchild];
                index = rchild;
            }
        }
        if ( a[start] < a[index] ) {
            temp = a[start];
            a[start] = a[index];
            a[index] = temp;
            downheap( a, index, finish );
        }
    }
}
void heapify( int a[], int n )
{
   int i, index;
   index = n / 2;
   for ( i = index; i >= 1; i-- )
       downheap( a, i, n );
}
```

Appendix B

Glossary

Learning Objectives

After reading this appendix, students will be able to answer almost every basic and conceptual question related to the topics studied in their syllabus.

B.2 *Data Structures*

Algorithm - A step-by-step procedure, written in a human-oriented language, to solve a particular problem.

Array - A collection of homogeneous data elements referred to by a common name where individual elements are accessed using a subscript.

AVL Tree - A height-balanced binary tree where for each node *R* of the tree, the height of the left subtree of *R* and height of the right subtree *R* differ by at most 1.

Base Address - The starting address of a data structure.

Binary Search - A search technique that is applied to a list of ordered keys. At each step of the search, the list is partitioned into two equal parts, with the selection of the appropriate partition to probe in the next iteration made on the basis of relative key values.

Binary Search Tree - A binary tree where for each node *R* of the tree, all keys in the left subtree of *R* are less than the key value of node *R* and all keys in the right subtree of *R* are greater than the key value of node *R*. A binary search tree is a special case of *m*-way search tree where $m = 2$. Also see *m*-way search tree.

Binary Tree - A tree where each node can have maximum out-degree of 2.

Bit - An acronym for a binary digit. A unit of information equals to one binary decision or one of the two possible states (on or off), true or false, (1 or 0) and represents the smallest piece of information in a binary system.

Bit String - A sequence of symbols derived from the alphabet {0,1}.

Boolean - A primitive data structure with values taken from the set {*false*, *true*} and with fundamental operators: *not*, *and*, and *or*. Also called *logical*.

Bubble Sort - An internal sort in which each key floats up to its proper position through a series of pairwise comparisons and exchanges with adjacent key values, require $O(n^2)$ comparisons to sort *n* key values. Also known as *exchange sort*.

Bug - A mistake in a computer program/software or a malfunction in a computer hardware component. To debug means to remove mistakes and correct malfunctions.

Circular Linked List - A linked list in which the last node points to the first node.

Code - A system of symbols or a set of rules for the representation of data in a digital computer. Some examples include binary, BCD, ASCII, EBCDIC, etc.

Column-Major Order - An array linearization technique that stores all the elements from one column, before storing any elements from the next column. Subscripts are varied left-to-right, *i.e.*, the left-most subscript is varied fastest. Compare with ***row-major order***.

Compiler - A program that translates the program written in a high level programming language into machine language that is understandable to the processor.

Complete Binary Tree - A binary tree that contains the maximum number of nodes possible for its height.

Data - Basic elements of information that can be processed or produced by a computer. Data represents any group of operands made up of numerals, letters, or symbols denoting any condition, value, or state. Current typical computer operand sizes include a word that contains 2 bytes, double word that contains 4 bytes, and a quad word that contains 8 bytes.

Data Structure - A class of data characterized by its logical organization and the operations that are defined on it. Also known as *data type*.

Data Type - See ***data structure***.

Debugging - The process of locating and correcting the bugs of a computer program or computer hardware component.

Doubly Linked List - A linked list in which each node points to both the next node and the prior node in the list.

B.4 *Data Structures*

Elementary Item - A field that is not decomposable to component fields.

Exchange Sort - One of a family of internal sort algorithms in which pairs of key values are compared and exchanged if they are not in proper relative positions.

Field - A specified area of a record used to represent a particular kind of information.

File - A collection of logically related records occurrences that are treated as a unit and are persistent, *i.e.*, independent of the execution of a particular run-unit.

First-In-First-Out (FIFO) - A method of linear management in which the first element into the list will be the first element taken out of the list; defines the mode of operation of a queue. Compare with ***Last-In-First-Out (LIFO)***. See also ***queue***.

Flowchart - A pictorial/graphical representation of the various processes performed to solve a particular problem on computer, where each pictorial symbol represents a distinct operation to be performed, and flow lines show the sequence of operations.

Front - The element that has been in the queue longest. Also, the next element to be removed from a queue.

Group Item - A field that is decomposable into component elementary and/or group items.

Infix Notation - A method of representing an arithmetic expression whereby a binary operator appears between its operands. Compare with ***postfix*** and ***prefix*** notations.

In-order Traversal - A method of visiting all the nodes of a binary tree, recursively defined by first traversing the left subtree in in-order, then visiting the root, then traversing the right subtree in in-order. Compare with ***pre-order*** and ***post-order*** traversals.

Insertion Sort – An internal sort in which the next entry in the unsorted list is inserted into its proper relative position in a growing sorted list.

Iterative Procedure - A procedure that repeatedly executes a series of steps but that does not invoke itself. Compare with ***recursive procedure***.

Key - The identifying field of a record. Also called a field whose value is used to place a collection of records into a sorted ordering.

Level - A characteristic of a node in a tree; a node's level is the length of the path from the root to that node.

Linear List - A general data structure comprised of an ordered set of nodes; for each node there is a single next node. Compare with ***tree***.

Linear Search - A technique applied to find the record of a collection with a particular key value; views the collection as a linear list and starts at the beginning of the linear list, sequentially comparing each record's key value with the sought key value until the target record is found or the end of the list is reached; requires O(n) comparisons to search a collection of n key values.

Linked List - A data structure in which the ordering of nodes is indicated by the use of direct or indirect pointers rather than by physically sequentially.

Lirst-In-First-Out (LIFO) - A method of linear management in which the element most recently added to the list will be the next element taken out of the list; defines the mode of operation of a stack. Compare with ***Fast-In-First-Out (FIFO)***. See also ***stack***.

Logical Error - Programming mistake that causes the wrong processing to take place even though there is no syntax error, *i.e.*, the program is syntactically correct.

Lower Triangular Array - An array in which all elements above diagonal are zero. If the diagonal is also zero, the array is strictly lower triangular. Compare with ***upper triangular***.

Max Heap - An almost complete binary tree, in which the key values are arranged such that for each node i, $key(i) \leq key(j)$, where j is the father of node i.

Merge - The combination of records in two or more sorted files to form one sorted file.

Min Heap - An almost complete binary tree, in which the key values are arranged such that for each node i, $key(i) \geq key(j)$, where j is the father of node i.

Node - An elementary component of a list, tree, or graph.

NULL - The value given to a pointer variable that is empty, *i.e.*, that points nowhere.

Partition-exchange Sort - An exchange sort. At each step of the sort, the list is partitioned into two parts such that the key values in one partition are less than a particular key value and key values in the other partition are greater than particular key value; the partitions are then treated independently in following steps of the sort. See ***quicksort***.

Pointer Variable - A variable whose value must be an address or NULL.

Postfix Notation - A method of representing an arithmetic expression whereby a binary operator appears after its operands. Compare with ***infix*** and ***prefix*** notations. Also known a ***reverse-polish*** notation.

Post-order Traversal - A method of visiting all the nodes of a binary tree, recursively defined by first traversing the left subtree in post-order, then traversing the right subtree in post-order, then visiting the root. Compare with ***pre-order*** and ***in-order*** traversals.

Prefix Notation - A method of representing an arithmetic expression whereby a binary operator appears before its operands. Compare with ***infix*** and ***postfix*** notations.

Pre-order Traversal - A method of visiting all the nodes of a binary tree, recursively defined by first visiting the root, then traversing the left subtree in pre-order, then traversing the right subtree in pre-order. Compare with ***in-order*** and ***post-order*** traversals.

Primary Key - The main key field of a multi-key file. In an alternate-key indexed sequential file, the field for which direct and sequential access are supported.

Primitive - A data structure that cannot be decomposed to other data structure. Also known as data structure or data type for which there is a built-in support.

Queue - A linear list in which elements are added only to the rear of the list and are removed only from the front of the list. See ***first-in-first-out (FIFO)***.

Quick Sort - See ***partition-exchange sort***.

Recursive Procedure - A procedure in which each step makes use of the results of the earlier steps, generally by invoking execution of some part of itself. Compare with ***iterative procedure***.

Reverse-polish Notation - See ***postfix notation***.

Right Thread - A link from a node in a binary tree to its successor node in the in-order traversal. Compare with ***left thread***.

Rooted Tree - A tree in which one node, called the root, is distinguished from other nodes.

Row-Major Order - An array linearization technique that stores all the elements from one row, before storing any elements from the next row. Subscripts are varied right-to-left, *i.e.*, the right-most subscript is varied fastest. Compare with ***column-major order***.

Searching - The process of trying to find the record or records that meets a given criterion.

Secondary Key - In a multi-key file, any field except the primary key.

Selection Sort - One of the family of internal sort algorithm in which the next logically sequential key in the unsorted list is selected and placed in the next position in a growing sorted list.

B.8 *Data Structures*

Similar Trees - Trees that have the same structure but not necessarily the same node contents. Compare with ***equivalent trees***.

Sorting - The process of arranging a collection of keys (and records) into a specified order.

Stack - A linear list in which the elements are added to and removed from only the top of the list. Also see ***last-in-first-out (LIFO)***.

String - A finite sequence of characters taken from an alphabet, *i.e.*, character set.

Syntax - Grammar rules for the formation of the allowable strings of a vocabulary.

Syntax Error - An error caused by the violation of the rules governing the structure of the programming language being used.

Table - A two-dimensional array. See also an ***array***.

Threaded Tree - A tree that includes a linked list of the nodes according to a tree traversal ordering.

Transpose - Transpose of a matrix is another matrix whose elements are obtained by reversing the subscript positions.

Upper Triangular Array - An array in which all elements below diagonal are zero. If the diagonal is also zero, the array is strictly upper triangular. Compare with ***lower triangular***.

Vector - A one-dimensional array. See ***array***.

❑ ❑ ❑

Index

G

H

I

J, K

L

M

N

O

P

Q

R

S

T

U

V

W